BREAKING THE CYCLE

BREAKING THE CYCLE

A Step-by-Step Guide to Healing
from Childhood Abuse, Neglect and Trauma

By Sandra P. Riggin

EVENING STAR PRESS

Sautee-Nacoochee, Georgia

Requests for permission to make copies of any part of this work should be mailed to:
Evening Star Press
Attention: Sandra P. Riggin
P. O. Box 357
Sautee, Georgia 30571

Copyright © 2005 by Sandra P. Riggin

ISBN 0-9742924-1-9

Library of Congress Catalog Card Number: 2004095234

Printed in the United States of America

First Evening Star Press Edition: 2005

Dedications

This book is dedicated first to God who helped me survive my own childhood abuse, neglect and trauma so I could help others to do the same. Secondly, to all of the people who were abused, neglected and/or traumatized as children. May this book help you find the path to healing and may your days ahead be filled with many blessings, hope and happiness.

Acknowledgements

Catherine Gibbs and Deana Wilbanks who were my friends and support during this second book. They spent countless hours proof reading and then reminding me of my calling to write this book. They provided me with the encouragement I needed to make this book possible.

Jane Grillo who came through for me again on this second book. Her editing skills were invaluable, as were her suggestions and unique point of view.

Linda Thagard and Bobbie Pethel who provided their fine-tuned proof reading skills.

Marlin Geiger for sharing his wonderful talents with designing the book cover and setting up the book. He was an invaluable resource in my quest to teach others how to heal. Without Marlin, this book would not have been possible.

Stan Crump for offering his fantastic and very professional recording skills.

John Serrie for allowing his powerful and popular music to be used in the background of the CD.

Words of Wisdom

The Spirit of the Sovereign LORD is on me,
because the LORD has anointed me
to preach good news to the poor.
He has sent me to bind up the brokenhearted,
to proclaim freedom for the captives
and release from darkness for the prisoners,
to proclaim the year of the LORD's favor
and the day of vengeance of our God,
to comfort all who mourn,
and provide for those who grieve in Zion—
to bestow on them a crown of beauty
instead of ashes,
the oil of gladness
instead of mourning,
and a garment of praise
instead of a spirit of despair.

Isaiah 61:1-3

Foreword

W<small>HAT IS IT IN PSYCHOTHERAPY</small> that cultivates healing? I ask myself that question almost daily, as I gaze into the faces of the clients who sit across from me, trusting that I will offer something to move them toward wholeness. On a recent day two clients offered lucid answers to my question. One had been molested and the other severely emotionally abused in childhood. They, like other survivors of childhood abuse, were wounded deeply and early. And their healing, like that of other survivors, would require the best of current psychotherapeutic understandings and techniques.

The first thing I noticed about twenty-one-year-old Barbara, after her warm smile, was the Alcoholics Anonymous medallion which she wore, like an Olympic gold medal, around her neck. Only moments after we began our first session she was telling me about her two years of sobriety from alcohol and a variety of drugs, including heroin.

"I was humiliated about the things I had done when I was using alcohol and drugs," she sighed. "But once I got into AA, I let go of all of that. Other people do those things too; so I know I'm okay." She went on to explain that she was coming to therapy at this time, because two years into her sobriety she didn't know how to overcome her fears and sadness, which were showing up all too often, against her will, as tearfulness.

"I was abused as a child, but I don't think that bothers me anymore. I don't know what it is," she pondered, knowing that she no longer felt ashamed of her abuse and no longer felt angry and unforgiving toward her perpetrator.

Barbara's pride in her AA friends reminded me that we need to discover early on a healing path where we can be heard, respected, and even loved, no matter what we have done, what others have done to us, or how much we have hated ourselves. We can open ourselves to this discovery in our relationships with friends and loved ones, with recovery group members, or with a therapist.

The loving respect present in Barbara's recovery group had done its work and now it was time for the inside job. It was time for Barbara to observe and replace her own subtle thoughts and beliefs, the states of being, which were triggering the unmanageable emotions.

Later in that same day another client, Jennifer, came in for her second psychotherapy session. She had come into therapy at the urging of her mother and friends who were concerned about her out-of-control rages, which were occurring whenever she felt fearful and jealous. Because Jennifer had defended her right to express her rage and because she had little idea that she could affect her own emotions and her actions, we had focused in the first session on changing the thoughts that fed her destructive emotions.

In this second session, Jennifer reported that she was pleased to discover that changing her thoughts was changing her emotions so much that her anger was now manageable. But she was ashamed to see how her earlier victimized thoughts had fanned the fires of her rage.

As I listened, I instinctively reached out to her with compassion and acceptance. And her earlier defensiveness, warmed by the acceptance, melted into revelations about her father's rage toward her. She recalled that his attacks had stopped only when she, too, had lost control. She had learned from his training to foster her own rage in order to protect herself.

As I recognized Barbara's need to see her own thoughts and beliefs clearly and Jennifer's need to accept herself just as she was, I remembered Tara Brach's book *Radical Acceptance*. She describes two parts of genuine self acceptance, which are as interdependent as the two wings of a great bird. Both are necessary for the survivor to fly free of old encumbrances. Those wings are clear seeing or understanding and self compassion. Either wing, without the other, is unbalanced. If we clearly see our ongoing role in creating the misery in our lives without holding ourselves with compassion, we get sidetracked in guilt and fear of our imperfections. If we have love and compassion for ourselves, without clear understanding of our own destructive patterns, we can lapse into self pity.

With *Breaking the Cycle*, Sandy Riggin joins the ranks of wise teachers who know we must strengthen both of these wings. For the clear seeing wing, she restates and revises existing psychological theories which can help survivors and healers understand patterns that are no longer necessary; and she gives us cognitive techniques for overcoming old thoughts and beliefs in particular. For the self-compassion wing, she offers guided imagery techniques for building self love and acceptance. As we follow her clearly presented steps, we find ourselves balanced and ready to take flight with her.

Sandy's own healing journey is infused into her words for survivors and for those who work with them. The words shine with empathy and with her commitment to the healing process. Her voice on the accompanying CD is the voice of an older sister who has been there and knows how to lead you home.

Those who have grown weary of self help formulas will find their faith renewed by Sandy's trust in the combination that worked for her and for the clients whose stories she tells. Therapists who read her work will be reminded of techniques which, used together, can complete the work of recovery. And they will have Sandy's life and her confident voice to assure them that full healing is possible.

Dr. Susan B. Lamb, Ph.D.
Clinical Psychologist

x

CONTENTS

SECTION III: APPENDICES

Disclaimer

THIS DISCLAIMER is being provided to make clear certain points. The most important being that this book was written for the lay person who is seeking a way to recover from the abuse, neglect and/or trauma they suffered as a child. It was NOT written as a means of defining psychological concepts in means of constructs or axioms or to illuminate the deep-rooted theoretical foundations behind these concepts. It was NOT intended to be used as a psychological text book or one that presents psychological theories as ordained by the originating psychologist. Instead, this book illustrates how various theories and psychological concepts may be applied to the issue of recovery in a very practical sense. I took the theories I deemed appropriate and necessary for the topic of childhood abuse, neglect and/or trauma and modified them to meet the topic of this book. This was not done to discredit the originator's intended use of the theory, but to help make the recovery process more attainable and understandable to the lay person.

I would encourage those who wish to understand any theories as they were originally intended to obtain writings by the originator of the theory.

You will also notice that on many occasions throughout this book the originator of certain theories was not mentioned. This was not done as a means of discrediting the originator, but because adequate information could not be obtained as to who originated that particular concept or theory.

In lieu of the originators name a symbol * was placed beside the name of the theory to make clear this author did NOT originate that particular concept or theory. Likewise, if a symbol does not appear next to a theory it denotes that the originator of the theory was credited or it was a theory this author conceptualized.

How To Use This Book

THE BOOK YOU HOLD IN YOUR HANDS isn't merely a written guide. It is, first and foremost, a workbook. It contains information and exercises to aid in your healing process and to help you grow as an individual. The recovery process isn't something you can rush through, but something you must work your way through. It will require diligence and a commitment on your part to do whatever it takes for you to heal. It will require not only reading the material in each chapter but also your willingness to give yourself all the time you need to thoroughly do what is asked of you.

Each chapter begins with an introduction and an explanation of concepts to help you understand how the recovery process works, and why. There are also exercises located at the end of each chapter for you to complete. Some of the exercises only require you to answer a few questions while others ask that you practice specific skills for a week or longer before forging ahead in the book. This is done so you will have the opportunity to master a particular concept or set of skills before acquiring new ones. Keep in mind that just because you are asked not to forge ahead doesn't mean you can't go back and review the material already covered.

It will be important for you to keep in mind that you will get out of this book, and more importantly the exercises, only what you put into them. Thus, I would suggest you take adequate time to ponder and think about the questions you are being asked before answering them. Then, answer the questions as specifically and as detailed as possible.

The exercises are being used as skill building tools and thus require that you complete them in order and without skipping around. You must master one skill before acquiring another. If you don't take the necessary time to master each skill in each new chapter, you won't be able to obtain the desired healing. So please allow yourself the time necessary to master each chapter of this guide before moving ahead.

As an added note, please be aware that you may not have enough room within the printed exercises to write out your answers in great detail. Feel free to use additional sheets of paper or to write out your answers in a notebook. In addition, the exercises, which require several days or weeks to complete, will need to be copied so you will be able to complete the assignment as asked of you.

It is also important for you to keep in mind that this book and your answers to the exercises are for your eyes only. So be honest with yourself and complete the exercises as genuinely as possible. The only way anyone will know what you have written in this book is if you choose to share it with someone else.

There is also a CD located in the back of this book. It is to be used in Section II of the book only. Please do NOT listen to any part of the CD until you are asked to do so. If you listen to it prematurely, it could hinder your ability to obtain recovery.

Finally, remember that recovery from years of abuse takes time, so please be willing to devote all the time you need to finding your way back to the person you were meant to be. Allow yourself to find the person you were meant to be in spite of the abuse, neglect and/or trauma...the person God intended you to be.

BREAKING THE CYCLE

Chapter 1

Beginnings

You MAY FEEL as if you are traveling down the road of recovery alone, with no one to guide or help you through this process. Even though you may feel this way, it isn't entirely true. The person guiding you through your journey of healing in this book, as in this author, has already traveled down the path you are on and has successfully recovered.

In many ways my childhood experiences were like yours, and so many others who will read and work their way to recovery using this book as a map. For me, my recovery began in a therapist's office. When I couldn't obtain the healing I was looking for through traditional counseling, I started writing my life story. I began looking for a way to help the little girl who still lived inside of me to heal from the hurt and pain she was still carrying around. As I wrote about the things that had happened to me, I was able to feel them and embrace them. I was able to find a way to recover. As I saw the words on the pages before me that graphically depicted the abuse, neglect and trauma I sustained as a child, I realized how it impacted my life as an adult, and how I recovered. I knew I had to share this with other survivors so they, too, could find healing. I had to break the silence of childhood abuse, so I published my personal story in my first book entitled, *Forbidden Memories: A Journey of Healing* (www.sandyriggin.com).

From there I was able to discover a better way of doing therapy and one that would help abuse survivors to resolve their past and to heal once and for all. What you hold in your hands is "that better way of doing therapy." It is what I believe will help lead you down that road of recovery to healing and resolution.

The key to your recovery, as you work your way through this book, is to never quit or give up on yourself. There will be points in your recovery process where you will feel challenged and maybe even overwhelmed.

There may come a time when you may even feel the need to put this book aside for a short while. If you do, this is more than all right. But don't quit and don't give up. Don't forget to pick this book back up again so you can continue traveling down your road of recovery and find resolution for the things that happened to you in your own childhood.

GETTING STARTED

Childhood abuse, neglect and trauma are some of the most difficult life experiences to overcome because there is very little effective information and support available to help anyone who is on this journey. Despite the fact bookstore shelves are filled with self-help books on this topic, very few of them treat the whole person or the original trauma itself. They only treat parts of the person, only the symptoms of the trauma. This, in turn, only allows for temporary relief of symptoms as opposed to recovery. Working with the symptoms and not the cause of the problem is like throwing a rock in a pond and only focusing on the ripples instead of the huge rock lying at the bottom of the pond. Until you can find and look at the rock that caused the ripples in your life, the ripples will always be there.

Another obstacle with treating abuse survivors is this: The techniques necessary to promote recovery are not being taught in post-secondary educational counseling programs. Therapists aren't being taught how to be therapists but merely theorists. I found this to be true even in my own educational pursuits. While going through undergraduate and graduate school, I was taught only theories, not how to help people recover from devastating life experiences. I was taught the systems of psychology and how to listen but not how to effectively help people recover.

Because of my own life experiences and personal struggle as an abuse survivor, I have dedicated my life to uncovering the answers to childhood abuse, neglect and trauma. My goal is to help those who have suffered to heal from the painful plight of their past. I don't want anyone else to have to suffer, to feel helpless or pray for death, not even for one more day.

Teaching survivors how to recover is of paramount importance because childhood abuse is passed on from one generation to the next. The abused tend to become abusers. The only way to save the next generation is by breaking the silence of abuse and ultimately the cycle of abuse here and now. It will require a sincere dedication and commitment on the part of all survivors today. It will require a change in life style and way of living. It will be necessary for schools to change how they teach future therapists; for child abuse organizations to become more effective; for therapists to become more knowledgeable; and for the world as a whole to become more aware of the effects childhood abuse, neglect and trauma have on the present generation and will have on generations to come.

As a result of my personal dedication to myself and other abuse survivors, I have developed a therapeutic technique that works—a system of therapy that actually leads to recovery. My goal is to share what I have learned with other abuse survivors and to teach therapists how to be more effective in the area of recovery.

An important thing to keep in mind as you read this book is there may come a point where you, as a survivor, may need the assistance of a therapist to help get you through some of the exercises. This will most likely be true with the emotional restructuring work you will be doing in Section II. Please make the choice to be kind to yourself and to seek whatever help you may need. It doesn't mean you are a weak person for asking for help. On the contrary, it reveals you have a keen awareness about yourself and one that will ultimately increase your chances of recovering.

As you go through this process an important thing to remember is not to compare or judge what happened to you with another abuse survivor. Nothing that happened to you as a child is too small or too insignificant not to be considered harmful. All that matters is how it impacted you. It's like the fairy tale about the lion that got a thorn stuck in his foot and in a place he couldn't reach. Even though the thorn wasn't a very big one, it still caused the lion a great deal of pain and suffering. All he could focus on was how bad he felt and on getting someone to pull the thorn out so the pain would stop. In the end, if the thorn, even though very small, wasn't pulled out it would have festered, become infected and would have eventually killed the poor lion.

This is how childhood abuse, neglect and trauma work. No matter how big or how small the abuse, it will eventually cause an emotional death if left to fester and get infected because it wasn't dealt with or pulled out. The size of what happened to you isn't important; it's the fact it got stuck inside of you and is breeding emotional infection and pain, causing misery and suffering.

Each abuse survivor, including you, holds their own thorn of pain deep inside of themselves. It is usually hidden so deep that no one, not even you, fully understands it. Equally true is that you also hold the answers to your own problems and pain. At this moment in time you may not be aware of exactly what the problems are or where the solutions lie, but it doesn't mean you can't find them. Through a sincere commitment to look deep inside of yourself and to know yourself intimately, you can learn to identify not only the places where you got hurt but also the path that will lead to your healing and recovery. Beware though, the path to healing may not look the way you think it should look, so be open-minded and be willing to do whatever it takes to obtain the healing you seek.

Finally, keep in mind recovery isn't always a tidy or straightforward process. It isn't always as simple as following the steps outlined in a seminar, book, or by a therapist. Many people would like to think recovery is like fording a creek with stepping-stones where one stone logically follows the next and there is steady progress being made as one crosses the creek. For most people, recovery involves taking two steps forward and then three steps backwards and then four steps forward again. The important thing is there are steps being taken in the right direction and ones that will eventually get you to the other side of the creek. So be patient with yourself and allow yourself to move through this book and your healing process at your own pace, knowing there will be strides of progress followed by momentary set backs. In the end, you will find yourself sitting in a sunny patch of grass on the other side of the creek, marveling at how you crossed the creek into a brand new world of happiness and wholeness.

SECTION I

COGNITIVE RETRAINING

Chapter 2

THE JOURNEY BEGINS

Dealing with childhood abuse, neglect and/or trauma is a very complicated task. It affects each person differently, and its effects tend to be multidimensional. Some of the effects lay on the surface for everyone to see, and some are buried so deep within that no one can see them, not even the abuse survivor. The damage is so individual that only the person who was abused, neglected and/or traumatized can fully understand the extent of it.

The healing process can only begin when you are willing to take an honest look at how the abuse affected you and how you tried to cope with it. Unfortunately, this isn't a quick or simple task. The memories and emotions are painful. Some people go for years trying to avoid the pain. They refuse to face the buried feelings and how they seep out into their adult life. Other people try to convince themselves the pain isn't important because on the surface they appear to be handling things well. Or, they try to cover up the pain with things like alcohol, gambling or food. But as time goes by they are forced to see their life isn't getting any better, only worse. Their methods of hiding aren't working because their hidden childhood wounds won't heal by themselves. They begin to notice their pain won't magically disappear with medication or by hiding in a habit or an addiction. Then the day comes when they must choose to either face what happened to them or be consumed by it. At that point, healing becomes a choice. This is true for you as well. If you choose recovery, it must involve a willingness on your part to acknowledge the depth to which the abuse impacted you.

Refusing to see how the abuse affected you and the damage it caused is nothing more than living in a world of denial. It is a place where you hide. It is a way of protecting yourself from your feelings and the truth. You become like the ostrich that buried its head in the sand, hoping no one can see you. Ironically, the only thing hidden in the sand is your ability to see yourself and your behavior, and that you are the only one who is perpetuating the abuse today by continuing to hide and hurt yourself. The same is true for the scars left behind from the abuse, neglect and/or trauma. No matter how much you try to deny or hide from them, they are there for everyone to see.

The pain, memories and scars are generally too much for any abuse survivor to carry around. So they try to hide their feelings from everyone. They become afraid of people and don't talk about what happened to them. They believe they are to blame for the abuse and for how people treated them. At some point this becomes too painful for them to carry around. The agony of their existence becomes too much to bear. The overwhelming feelings begin making their way to the surface, but they don't know what to do with them. So they try to stuff them back down inside of themselves and try to make the pain tolerable. They might start drinking or over-eating to soothe themselves. Or, they begin acting out, unconsciously hoping others will see how much they are suffering. Whatever they do it falls in the category of self-destructive behavior and on some level it's their way of crying out for help.

What was just described may be you. You may be at the point in your life where you can't continue hiding or carrying around your pain any longer. Maybe you are tired of acting out and self-destructing. So your first lesson is to learn that the self-destructive behaviors you engage in, in psychological terms, are referred to as identifiable negative responses to the abuse or what I like to call **adverse reactions**. These adverse reactions come in many sizes and shapes. There is no pattern to who chooses which unhealthy behavior. Some of the most common adverse reactions are:

- Alcoholism and drug addictions
- Eating Disorders
- Self-Mutilation
- Frequent suicide attempts
- Psychiatric problems (depression, anxiety disorders, panic attacks, Post Traumatic Stress Disorder)
- People pleasing
- Sexual addictions/promiscuity
- Underachieving.

These adverse reactions are nothing more than symptoms that you, the abuse survivor, display to the world. They are a sign that something is going on inside of you on a much deeper level. It's like having the flu.

The virus is living in your body, but it's your fever and runny nose that tells others you are sick. Thus, these adverse reactions are just symptoms and not the cause of the problem, just like the fever and runny nose are not the cause of the flu. They are the ripples in the pond, not the rock lying at the bottom of the pond.

People who know you and who live with your symptoms may think your behavior is the problem because they can't see what is hidden deep inside of you. They don't understand your self-destructive behavior is only a manifestation of the unresolved pain that festers inside of you. They can't see this is your cry for help. They don't understand this is your way of telling the world there is still a thorn stuck in your foot and you need help pulling it out. This is why your recovery is so important. Until you can face what happened to you and how it impacted you, you can't share it with anyone else or get the help you need. So your opportunity to heal and recover starts now, should you choose it.

When talking about adverse reactions, something to keep in mind is that some abuse survivors, not many, are able to cope with the abuse in what appears to be a positive manner. They don't handle their pain through self-destructive behaviors. Instead, they disconnect themselves from their pain and their emotions by becoming intellectuals, studying hard and becoming overachievers. On the surface they look successful. It seems to the casual observer that they are well-adjusted and are doing well in life. However, underneath the surface, deep in their hearts, they carry their pain and hurtful memories around just like everyone else.

Survivors who disconnect themselves from their feelings by intellectualizing don't realize they are creating additional problems for themselves and ones that are hard to rectify. By disconnecting themselves from their feelings, they are also inadvertently disconnecting themselves from people. Their capacity to experience new, positive emotions and to connect with people disappears over time. They lose their ability to emotionally connect in relationships and even friendships. Over time, they develop a type of emotional insulation that becomes impenetrable. As the emotional insulation grows, it pushes people away. It eventually gets so thick that it keeps people out and the person who is intellectualizing emotionally isolated and disconnected.

Intellectualizing and disconnecting from the pain of their abuse provides only a temporary means of escape. It only helps the feelings about the abuse disappear for a finite period of time. Then the day comes when their ability to overachieve and to intellectualize everything ends and the emotional insulation leads to nothing but isolation and emotional unrest. At this point these survivors, too, will need to face their abuse. They won't be able to continue running from what happened to them and how it made them feel. If they don't stop and look at the abuse, they, too, will become just like all other abuse survivors. They will move away from what seems like a positive means of escape and fall into a pit of self-destructive behaviors to get away from the pain that is seeping through to the surface and the loneliness that surrounds them.

The lesson here is this: No matter who you are and no matter what you have tried to do to run away from the things you suffered as a child, they will always resurface at some point in your life to give you a second chance to deal with them. If you don't deal with what happened to you, then your life will continue to be filled with one adverse reaction after another until there is nothing left but for you to look at the abuse. You can either face what happened to you now and have the rest of your life to be happy, or you can continue running and hiding for the next 20, 30 or even 40 years and still be left with the same decision to make. Have faith in yourself and love yourself enough today to choose to heal. You can do it.

ADVERSE REACTIONS AND MISPERCEPTIONS

The adverse reactions, or self-destructive behaviors, you carry around are nothing more than symptoms of a deeper, underlying problem. They cover up the memories of the abuse and how you were left feeling about yourself.

You ended up self-destructing because the abuse, neglect and/or trauma caused you to view yourself and the world differently than those who grew up in a nurturing home. It caused you to develop a very negative and distorted sense of who you are and an unhealthy set of core beliefs about who you are as a person.

Most abuse survivors who live long enough to become adults think they are to blame for everything that happened to them as a child and everything that happens in their adult life. They take everything personally. They believe they are bad and can't do anything right. They feel inadequate and different. They believe everyone is better than they are. These distorted thoughts and feelings they have about themselves are called **misperceptions**. To help you better understand this, let's look at an example of woman who developed a negative set of core beliefs and misperceptions about herself and who takes everything personally.

Martha is a 35-year-old woman. While Martha was growing up, her mother constantly criticized her. She would yell, "You are stupid and can't do anything right. I don't know why I even bother with you. You won't ever amount to anything. You're just a dumb girl who can't think for herself."

Each time Martha heard her mother yelling these words, her heart broke with sadness. She felt unlovable and inadequate. It made her wonder what her life would amount to if she were truly stupid.

As the years passed, Martha began believing the things her mother had said to her. So she dropped out of high school and got a minimum wage job working in a restaurant. She didn't have any friends and didn't go out to meet people because she believed everyone was better than her.

Then one day at the restaurant, Martha met a man named Larry. For both of them it was love at first sight. Larry asked Martha out on a date and they became the best of friends. Martha really liked being around Larry because he was always telling her, "You are so special to me. I really love you. You are so smart and beautiful. I really enjoy being with you so much. One day I will spend the rest of my life with you."

Two years later, Martha and Larry got married and had several children.

Then one day Larry went to work and had an argument with his boss because of a negative performance review. He felt he was being unfairly judged. By the end of the day, Larry was tired and grouchy. He was also embarrassed and wondered how he was going to tell Martha he didn't get the raise they so desperately needed.

Larry drove home and walked into the house acting as if everything was fine. Martha, not knowing what kind of a day Larry had, greeted him with a smile and asked him a benign question about the flickering light in the refrigerator. Larry just looked at her in a frustrated manner and yelled in a short, gruff tone of voice, "What's the matter with you? Can't you handle anything by yourself? Can't you see I've worked hard all day and don't need you playing stupid and not being able to think for yourself?"

Martha just stood there bewildered and crying. She didn't understand what had just happened. She didn't know why Larry was yelling at her. She ran into her bedroom and emotionally fell apart. She wanted to crawl up in a ball and disappear.

So the question becomes, "What happened to Martha and why did she respond this way?"

The first thing that happened was this: The things Larry had screamed at Martha reminded her of all the things her mother had said to her when she was a little girl. This tapped into her negative thoughts and feelings about herself (misperceptions) and the negative set of core beliefs she learned as a child. It reminded her of how she felt stupid and inadequate. Because Martha believed everything her mother had said about her, she took what Larry said personally. She made the entire situation about her. She believed Larry said those things because she had done something wrong. So, in essence, what Martha did was take Larry's mood and his words, mixed them with how she already felt about herself and then turned the situation into something personal. She made herself out to be inadequate rather than stepping back to see that Larry acted the way he did because of something that was going on with him—because of his negative performance review and not getting his raise.

Let's stop here for a moment to summarize what has been covered so far. People with a distorted, negative set of core beliefs feel they are to blame for everything that happens. They take everything personally, don't feel as if they are as good as everyone else, and feel needy (misperceptions). To cover up how they feel about themselves and the pain they endured as a child, they fall into myriad self-destructive behaviors (adverse reactions), such as alcoholism, gambling, etc. This pattern of behavior looks something like this:

Misperceptions (What you *think and feel* inside) lead to ⟶
Blame yourself for everything
Take everything personally
Don't feel as if you are as good as everyone else
Feel needy for love and attention, etc.

Adverse Reactions (What you show to the world)
Alcoholism
Addictions
Depression
Anger Problems
Eating disorders, etc.

So the question becomes, "How and why did you develop the distorted thoughts and feelings in the first place?"

To answer this, you have to go back to an earlier time in your life and understand a little bit about child development. Until about the age of 11 or 12 everyone is neurologically wired to operate out of what is called a state of **egocentricity**. The concept of egocentricity was developed by a Swiss scientist named Jean Piaget. The word ego means self and centricity means central. Piaget stated in numerous writings that children tend to view the world from their own perspective and thus have a difficult time seeing things from someone else's perspective. This means that as a child you thought, observed, and regarded yourself as the object of all of your experiences. You saw yourself as the center of the universe and believed everything that happened in your world was because of you. Obviously these weren't conscious but unconscious thoughts. For example, if your Mom or Dad lost their job you believed it was because "I was a bad little girl/boy." If your Mom got a promotion, it was because "I was a good little girl/boy." If your Mom and Dad got a divorce, it was because "I was a bad little girl/boy." To take this one step further, "If my Mom or Dad beat me, sexually abuse me, or neglect me then I must be a bad little girl/boy."

Children make the assumption that their parents and other perpetrators abuse them because of who they are as a person, because of their worth as an individual and because of what they did or did not do (their behavior). They don't understand they didn't cause the abuse, neglect and/or trauma to happen. They can't see the abuse was about the people who hurt them, and not about them because they aren't neurologically able to do so.

Children operate out of a state of egocentricity and believe the abuse is somehow their fault. This belief alone is enough to cause deep emotional wounds, and ones that can be carried into adulthood; ones that can be acted out through adverse reactions. However, there is something else that complicates things even further. It is that of **being given the responsibility but without the authority***.

It is very common for abusive and neglectful parents to assign their children the role of being responsible for things that as children they have no control over and no authority to change. However, they aren't usually aware they are doing this. They give their children this responsibility because this is what their parents had done with them when they were growing up. They learned to be this way from their parents.

Children who are abused are frequently given the responsibility to step in and take care of family members when a parent is unable, or refuses to do so themselves. In some situations they are expected to care for the abusive parent and/or their siblings.

Let's look at an example with Kathy who is a five-year-old girl. Her step-father is an alcoholic. Domestic violence is rampant in Kathy's family. Kathy's mother takes out her frustrations on her by physically abusing her. Because Kathy's mother is so caught up in her own abusive relationship with her alcoholic husband, she assigns Kathy the role of rescuing her when the fighting becomes too explosive. She also gives Kathy the responsibility of making sure her younger brothers are safe and taken care of, as are the household chores. However, when Kathy tries to protect and take care of her mother and brothers, tries to make her step-father stop drinking, or tries to make the fighting stop, she is unable to do so. She wants to do what has been asked of her and to fulfill the role her mother assigned her, but she isn't capable of doing so because she is just a child who doesn't have the authority to make the needed changes in her family. Kathy's inability to make the bad things stop causes her to feel helpless and ineffective. It causes her to begin developing a number of misperceptions (distorted thoughts and feelings) about herself. She begins to believe she is worthless and can't do anything right. Unfortunately for Kathy, she will eventually carry these misperceptions into her adult life and they will shape who she is as an adult. She will likely try to cover up the negative feelings she has about herself with some type of adverse reaction (alcohol, drugs, food, etc).

Like Kathy, many people who were abused develop an overwhelming number of misperceptions about themselves and the world they live in as a result of egocentricity and being given the responsibility without the authority. Some of the most common misperceptions are:

- I am to blame for everything that happened in our family and everything that happens in the world.
- I am not good enough/ I am bad.
- I have to do what I can to keep people happy. This will keep them from getting mad at me and will ensure that they like me.
- I am defective somehow.
- I can't trust anyone, if I did I would get hurt again.
- If anything bad is going to happen, it will happen to me.
- I can't let anyone see how I feel or know my pain.
- I have to be perfect.
- It's not safe to let anyone close to me.
- I have to keep the past a secret.

Let's take a moment to put all of this together. The abuse, neglect and/or trauma you endured as a child was filtered through your belief that you were to blame for everything that happened to you and your family (egocentricity) and the fact that you were given the responsibility to change things but without the authority do so. Because you felt responsible for the things that happened and couldn't make things change, you began feeling badly about yourself. You began feeling frustrated, incapable and unlovable. You began telling yourself negative things about yourself and believed them to be true (misperceptions). As the years passed and you became an adult, those distorted thoughts and feelings about yourself became too much to bear. So you acted your feelings out and/or fell into a cycle of self-destructive behaviors (adverse reactions). To you, this was your only way of letting the world know of your pain. It was your unconscious cry for help.

The following diagram has been provided to help you better understand the complete cycle:

Child abuse, neglect, and trauma are filtered through

Egocentricity and **being given
the responsibility but without the authority** lead to ———

Misperceptions (What you think and feel inside) lead to ———
Blame yourself for everything
Take everything personally
Don't feel as if you are as good as everyone else
Feel needy for love and attention, etc.

Adverse Reactions (What you show to the world)
Alcoholism
Addictions
Depression
Anger Problems
Eating disorders, etc.

Incorporated into this book are several sets of exercises. They were designed to help you develop an intimate knowledge of yourself and to help you connect with yourself in a way you may never have thought possible. The next page contains the first exercise. Please complete Exercise A before reading any further.

Exercise A:

Adverse Reactions and Misperceptions
Egocentricity and Responsibility Without the Authority

Take a moment and think about the following questions and answer them to the best of your ability:

1. What adverse reactions do I maintain today as a result of my childhood, i.e. alcohol abuse, addictions, eating disorders, depression, gambling, promiscuity, workaholic, perfectionism, etc.?

Depression, perfectionism
workaholic,

2. What misperceptions (distorted thoughts/feelings) do I maintain today as a result of my childhood?

Take everything personally, feel
worthless, take on blame
do what I can to keep the place,
I have to be perfect, don't let anyone
Too close, take the blame

3. What caused you to develop the misperceptions you maintain today?

Alot was due to responsibility w/o
authority. Sexual abuse,
emotional abuse, verbal abuse
and the total lack of nuturing

4. As a child what did you feel you were to blame for, i.e. parent's divorce, being abused, not being paid attention to, moving around a lot, being criticized , etc.?

Not keeping my sisters in
line so that they would be
good + quiet and we could
disappear - not be noticed.

5. What responsibilities, but without the authority, were you given as a child, i.e. to make your mom stop drinking, to make your dad stop hitting your mom, to take care of your siblings, etc.?

To take care of my sisters,
to make sure they behaved.
Later, to keep the house, cook,
grocery shop, laundry, baby sit
to try to protect them from
my father.

6. What were the things that happened to you as a child that caused you to feel bad about yourself?

Sexual abuse caused shame, made
me feel different. Witness physical
abuse to Maryan + couldn't stop it,
witnessed sexual abuse to Sister
and couldn't stop it. Verbal abuse
to self + sister.

7. How were you abused, neglected and/or traumatized?

Sexual abuse + molestation.
Lack of love, threats, made to
watch physical + moral abuse
to sister; never allowed to talk
or go out except to school.
Verbal abuse, humiliated
publicly and alone.

RECREATING VS. OVERCOMPENSATING

A large segment of our society is made up of people who have suffered some form of abuse, neglect and/or trauma. In order for the cycle of abuse to be broken and for our society as a whole to stop self-destructing, each abuse survivor must take on the responsibility of looking at the misperceptions they developed as a result of the abuse and to then deal with the abuse itself.

When abuse survivors fall into a lifestyle of self-destruction rather than looking at what happened to them and changing what they believe about themselves they perpetuate the cycle of abuse. When they don't resolve the misperceptions they developed as children, and still maintain as adults, they end up either **recreating** what happened to them as a child or **overcompensating** for it. It has been my experience as a therapist that people who hold onto the abuse emotionally tend to recreate it, while those who intellectualize the abuse tend to overcompensate. It is important to keep in mind that recreating and overcompensating are unconscious acts.

Recreating happens when you repeat, in your own family, the abuse you received as a child while overcompensating means you do the exact opposite of what your parents did to you. Let's look at an example of someone who re-creates.

Betty grew up in a family where she was constantly told she would never amount to anything and was berated by her parents. Every time she tried to prove her parents wrong and tried something new, she was told, "Why do you keep trying to do things? Don't you know by now you will fail at anything you try? You just aren't good at anything. You just need to get married and let a man take care of you."

By the time Betty became a teenager, she didn't think she could do anything right. So she started skipping school, hanging out with the wrong crowd and was frequently suspended from school for truancy.

As an adult, Betty married a man who could only perform manual labor jobs. She didn't work, but instead stayed at home with her three children. They could barely afford to support their children, much less themselves. Eventually, Betty and her family ended up on welfare.

Betty's life turned out like it did because she believed all the things her parents had instilled in her as a child and all the misperceptions she subsequently developed about herself. She carried those misperceptions about herself into her adult life and ultimately fulfilled the expectations her parents set before her.

As Betty's children grew up, she did with them what her parents had done with her. She re-created her childhood by degrading her children, never encouraging them to do well in school and constantly telling them they would never get ahead in life.

If Betty had been a survivor who overcompensated rather than re-created her childhood, she would have developed a strong determination to do just the opposite of what her parents had done with her. No matter what, she would have encouraged her children to do well in school and may have even pushed them a little too hard at times. It would have been her primary goal to make sure that her children believed in themselves and their lives turned out better than hers did.

Let's look at one more example. As a child, Bill's father violently beat him when he misbehaved. Bill wasn't allowed to participate in school activities, have friends over to his house or go out on dates. As an adult, Bill could have chosen to re-create his childhood by beating his own children when they misbehaved and by keeping them socially isolated. Or, he could have overcompensated by allowing his children to run free without any form of discipline whatsoever.

Recreating and overcompensating perpetuates the cycle of abuse being passed down from one generation to the next. This cycle will persist until each and every abuse survivor makes the commitment to do whatever it takes to heal from their own childhood wounds and to complete their recovery process. Then and only then will they be able to walk down the middle of the road called compromise and structure, which lies between re-creation and overcompensation.

It is also worth mentioning there is one other way a survivor can re-create their past. Most therapists have been aware of this form of recreating for a long time, but it was Harville Hendrix who actually wrote a book about it, "Getting the Love You Want"(Henry Holt and Company, LLC, 1988). What will be provided to you is my perception of how this form of recreating goes back to childhood abuse, neglect and/or trauma.

This second form of recreating involves the people you choose to be in relationships with or to marry. It interferes with your relationships and creates an unstable basis for partnering and marriage. It is also much more prevalent than you might think. It is happening in rapid succession these days because of the level of dysfunction and the volume of child abuse that is so rampant in today's society.

Children who are abused tend to grow up into adults who have many unresolved issues and many needs that were never met, such as the need to be loved and cared for. So when they grow up, they tend to seek out partners who they think can love them and meet their needs. However, what usually happens is they choose people who have the same traits as their abusive parents, but they don't recognize these traits until after they are married.

You might be wondering why anyone would do such a thing. The answer is quite simple, yet complicated and sad. Most abuse survivors marry people who are just like their parents as an unconscious means of having another opportunity to resolve the issues they didn't get to resolve when they were growing up; to get the love they never got; and to get their unmet childhood needs met. Unfortunately, this doesn't work and their needs remain unmet. After the marriage fails, they look for someone else to meet those same needs and keep marrying the same people over and over again, hoping things will be different. Thus, the cycle of recreating persists.

When the survivor realizes the person they married is incapable of healing their buried childhood wounds their relationship will either end or they will seek help. Most survivors end up in one dysfunctional relationship after another, thinking it is simply a matter of not having met the right person. They don't understand that they will never meet the right person as long as they are unconsciously looking for their parents. This will always be the case for them and for you until you make the choice to go back and resolve the original issues with the original people who hurt you. The cycle of interacting with and marrying people who are just like your parents/perpetrators will continue until you break the cycle. Your wounds cannot be healed by a partner, no matter how wonderful he/she may be, because they were not the creator of your wounds. The cycle can only be broken by you and by you dealing with the people who hurt you as a child.

Going back to the original cause of your wounds, and going back to the misperceptions created by the abuse, neglect and/or trauma is the only way to recovery. Recovery requires hard work, but it is undoubtedly the most important work you will ever do for yourself.

To help you better understand if you recreate or overcompensate for your childhood, please turn the page and complete Exercise B.

Exercise B:

Recreating and Overcompensating

Take a moment and think about the following questions and answer them to the best of your ability:

1. Do you recreate or overcompensate, and how?

I overcompensated - I vowed not to be like my parents and was just the opposite, I didn't & couldn't understand that discipline & abuse are not the same.

2. What type of people do you choose to have relationships with? Describe them.

my first husband & Frank were both abusive, sexually and verbally. - like my father, Glenn was more like my mother, unable to handle life unable to lead.

3. What negative characteristics do your partners/spouses have in common and list them. *Billy & Frank / sometimes Glenn*

Sexually abusive, demanding, demeaning, lack of motivation, unable to be supportive, selfish

4. What issues are you trying to resolve from your past with your partner?

Being nurtured, having someone to depend on

5. What unmet needs are you trying to get met?

To be loved, unconditionally to be taken care of to have someone else carry the burdens and worries

6. How are you recreating or overcompensating your childhood with your partner?

I overcompensate by trying to be all things

7. What kind of a partner would you choose if you were NOT recreating or overcompensating?

Someone that would be a partner in all things. Someone to share with, that was emotionally stable

Chapter 3

The Basics

EVERYTHING MENTIONED THUS FAR has centered around the abuse you endured, how it impacted you and how you dealt with it. You now understand how the abuse created misperceptions in your mind about who you were as a child and how you have tried to cope with the abuse and negative core beliefs through adverse reactions and/or self-destructive behaviors. You have learned that the way your parents treated you shaped how you thought and felt about yourself, and how it still does even though you are now an adult. You also know that your parents either recreated or overcompensated what happened to them and that you are doing the same with your family today.

Equally true is the fact that you watched your family as they tried to cope with their dysfunction through their own set of adverse reactions, such as domestic violence, alcoholism or physical/emotional/sexual abuse. Consequently, when you became older the only coping skills you possessed were the ones you had learned from your family. The only way you knew how to deal with what happened to you was by acting out or hiding in those same self-destructive behaviors your family had maintained.

What is different now is that you are an adult. You now have the right to do something different with your life. You have the right to heal and to let go of your past. The decision is now yours. So the questions become: Do you want to continue recreating and/or overcompensating for what happened to you as a child? Do you want to treat your family the way your parents treated you? Do you want to maintain the misperceptions you developed as a result of the abuse, neglect and/or trauma you sustained? Do you want to continue hiding behind your self-destructive behaviors (adverse reactions)? If not, then make the decision right now to do something different and then allow this decision to be one of many steps toward your healing and recovery.

Recovery begins with you learning the things you should have been taught as a child and the things that would have made being an adult easier and more understandable; learning the lessons that would have prepared you for life in general. Thus, your education begins with you learning how to identify the way you respond to your world, who is in control of your life, and what role you tend to play with other people.

Your job is to study and learn the concepts presented, and then to incorporate them into your daily life. It won't be enough just to be exposed to these concepts. You will have to understand and live by them. You will need to apply them to your daily life so you can see and understand your behavior and why you maintain that behavior. So you can understand yourself and begin recognizing how you interact with your world and the people in your world. Only then will you know who you are as a person. Without this knowledge you will never be able to change your behavior or change what you don't like about yourself. You will never be able to let go of your past and the impact it has had on you.

Take a moment and ask yourself these questions, "How can I change something I'm not aware of? How can I change what I don't like about myself unless I am willing to replace it with something I do like and then practice it?"

The answer is, you can't. Imagine someone being abused for 18 years and it taking them another 20 years to get into therapy and/or recovery. That is 38 years worth of habits and learned behavior they have to dissect and then change. The only way that person can successfully do this is through a conscious effort and daily practice. The more they, and you the abuse survivor, practice your new behaviors the greater chance you will have of succeeding and of being free from your past.

THE FOUR BASIC CONCEPTS

As children grow up, they rely on their parents to teach them certain truths, certain facts about life and certain concepts to live by. They rely on their parents to love them and to teach them how to take care of themselves. They depend on them to teach them how to solve problems and how to think and fend for themselves in difficult situations.

What parents teach their children will ultimately shape how they view themselves, the world around them and the people they come in contact with. It will determine whether they will be able to respond to the world in a constructive, appropriate way or in one that is reactive and/or self-destructive.

For children who grow up in positive, functional families, the truths they are taught allow them to know and feel they are all right and so is everyone else. They understand they are good people and deserve the good things in life. They feel confident in their ability to take care of themselves. They view themselves and the world positively. They believe they can change things they don't like about their lives. They believe things happen for a reason and can trust what people say and do.

These truths their parents taught them are called the **four basic concepts** *. Summarized the four basic concepts state:

1. I am a good person;
2. The world is a trustworthy place;
3. There is order in the universe (there is a reason why things happen and that reason is ordered);
4. I have a certain amount of invulnerability (things happen to other people, not to me).

Children who were taught these truths are the fortunate ones. They were the ones who had parents who were consistent with their love and affection. Their parents were generous with their nurturing and protection, and communicated how they felt about their children regularly and in a positive manner. They sheltered their children from fighting and/or negative behavior. Most importantly, they allowed their children to test the world without harsh consequences. In the end, these children grow up into adults who like themselves and have the ability to successfully interact with the world.

Unfortunately, not all children come from loving homes where the parents are consistent and nurturing, where they can be taught the four basic concepts. On the contrary, a large percentage of today's children and adults are abuse survivors who grew up in homes where they were abused, neglected and/or traumatized. They didn't have the opportunity, or the parents who could teach them how to survive more effectively in their world. They didn't have the love and/or attention they needed to believe they are good people and deserve to be loved. On the contrary, they were taught that standing up for themselves was unacceptable and speaking their truth was even more unconscionable. They came to believe they were helpless and powerless because nothing they did was effective. They were taught that people and situations cannot be trusted. They ended up confused because the rules of the family changed from one day to the next. They were taught every one else in their life was in control and they had no control at all.

So the question becomes, "Why couldn't the parents who were

abusing, neglecting and/or traumatizing their children teach or instill in them the same basic concepts functional parents teach their children?" The answer is this: The abusive parents probably came from abusive families themselves. They likely came from families who didn't know the four basic concepts or what a child should be taught in order to ensure success in them as adults. Because their parents were never taught the four basic concepts, they couldn't pass them on to their children. As a result, the cycle of defeat and abuse continued.

Abuse survivors who were never taught the four basic concepts usually suffer from low self-esteem, don't trust people, take everything personally, don't believe there is a rhyme or reason for why things happen, and believe that if something bad is going to happen it will happen to them. They feel incapable of dealing with the world on its terms and still operate out of a state of egocentricity (believing everything is about them and is their fault). Even in adulthood, they still feel helpless. They still don't feel they have control over their world because they don't understand the rules or the concepts of life.

Despite the fact that as an abuse survivor you probably weren't taught these basic concepts, and your parents weren't taught them either, it isn't too late to learn them now. It is never too late to learn these concepts and to apply them. For that matter, it isn't too late to learn any of the concepts in this book or to begin your journey of healing.

The goal, now that you are in recovery, is to learn the four basic concepts and to understand them so you can incorporate them into your life and change your view of yourself and the world around you. Your first opportunity to do this is located on the next page. Please complete Exercise C before reading any further.

Exercise C:

The Four Basic Concepts

Step I: Evaluate which of the four basic concepts you feel you learned as a child and circle them:
  1. I am a good person;
  2. The world is a trustworthy place;
  3. There is order in the universe (there is a reason why things happened and that reasoned is ordered;
  4. I have a certain amount of invulnerability (things happen to other people, not to me).

Write out how they manifest in your daily adult life:
*Example: I interact well with people because I **trust** them.*

_____

_____

_____

_____

_____

_____

_____

_____

Step II: Circle the concepts you don't feel you learned as a child:
  1. I am a good person;
  2. The world is a trustworthy place;
  3. There is order in the universe (there is a reason why things happened and that reasoned is ordered);
  4. I have a certain amount of invulnerability (things happen to other people, not to me).

Write out how not learning these concepts has impacted your life.
Example: I don't interact well with people because I don't trust them.
I feel scared and lonely all the time because I am afraid of people.

_____

_____

_____

_____

_____

_____

_____

_____

_____

_____

Step III: Think about and then write out how those things in Step II would change if you could learn the basic concepts you didn't learn as a child. Would you feel differently? Would you view the world more positively? Would you trust more?

_____

_____

_____

_____

_____

_____

_____

_____

EXTERNAL VS. INTERNAL LOCUS OF CONTROL

Have you ever wondered why some people seem so together, and act as if nothing bothers or upsets them? And then there are those who seem to be affected by every little thing that happens to them. An explanation for this can be found in a concept developed by Julian Rotter, a psychologist, in the 1950s. Even though his declaration that each of us operates out of either an Internal or External Locus of Control originated such a long time ago, it is still very applicable today. It is an essential concept to the recovery process and one that needs to be learned and practiced in each survivor's life. The important thing to remember about one's locus of control is that it is belief system.

A person who operates out of an **external locus of control** believes they have to rely on people and situations outside of themselves to make them feel good about themselves inside: a boss giving them a compliment; winning a prestigious award; or having their spouse lavish them with constant attention. Without this positive attention from other people, they experience low self-esteem and question their self-worth. They believe they aren't a good person and there is no worth to their life.

People with an external locus of control also believe they don't have control over their life or what happens to them. If something unpleasant or harmful is happening to them, they don't feel as if they have the ability or power to change it or to make it stop. They believe if something bad is going to happen, it will happen to them. They believe everyone else is okay but they are not.

This person's daily life tends to be filled with many emotional peaks and valleys. Let's look at Joe as an example. Like any ordinary day, Joe gets up and goes to work first thing in the morning. As he walks in the door of his office his boss starts clapping his hands and complimenting him. His boss then turns around to the rest of the office and announces Joe has been elected employee of the month. Because of Joe's new-found status at work, he believes he is a valuable member of his work team. Thus, his day starts off with him feeling good about himself. He feels wonderful and like life is grand. However, at lunch, someone shoots a jealous look at Joe and makes a snide comment about him. Because Joe operates out of an external locus of control his feelings of elation are replaced with self-doubt. Depression begins setting in. At the end of the work day, Joe receives a call that he has won the church raffle. He smiles and believes he is lucky. Thus, he starts climbing the self-esteem ladder once again with positive feelings about himself. On his way home, Joe can't wait to tell his wife about his award and winning the raffle. However, when he walks in the door he finds his wife upset about the bills. Joe begins to blame himself for their financial problems and believes his wife is doing the same, even though she isn't. Thus begins his spiral back down the self-esteem ladder and his depression returns.

This example helps illustrate how people who operate out of an external locus of control usually feel ungrounded. It also shows how the events in their everyday life cause them to bounce around emotionally and leaves them feeling emotionally out of control.

On the other hand, there are people who operate out of an **internal locus of control**. They tend to be the exact opposite of those who operate out of an external locus of control. They rely only on themselves, not people or situations, to make them feel good about themselves. They feel in control of their lives and believe they can change anything they don't like about it. They believe they are okay and so is everyone else. They are convinced good things can and will happen to them. And, if something negative happens, they believe they have the power and ability to accept it and/or make something good come out of it. They also understand they have the ability to seek out resources, if necessary, to deal with any negative situations more effectively. They tend to be very centered and grounded. They rely only upon themselves to meet their needs, thus they take responsibility for themselves and their actions.

You might be wondering, "How do the loci of control apply to someone who was abused, neglected and/or traumatized?"

Most people who were abused, neglected and/or traumatized as children tend to operate out of an external locus of control. They rely on others to make them feel good about themselves and to feel safe. They look to other people to meet their need for love and attention. Their feelings get hurt easily because they take everything personally. They avoid confrontation because they don't believe they can handle it without feeling frightened or falling apart emotionally. They believe everyone else is always doing great, is making the best out of their lives and is always feeling good about themselves. They believe they can't speak their truth or stand up for themselves because they might hurt someone else's feelings. And, if they hurt someone else's feelings they will end up being abandoned. They see everyone else as having power and control, and they have neither.

One of the biggest problems with an abuse survivor operating out of an external locus of control is it greatly interferes with their ability to recover. They believe the pain of their wounds is so deep and so hurtful that they can't recover unless someone helps them. They fear they will be consumed by their pain if they are left to look at it and feel it by themselves. In essence, they still feel as if they are the small, helpless child who needs a parent to take care of them, to make the pain stop and to show them how to be okay. Without realizing it, they want this parent figure to rescue them and take care of them, as their parents should have done when they were a child. So they pick someone they feel safe with and then assign them the responsibility of taking care of them while they heal; responsibility for loving them through the recovery process; and responsibility for nurturing them when the pain gets to be too much. The problem becomes this: They are so busy looking to the other person to meet their needs that it prevents them from looking at themselves and their own pain. Thus, they can't get their eyes on themselves long enough to face what happened in their childhood so they can recover.

Until you, the survivor, deal with what happened to you as a child and look to yourself for comforting and parenting, you will never find the resolution you are looking for in relation to your childhood. The irony of all of this is there is a part of you who believes you need to be rescued, but somewhere inside there is also a voice telling you that you have the ability to do what it takes to recover, to face your past and to take care of yourself. Listen to the latter voice that is inside of you because it is right.

Finally, it is important for you to identify which locus of control you primarily operate out of. It will help you to understand how you see yourself and the world around you. It will tell you if you believe and feel as if you are in control of your life or if you believe and feel you are being controlled.

One of the primary purposes of this book is to help you to identify which locus of control you are operating out of and to help you develop an internal locus of control. It is through the internal locus of control that you will learn to understand that you, not your past, your parents, or anyone else, is in charge of you; and no one is responsible for how your life turns out except you. You are no longer the child who is being abused, neglected or traumatized, but an adult who can take control of your life and heal. So turn to the next page and continue your recovery process by completing Exercise D. Please complete the exercise before reading any further.

Exercise D:

External vs. Internal Locus of Control

Step I: As you go through your day, start noticing in what situations you are operating out of an External Locus of Control (ELOC) vs. an Internal Locus of Control (ILOC). Write down a brief description of each situation as it occurs and then circle which locus of control you are operating out of. Then write a brief note about how it felt to operate out of that locus of control.

Situation 1:
Description of event:

_____

_____

_____

_____ ILOC / ELOC

How it felt:

_____

_____

_____

Situation 2:
Description of event:

_____

_____

_____ ILOC / ELOC

How it felt:

_____

_____

_____

Situation 3:
Description of event:

_____

_____

_____

_____ ILOC / ELOC

How it felt:

_____

_____

_____

_____

Step II: At the end of each day, review the list. In the situations where you operated out of the ELOC, ask yourself this question, "What could I have done differently so I could have operated out of an ILOC" and write it down.

_____

_____

_____

_____

_____

_____

Step III: Take a moment and think about whether you have assigned other people in your life responsibility for your recovery and for rescuing you. Then write down who those people are and how you are wanting them to rescue you.

_____

_____

_____

_____

_____

_____

Step IV: Take a moment and think about how you can take charge of your own recovery process and rescue yourself. Then write down how you think you can achieve this.

_____

_____

_____

_____

_____

_____

_____

_____

_____

_____

TRANSACTIONAL ANALYSIS

If you operate out of an external locus of control and want to understand why you need people to rescue you, why you want them to take care of you, and why you assign them responsibility for your recovery, then you need to study and understand the concept of Transactional Analysis.

Eric Berne, a world renowned psychologist, developed Transactional Analysis to help people understand what roles they play with each other, and the purpose those roles serve. He called the roles people play **ego states**. Everyone in life operates out of a particular ego state. There is one primary ego state each person identifies with and one that matches who they feel they are as a person deep inside themselves. Thus, they tend to operate out of that ego state most of the time. However, occasions arise, such as during difficult or stressful situations where someone may move from one ego state to another and may play several different roles at one time.

There are also those who feel as if they are one ego state inside themselves but they portray a different ego state to the world. They usually do this as a means of hiding their true thoughts and feelings from other people. They do it to protect themselves from getting hurt. Picture a person who goes to a party and tries to convince everyone they are extroverted by being the life of the party and acting like a social butterfly. However, deep inside themselves they are really shy, introverted and feel terribly uncomfortable in large crowds of people. The extroversion is done as a means of protecting the fragile person who hides inside of them. It keeps people from teasing them about being shy.

It is important to understand that Eric Berne developed the concept of Transactional Analysis, but I have changed parts of it to coincide with the way I see the recovery process and how it relates to childhood abuse, neglect and trauma. I have modified the meanings of the ego states and what they represent.

The first ego state, or role a person can play, is called the **Parent** (**P**). The parent ego state is the thinking part of ourselves we developed as children. There are two parts to the parent ego state: the critical parent and the chronic caregiver.

People who operate out of the critical parent ego state tend to berate and criticize other people. They constantly think and verbalize critical thoughts, such as "She's no good. He's too fat and ugly. She'll never amount to anything. Why can't she do anything right? He's just plain stupid."

The problem with people who operate out of this critical parent ego state is they don't only criticize other people but they also maintain a critical internal dialogue about themselves. They say, "I'm no good. I'm too fat and ugly. I'll never amount to anything. I can't do anything right. I'm just plain stupid."

The person who maintains this ego state usually has an issue with control and low self-esteem. As a child, they didn't feel as if they could control anything that was happening to them. They couldn't make the abuse stop, make their uncle stop criticizing them, make mom and dad stop fighting or stop the divorce. This left them feeling helpless and worthless—as if they couldn't affect or change anything happening in their life. They lived with this feeling of helplessness and worthlessness throughout their childhood until it slowly mutated into frustration and low self-esteem. By the time they became an adult they felt a need to control themselves and everyone around them so they could control how they felt and prevent them feeling helpless and worthless again. Being critical and degrading is the weapon they discovered they could wield to obtain and maintain this needed control over people and situations in their life.

Criticizing and degrading other people makes the survivor who operates out of the critical parent ego state not only feel as if they are in control but also superior. They believe, unconsciously, that if they can make other people look and feel bad about themselves, then it will make them look and feel good about themselves. To them, it dispels whatever lack of control they felt as a child and the negative comments made to them by their parents or caregivers. The message, "you are worthless" magically fades away.

What they don't understand is that it is only temporary. It only lasts until the next critical and berating comment can be made. Thus, a cycle is born in which this survivor only feels good about him/herself as long as they are putting someone else down.

Lets look at an example of someone who plays the critical parent ego state as a means of maintaining control.

When Brett was growing up, his father constantly berated him. He told him, "You are worthless and will never amount to anything. I don't know why I couldn't have had a son who had an ounce of common sense and who could think for himself."

Brett wanted to tell his father he was wrong, but he was afraid of him. His fear was justified as he watched his father beat on his mother. He was afraid the day would come when his father would hit him, too.

Brett tried his best to be a good son and to be smart. He tried to be strong, but ended up feeling helpless as he watched his father beat his mother. As he stood there feeling powerless, he became angry and then remembered what his father had told him, "You are worthless and will never amount to anything". In Brett's mind his father was already right. After all, he couldn't save his mother from the horrible beatings.

Brett carried his anger and his father's critical words into his adult life. At the age of 30 Brett married a lovely woman, named Cindy. Brett really loved her, but soon learned he had difficulty being the person he wanted to be when he was around her, especially when they were arguing. Their marriage was filled with a lot of financial stressors. Brett felt responsible for the financial difficulties and wondered, "Why can't I seem to get ahead of these bills?"

As he pondered this question, his father's words, "You are worthless" began playing over and over in his mind again.

As Brett remembered his father's words, he remembered how worthless he felt as a child and how he still felt that way as an adult. However, instead of recognizing what was going on with himself, Brett took out his frustrations on Cindy. Each time Brett and Cindy started talking about their finances, he would criticize her, put her down, and would tell her, "You are a lousy wife. I don't know how I ever ended up with you. Why can't you do something to make things better?"

As the years passed, Brett continued criticizing Cindy about their finances and then about everything she did. Nothing she did was right or good enough. Then the day came when they had an argument and Brett snapped. He began degrading Cindy again and then became so rageful that he slapped her. As he hit Cindy, his father's words rang in his head once again. He saw himself as he had seen his father, as an abuser. Brett didn't like what was happening to him but he didn't understand it either. He didn't understand he was recreating his childhood and was acting out of the critical parent ego state. He only understood that Cindy didn't spend a penny of their money as long as he was criticizing and hitting her. Thus, he was the one who was in control.

Brett controlled Cindy by constantly criticizing and hitting her. As long as he could maintain this needed control, he could feel good about himself and as if his life was manageable. He could maintain the role of the parent in this relationship and be the one who was in charge. In Brett's mind his behavior was normal and would keep him from getting hurt by his wife. After all, he had learned this from his father as he watched his father do the same thing with his mother.

THE BASICS   3 7

The second aspect of the parent ego state is the **chronic caregiver**. The chronic caregiver part of the parent ego state has nothing to do with control. Instead, it has to do with responsibility. Some children who were abused, neglected and/or traumatized were given the responsibility of taking care of a parent, a sibling, or someone else. They were given the responsibility of cleaning up after their alcoholic mother, throwing out the liquor bottles and then making sure Mom's boss knew she would be out of work because she was "sick". They were given the responsibility of taking care of their baby brother, fixing his breakfast, getting him off to school, and helping him with his homework because no one else was around to do so. Because their mother was off carousing at a local bar, they were given the responsibility of taking care of an ailing father who had terminal lung cancer. Whatever the case may have been, this child was placed in the role of being the caretaker.

Unfortunately, many of these children grow up to become chronic caretakers and only feel good about themselves when they are functioning in this role. The problem with this role is that their lives are filled with guilt and a sense of over-responsibility that usually last a lifetime unless looked at carefully. They don't stop to think about their own needs and usually end up ignoring themselves and their own basic needs.   Thus, they usually end up marrying someone who needs to be taken care of and they perpetuate the cycle they grew up in.

The second ego state is called the **Child** (**C**). The child ego state is the feeling part of ourselves we developed as a child, not the thinking part. The thinking part only pertains to the parent ego state.

The child ego state is also made up of many components but we will focus only on two them. The first is called the **defiant teenager**.

Have you ever met someone who gets frustrated easily and then has a temper tantrum, even though they are an adult? If so, you have met someone who plays the defiant teenager part of the child ego state.

Just imagine how a defiant adolescent acts and you have the defiant teenager. They tend to deal with situations through anger, hostility and defiance. They have emotional and physical temper tantrums. They feel the need to always get their way but have difficulty communicating what their needs are. They have difficulty putting their feelings into words. They believe they have to constantly be in a defensive mode to ensure no one hurts them first. They tend to be difficult to work out problems with because they see talking about problems as a means of pointing a blaming finger.   In their mind, they have to point the finger first in an effort to keep others from hurting them. They don't feel safe so they don't talk about things but act them out instead. They don't feel safe enough to speak their truth, but hope people can decipher what they are saying through their actions.

An example of someone who operates out of the defiant teenager ego would be John, a 34-year-old man. As a little boy, John lived with his father, who was an alcoholic. He only lived with his father because his mother died of alcoholic cirrhosis of the liver when he was four years old. Because his father was always drunk and never worked, they could afford only to live in the projects or in cheesy trailer parks. This embarrassed John and left all the kids at school teasing him. John tried to make his father stop drinking so they could have some money to eat and buy clothes, but nothing he did worked.

As John grew into a teenager, he became angry. He couldn't understand why his father didn't love him enough to stop drinking so they could live better. Even though somewhere inside himself John knew he loved his father, he grew to hate him because he wouldn't stop drinking. So on his eighteenth birthday, John dropped out of high school, packed his bags and left home. He intended never to return.

John got a minimum wage job and found a one-bedroom efficiency apartment. He was able to support himself for quite some time and deemed he would never end up like his father.

Several years later, John met Kim and fell in love with her. They dated for several months and then got married. Because neither one of them made much money, they could afford only to move into a trailer. In the beginning this was all right with John because he believed it was only temporary. However, months and then years passed by and they were still living in the trailer. They couldn't seem to save enough money to buy their dream house. This made John feel terrible about himself and made him feel like he was going to end up just like his father, trapped and broke.

Each time Kim tried to talk to John about buying a new house, he became angry and defensive. He would get so angry that he would yell at her and would throw things. She would end up crying and asking him, "Why are you getting so angry with me? What is going on with you? I just want us to be able to talk about things."

Instead of answering her, John would storm out of the trailer and go to the local bar to get drunk.

So the question becomes, "Why did John respond to Kim this way?"

John yelled at Kim because he believed she was blaming him for their living in a run down mobile home and for not being able to afford their dream home. For Kim, this wasn't true at all. All she was trying to do was talk about things so they could find a way to earn enough money to buy their dream house one day.

Because John believed Kim was blaming him for their financial problems, it reminded him of how he had felt as a child and how his father didn't love him enough to stop drinking so they could have enough money to move out of their poverty stricken neighborhood. He felt just like his father, unable to provide for his family.

Instead of telling Kim what all of this was reminding him of, how the pressure of a new house was affecting him, and how he felt like a bad little boy who can't afford anything, John continued becoming defensive and getting drunk. He did this as a means of protecting himself from what he perceived to be criticism. What John was ultimately doing, unconsciously, was putting his wife in the role of the parent (parent ego state) and assigning himself the role of the defiant teenager (child ego state). He was acting out what he didn't feel safe enough to say.

The second aspect of the child ego state is the **wounded child**. The person who plays the role of the wounded child tends to feel emotionally small and helpless. They feel fragile and vulnerable. They feel as if they have been hurt a lot and are incapable of taking care of their own emotional needs. They feel like victims and believe people, if given the chance, will hurt them. They feel as if they have no way of defending themselves against the pain other people inflict. They are convinced the world is not a safe place. They don't trust people yet they feel as if they need others to take care of them; to provide them with the love and nurturing they didn't receive as a child.

Carla is someone who plays the role of the victim and who operates out of the wounded child ego state. She is 45-year-old woman who is single and works full time at a furniture store. One day Carla goes to work. She walks into her office and finds her boss sitting in a chair waiting for her. She becomes frightened and tells herself, "I don't know what I did wrong, but I must be in trouble for something."

She really believes she is in trouble, but she can't remember what she did wrong. Even though Carla is nervous, she forces herself to sit down.

As Carla sits behind her desk, her boss proceeds to stand up and yell at her for the company's financial loss over the past year. She doesn't understand what this has to do with her since she is just the secretary. Because Carla is afraid her boss will fire her, she just sits there and takes the verbal beating. When her boss is finished, he turns around and walks out her office.

After he leaves, Carla emotionally falls apart. She wonders why her boss was so mean to her. She tells herself, "He yelled at me because I am a bad employee."

Carla becomes small and helpless inside. She stares at the floor and begins crying. Her feelings are hurt. She feels just like she did when her mother used to tell her, "You are to blame for everything bad that happens. Why can't you be a good little girl?"

Carla was so upset she spent the rest of the day hiding out in her office.

So the question is this, "What happened to Carla and why did she respond this way?"

Carla took the whole situation personally and became the wounded child. She didn't stop to consider that her boss was only yelling at her because he was having a bad morning. She allowed her boss to talk to her in a disrespectful manner and didn't stand up for herself. Thus, she continued playing the role her mother had assigned her a long time ago— that of being responsible for everything bad that happens. Thus, Carla assigned her boss the role of the parent while she played the role of the wounded child.

There is one thing I would like for you to consider in relation to the defiant teenager and wounded child. It is the defiant teenager who acts out what the wounded child is too afraid to say. The defiant teenager is the behavior the wounded child is too afraid to demonstrate. It is the defiant teenager who tries to protect the fragile wounded child.

The last and most desirable role to play is that of the **Adult (A)**. The adult ego state is the healthy balance between the thought and feeling side of ourselves. The person who primarily operates out of the adult ego state understands that in difficult situations it is neither necessary to crawl into their thoughts to become critical, nor delve into their emotions to become defiant or wounded. To them it is acceptable that each person have their own point of view. They feel in control of their thoughts and feelings, and believe in their ability to act appropriately in difficult situations. They know it is all right for them to stand up for themselves and to speak their truth. They realize they are not responsible for how other people think or feel, only for how they let other people treat them. Their perspective of themselves and the world in general is positive. They believe in their ability to solve their own problems and experience their own pain without having to become self-destructive (wounded child/adverse reactions). They are tolerant of themselves and thus are tolerant of others. They live by the philosophy that everyone, including themselves, is trustworthy and okay.

In the previous example with Carla she could have played the role of the adult by acknowledging that her boss was taking his anger out on her to make himself feel better. She could have realized there wasn't any way she could have been responsible for the company's loss. She could have told her boss she would appreciate it if he wouldn't talk to her in that manner. She also could have chosen not to take the verbal bashing personally. She could have understood that what was going on with her boss was about him and not about her. This would have kept Carla from delving back into her childhood and becoming the wounded child all over again. She could have recognized her boss was playing the role of the critical parent and this would have given her the choice as to whether she wanted to play the role of the child or not.

Now that you have an understanding of the different ego states, I would like to provide you with a visual representation of them as well:

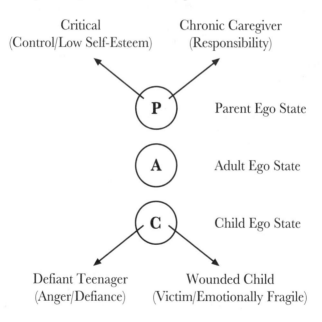

Critical
(Control/Low Self-Esteem)

Chronic Caregiver
(Responsibility)

P — Parent Ego State

A — Adult Ego State

C — Child Ego State

Defiant Teenager
(Anger/Defiance)

Wounded Child
(Victim/Emotionally Fragile)

WHAT'S BEHIND THE ROLE

Some questions you might be asking yourself are, "Why do people choose a particular ego state and what would they get out of playing a role other than that of the adult?"

People generally chose an ego state, unconsciously, because they believe that ego state will protect them better than any of the other ego states. They also choose that ego state and play that role out of habit. The habit develops in childhood and is carried over into adulthood. They continue playing whatever role was assigned to them by their parents, even though they are now an adult. For example, if Steve was given the role of taking care of his alcoholic mother, then he will more than likely grow up to be a chronic caregiver (parent ego state). If Joe was told he was stupid and was never allowed to talk about how he felt as a child, he will likely grow up to play the role of the defiant teenager or wounded child (child ego state).

People also play these roles because they believe it is the best and most consistent way in which they can get their needs met. A person who feels the need to be in control will maintain the parent ego state while someone who feels the need to be taken care of will maintain the child ego state.

In my professional experience, survivors most frequently choose the role of the child ego state. They hope somewhere deep inside themselves that acting out or emotionally shrinking away will protect them from people. Yet, they simultaneously hope it will cause someone to step into the role of being their parent so they can get from them the love they had needed from their parents; so they can finally get their unmet childhood needs fulfilled by someone.

For example, lets say Marie, as a child, was neglected by her mother. As an adult, Marie isolates herself from everyone yet she wishes she felt safe enough to allow someone in so she can feel loved. In order to cover up her loneliness, Marie secretly, so she thinks, drinks a lot of alcohol. Without realizing it, she becomes an alcoholic. She thinks no one notices that she drinks all the time, but her co-workers do. They can smell the alcohol on her and become concerned. They start asking Marie if she is all right. This unsolicited attention makes Marie feel good. After much thought she comes to believe it is her drinking that is getting her the attention she so desperately needs. So Marie unconsciously continues playing the role of the wounded child by drinking too much so her co-workers will continue playing the role of the caregiver (parent ego state). She does this hoping it will cause them to continue taking care of her so she can get the love and attention she is so starved for. Thus, Marie's playing the role of the wounded child is the ego state that allows her to get her needs met, even though in a very unhealthy way.

ASSIGNING ROLES

As you have already seen, when you operate out of a particular ego state you aren't the only one playing a role. You are inherently assigning whoever you are interacting with a role as well, the role opposite the ego state you are playing. So if you are playing the role of the child, then you are likely assigning the other person the role of the parent.

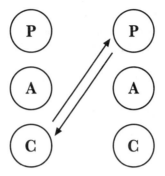

If you are playing the role of the parent, then you are likely assigning the other person the role of the child.

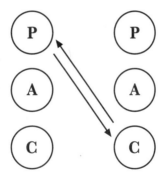

If you are playing the role of the adult, then you are likely assigning the other person the role of the adult.

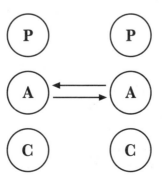

There are endless combinations of roles you can play and roles you can assign other people. We will be focusing primarily on the child-to-parent role because this is the way most survivors tend to interact with other people.

What most survivors don't understand is that healthy adults instinctively interact with people through the adult-to-adult ego state. Healthy adults assume this is how everyone interacts. They aren't aware there is any other role to play other than that of the adult because this was all they were exposed to as children. This becomes a problem for people who were abused, neglected and/or traumatized.

Most survivors assign people roles to play and it tends to be a role the other person doesn't know exist. In their mind it doesn't matter that the other person is unaware they are being assigned this role. All that matters is that the other person is meeting their needs. Because the other person doesn't understand they have been assigned the role of being the parent, as a means of making the survivor feel loved and cared for, they don't give them what they are looking for. Maybe this is true for you as well. Maybe you assign other people the role of being your parent so you can get your need for love and attention met. However, your needs go unmet because the other person doesn't know you have assigned them this role. Ultimately, it reinforces you feeling unlovable and incapable of getting your needs met.

For example, look at Betty and Todd who got married this past year. They had a great courtship and a beautiful wedding. As a couple, they were very much in love. But what Todd didn't know was that Betty grew up in a family where her father didn't pay much attention to her and it left her feeling emotionally neglected and needy. Todd on the other hand grew up in a loving, healthy family.

About six months after Todd and Betty got married, the differences in how they were raised began showing up. Todd got a new job that demanded many of hours. His new job was important to him because he believed it would afford Betty the lifestyle she deserved. However, each night after Todd got home from work, Betty was distant and moody. She acted sad and depressed. She acted like she didn't want to be around Todd. Todd didn't understand why she was treating him this way and how she could be so unappreciative of his hard work. Todd became angry and frustrated, but kept his concerns to himself because he didn't want to hurt Betty's feelings. Consequently though he began working longer hours because didn't feel wanted at home.

So the questions become, "What happened to Betty and what role was she playing? What role was she assigning to Todd? Could Todd

understand what role was being assigned to him and meet Betty's needs?"
Betty wanted Todd to pay attention to her and to spend time with
her. When she couldn't get these need met, she felt neglected and ignored,
just as she had as a little girl. She was appreciative of Todd's hard work,
but she couldn't show it because her feelings were hurt. His working all
those hours reminded her of how her father was never there and how he
had neglected her. Thus, Betty dropped down into the wounded child
ego state, hoping it would cause Todd to be home more and to love her.
However, Todd didn't know about Betty's childhood, didn't understand
how his long hours were creating a void in her life and were reminding
her of her father's neglect. Thus he couldn't understand why she was
treating him like she was. He didn't understand Betty was playing the
role of the child and was assigning him the role of the parent, hoping he
would take care of her emotional needs. Todd couldn't recognize this
because he had grown up in a family where everyone operated out of the
adult ego state, where everyone asked for what they needed and talked
about their feelings. Thus, Betty was assigning Todd a role he didn't know
existed, so he couldn't recognize it and meet her needs. In the end, Betty's
needs went unmet.

Betty could have resolved this situation and could have gotten her
needs met if she had played the role of the adult, had told Todd how she
felt and explained what she had needed from him. This would have given
Todd the opportunity to do something different and to have met Betty's
needs.

This isn't only true for Betty but for everyone and for you as well.
No one can read your mind, guess how you feel or instinctively know what
your needs are. It is your responsibility to recognize what role you are
playing and to then pursue the adult ego state so you can get your needs
met in a healthy way. When you are able to do this, your interactions
with other people will be on an adult-to-adult level. This will be a very
positive thing in your life. At this point you will begin to realize you have
the ability to meet your own needs just as well as anyone else does.

BLEEDING OVER

There is a common pitfall survivors experience as they are learning
how to operate out of the adult ego state. It is still based in Transactional
Analysis but I call it **Bleeding Over**.

When you, as the survivor, are recovering you may notice you have
difficulty putting aside your need for control, care giving, defiance, or

feeling like a victim. You may try to act like the adult, but find those old thoughts and feelings seeping through to the surface. You want to believe, "No one can hurt me again," but still feel overwhelmingly afraid and fragile inside (child). You try to tell yourself, "Everyone has the right to their own opinions," but still hear the voice, "You have to be in control because everyone else is inept" (parent).

In difficult situations you try to act like an adult, but end up crying and feeling fragile. This happens because one ego state is bleeding over into another. For example, Diane is an adult abuse survivor who has a hard time standing up for herself. As a child, she learned it wasn't okay to speak her truth or stand up for herself. Each time she tried, her father criticized her unmercifully and told her, "You're just a girl, your opinions don't matter".

Sometimes he would even slap her across the face just to show her he was the one who was in charge and that his opinions were the only ones that mattered.

As Diane became an adult, she realized she was an emotional door mat and she allowed everyone to treat her any way they wanted to. She hated herself when she did this. It caused her to overeat and to become overweight. Because she hated her obesity and fear of people, she got into therapy. She learned about ego states and how to speak her truth. Then the day came when Diane was ready to start testing her ability to stand up for herself. The first time she tried, she couldn't do it without feeling small and helpless again; feeling just like she did when she was a little girl. She cried and became afraid. No matter what she did she couldn't seem to quit crying so she could act like an adult in this difficult situation.

The reason this happened to Diane was because her child was bleeding over into her adult. The fears and feelings her child had been carrying around all those years about her father were bleeding over into her adult. This prevented her adult self from being able to stand up for herself and from being able to take care of her child self.

When your child bleeds over into your adult, you will feel all the things you felt as a child. You will feel like the small, helpless child all over again who can't take care of yourself, even though this isn't true today. It will look like this:

If you allow your child to bleed over into your adult, it will diminish your capacity to deal with the world as an adult. It will leave very little room for you to handle life with anything other than raw emotions that will overwhelm you and will stunt your emotional growth.

If your parent is bleeding over into your adult, it will also diminish your capacity to deal with the world as an adult. It will allow little room for anything else in your life except for being critical or feeling overly responsible for everyone. It will look like this:

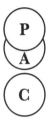

What then is the goal of Transactional Analysis? It is to learn how to move the ego states that are bleeding over into your adult out so you can operate in the adult ego state. This will help you to possess three separate ego states that function independently of each other and as a part of who you are, but not be in control of who you are. It will look like this:

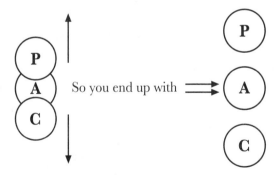

So you end up with

When you have mastered operating out of the adult ego state, your life will drastically change for the better. You will have the ability to choose how you want to respond to the people and situations around you. You will feel in control of yourself and what happens in your world. You will have the opportunity to meet your own needs or will have the ability to allow someone else to meet your needs in a healthy way. You will believe you are okay and so is everyone else. You will understand and believe you and only you are responsible for your own recovery. You will feel confident in your ability to handle difficult situations.

When you start operating out of the adult ego state, there is something you need to be aware of: Other people in your life might not know how to respond to the new you, to the new adult. They might not like the changes you have made because they were comfortable with roles you had been playing with each other. Changing your role might cause them to have to look at themselves and examine why they act like they do. Thus, there may be some repercussions as a result of your growth. I have discovered one of three things will usually happen when a survivor assumes the role of the adult:

1. The other person will respond back to you in the adult ego state (most desired outcome).
2. The other person will remain in their parent or child ego state hoping they can push you back down into the ego state they are used to you playing so your relationship with them will go back to the way it used to be.
3. Someone will leave because the ego states that are being maintained in this relationship are incompatible, such as adult-to-child, and adult-to-parent.

If a relationship or friendship you have been in dissolves because you begin playing the role of the adult, I would encourage you not to look at it as something negative or bad. It just means you are making so much progress that you are outgrowing certain people in your life. These are usually people who aren't capable of playing the role of the adult. When you make this type of progress and are able to maintain the adult ego state, something very positive will start happening. You will start attracting people who operate out of the same ego state as you. You will start attracting people who are emotionally healthy. So be aware that outgrowing people may be painful, but in the end you will likely be much happier with the healthy people you are attracting and with whom you are developing new relationships and friendships.

INCORPORATING TRANSACTIONAL ANALYSIS

Transactional Analysis alone is not the answer to everything that you, the survivor went through as a child. It must be incorporated with other concepts you have already been exposed to and new ones that are to come. Thus, it is time to incorporate the theory of Transactional Analysis in with the concepts of internal vs. external locus of control and with aggressiveness/assertiveness/passiveness. The only ego state which operates out of an internal locus of control and is assertive is the adult ego state. The parent and child ego states both operate out of an external locus of control, while the parent ego state tends to be the aggressive one and the child ego state tends to be the passive one. It looks like this:

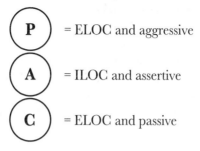

P = ELOC and aggressive

A = ILOC and assertive

C = ELOC and passive

You might be asking yourself, "How can the defiant teenager be considered passive?"

The defiant teenager portion of the child ego state is said to be passive because the defiant teenager acts angry only because he/she doesn't feel safe enough to speak his/her truth and thus acts it out. This person may throw things when angry or pout instead of verbalizing what is wrong. It's the act of not speaking one's truth (hiding verbally) that makes this ego state and person deemed passive.

It is important to understand that the concept of Transactional Analysis is not meant solely for the abused, neglected or traumatized. It is a universal concept of truth that can make anyone's life better and more satisfying. So when you are interacting with other people, remember they are dealing with the same issues as you. They are dealing with roles, loci of control, and aggressiveness/assertiveness/passiveness. Remember that these concepts apply to other people just as much as they do you. It may help you to visualize it this way:

	You	*Other Person*	
ELOC and aggressive	P	P	ELOC and aggressive
ILOC and assertive	A	A	ILOC and assertive
ELOC and passive	C	C	ELOC and passive

There is an exercise on the next page which will help you better understand these concepts in relation to yourself and others. Please turn the page and complete Exercise E before reading any further.

Exercise E:

Transactional Analysis
Internal Locus of Control/External Locus of Control
Aggressiveness/Assertiveness/Passiveness

Step I: For the next week, observe what ego state you are playing and what role you are assigning other people. Write a brief description of those situations where you are NOT playing the role of the adult and draw out what role each person is playing. (For example, I started crying and went home from work when my co-worker degraded me in front of other people. Child-to-parent.)

Description:

_____

_____

_____

_____

    Me   Other Person

   (P)   (P)   Internal Locus of Control or External Locus of Control

   (A)   (A)   Aggressive or Assertive or Passive

   (C)   (C)

Step II: Determine if you were operating out of an Internal Locus of Control or External Locus of Control, and were being Aggressiveness/Assertiveness/Passiveness and circle it.

Step III: Write out what you could have done differently in that situation so you would have been playing the role of the adult, operating out of an Internal Locus of Control and how that would have changed the situation.

_____

_____

_____

_____

_____

_____

_____

Please do not read any further until you have practiced this exercise for at least one week.

THE CHILD EGO STATE VS. THE INNER CHILD

When dealing with Transactional Analysis it is important to keep in mind that it only pertains to the roles you play and the way you respond to the world, as a result of the way you were raised. The role you play serves a purpose: to protect your fragile core self and to get your needs met. When you reach the place where you don't feel the need to protect or defend what is inside of you and you can meet your own needs, then you will have mastered operating out of the adult ego state.

Having said all of this, it's time to understand the difference between the child ego state and your inner child. The child ego state is very different from your inner child or child self. The child ego state is the part of you that you show to the world. It is a role you play with other people. On the other hand, your inner child is the person who lives inside of you who represents the child you were when you were growing up. It is important to understand that everyone has an inner child, not just the abused, neglected or traumatized.

Your inner child holds all of the feelings you felt, the memories of the events you experienced, and the thoughts you had as a child. Your inner child isn't just the negative aspects of your childhood, but also the positive ones as well.

Holding onto these positive memories and remembering this part of who you were is important, so please take a moment right now and try to remember those happy times you had as a child. Remember who you were when you were having fun and feeling free. Remember who you were when you weren't' being hurt. Ask yourself, "What did I like to do? What were my favorite things growing up? Did I have a favorite television show, game I liked to play, or special occasion I remember fondly?" Then write out your memories here:

_____

_____

_____

_____

_____

_____

_____

_____

Unfortunately, not all of your childhood memories are happy ones. Many of them are filled with the pain of the abuse, neglect and/or trauma you endured. As a result, it's not those happy memories you will be dealing with in your recovery process. It will be your inner child who suffered through those painful events. Thus, it will be your inner child you will be focusing on in your recovery process because it was your inner child who was hurt and wounded.

It is your inner child you will need the most now because he/she is your only link to the past. Your adult self cannot provide the answers or memories to what happened to you because your adult wasn't there when you were being hurt, only your inner child was. Without your inner child and his/her memories you will never be able to remember what happened to you so you can heal.

It's like your inner child is standing on one side of a river and your adult self is standing on the other side. The bridge that separates you is supported by your inner child's memories, thoughts, feelings, and perceptions of what happened to you and the things in your past that still hold you captive. It is only by acknowledging, experiencing, and understanding the bridge that will set you free and allow you to start responding to the world out of the adult ego state.

So, just like it was important to remember the good things that happened to you as a child, it is equally important to remember the abuse, neglect and/or trauma and who you were as a child. How did it feel to be you growing up in your house? What were the things you dreaded or hated about your life back then? Were you sad, frustrated, confused or angry? Did you cry a lot? What did the pain on your face look like?

Feel what your inner child felt because it is this child you will be dealing with throughout the rest of this book; the child you will be helping to recover. Take a moment and write your responses here:

Many survivors still have this inner child living inside of them. A child crying out for love, understanding, and attention. A child who wants be held, taken care of and told that everything is going to be all right. This creates huge problems in any survivors adult life. It creates problems in your life. You may be 40 years old but have a six, eight, or even ten-year-old child running around inside of you. This is a very difficult thing for you and any survivor to live with. In the end it causes you to respond to the world like a child, to assign everyone in your life the role of being your parent, and gives everyone the responsibility of meeting your needs. Again, the problem with this is that no one else knows you have assigned them the role of being your parent and it's inappropriate for one adult to expect another adult to comfort them as they had needed their parents to do when they were a child. In turn, this always leaves you, as an adult survivor carrying around a wounded inner child who feels unloved, frustrated, misunderstood, and always lacking. This is why your inner child cannot be ignored in the recovery or therapy process. The bridge, as well as the heart of the inner child, must be repaired so the inner child can heal and grow up into a healthy adult and stop running your life.

Chapter 4

Automatic Responses

As a little girl, Regina was expected to be perfect with anything and everything she did. Her mother sent her to ballet, art, swimming and piano lessons. She was expected to be the best in all of her recitals and to win no matter what. Her mother constantly told her, "You need to shape up and do everything the way I tell you to do it. You must be perfect. We want everyone to see how perfect you are and how perfect we are as a family."

With the expectation of perfection also came the constant criticism from her mother, "Why can't you do things the way you are taught? What's the matter with you? Can't you do anything right? You need to make sure everyone sees how wonderful you are so stop crying! When you don't win, I think you are just trying to embarrass me in front of the whole community."

Every time Regina tried to do her best, but couldn't be the best, she cried. She wondered what was wrong with her and why she couldn't live up to her mother's expectations. She began to hate who she was and the way her mother disapprovingly looked at her. The constant pressure to perform was too much for this little girl to handle. She felt suffocated and unworthy.

To make matters worse, Regina also had a father who had a problem with alcohol and drugs. He was also extremely passive. She wanted him to see how her mother was treating her, but he wouldn't stop drinking and doing drugs long enough to pay attention. This made Regina feel even more hopeless and unlovable.

As a teenager, Regina believed it wasn't all right for her to have an opinion or to stand up for herself, especially with her mother. She didn't believe anyone loved her. She didn't believe anyone would come to her rescue since her father just sat and watched what was happening to her day after day. Thus, Regina grew quiet and timid. She didn't talk about her thoughts or how she felt. She remained silent out of fear of getting in trouble and making her mother so angry she would be disappointed with her again.

By the time Regina became a young woman, she unexpectedly got pregnant and was forced to drop out of college. She ended up marrying a man she didn't love in order to keep her family, especially her mother, from being embarrassed about her pregnancy. What Regina didn't realize was she had married a man who was just like her father, passive and emotionally unavailable. He was a man who only looked out for himself.

As the years passed, Regina grew terribly unhappy. Her husband started spending long hours at work while she tried to be the perfect wife. She worked a fulltime job, took care of the children, and maintained the household affairs. She thought this would make her husband happy and would make him love her. She thought this would make her perfect in his eyes. However, he never stopped long enough to notice anything she was doing.

Regina worked in a place where there was a great deal of pressure to perform. Her boss believed in micromanaging and kept a close eye on all of his employees. He was just waiting for them to make a mistake. Without realizing it, Regina had placed herself in another situation where she had to be perfect; where she had to perform or be judged harshly.

Regina began feeling smothered all over again and incapable of doing anything right. This reminded her of her childhood and how her mother had treated her. It reminded her of how she could never be prefect enough or make anyone happy. She grew lonely and discontented with her life and her marriage.

While all of this was going on in Regina's life and marriage, her mother constantly called and showed up at her house unannounced. She continued trying to run Regina's life, treating her the same way she had when Regina was a little girl. Her father maintained his patterns as well, anesthetizing himself and remaining passive.

Regina became so unhappy with everything about her life that she fell into a pit of depression. All she could focus on was how she felt emotionally overwhelmed; how she felt like a failure. She hated herself. Those feelings began seeping their way to the surface in the form of panic attacks. Her body was trying to tell her something was wrong. Because Regina didn't understand herself or why she was acting the way she was, she couldn't make the panic attacks stop and this, in turn, caused her to feel even more helpless and out of control.

One day at work, Regina had a panic attack that was so severe she had to be sent home. This frightened her. She feared her boss would realize she wasn't perfect and would fire her. This caused Regina even more panic because being fired would ultimately make her husband mad and her mother disappointed. So Regina called a therapist and started counseling.

After several months of therapy Regina came to understand she was recreating her childhood by recreating the same situations over and over again in her adult life. She was doing this as a means of giving herself an opportunity to resolve the issues with her mother she never had a chance to resolve when she was a child. She learned that she was playing the role of the passive, wounded child and was assigning everyone else in her life the role of the critical parent. She recognized how she was operating out of an external locus of control.

Then the day came when she felt she was ready to apply what she had learned to the people in her life. Several situations presented themselves where Regina had the opportunity to practice her new tools and to operate out of the adult ego state. However, she wasn't successful. Instead, she found herself sitting in her therapist's office, crying and declaring she was a failure because she continued to let people treat her the way she had always let them treat her.

After reading all of this, what do you think went wrong? Why wasn't Regina able to apply the concepts she had learned in therapy? Why couldn't she speak her truth to her parents and her husband? Why couldn't she play the role of the adult? Why didn't she feel safe enough to let other people see her differently? What was she afraid of?

To start with, Regina reacted the same way she always had because she was afraid of what would happen if she truly stood up for herself and spoke her truth. She was terrified it would hurt the other person's feelings. And if their feelings had gotten hurt then they would get angry with her. And if they had gotten angry with her then they would leave her; they would abandon her just like her mother had done all her life. Just like her husband had already done by spending excessive hours at work. Just like her boss did every time she wasn't perfect. This was Regina's external locus of control. It was her fear of abandonment that kept her from stepping into the adult ego state and speaking her truth. She didn't fully understand it was her silence that gave everyone in her life permission to continue playing the role they had always played with her, the role of the critical parent.

Secondly, Regina's child was bleeding over into her adult. When Regina was around her mother or other critical parent figures, she instinctively became the small, helpless child again who couldn't stand up for herself out of fear of being abandoned. This response was so automatic that Regina couldn't see when it was happening. I liken this automatic response Regina experienced to driving a car. When Regina, and you, first started learning how to drive you had to think, "Red means stop and green means go." Then, after you had been driving for several years, you didn't have to think about driving through a green light. You automatically pressed on the accelerator without thinking about it. You did it out of habit.

The same thing happened with Regina every time she got into a difficult situation with a critical parent figure, especially one who reminded her of her mother. Just like driving through a green light without thinking about it, Regina instinctively jumped into the child ego state. Her inner child's fears and feelings would rush to the surface so quickly that she would become frightened and panicked without warning. She would instinctively become the small child who needed to protect herself from being hurt and abandoned again. Thus, Regina reacted to whatever difficult situation she was in just like she had done as a child. She didn't have to think about it. She resorted back to the child who had to remain silent and who couldn't stand up for herself. It had become second nature for her to be the same small and helpless child she had always been with her mother.

So the question becomes, "What does Regina and any other survivor need to do to stop this automatic response so they can apply the tools and concepts learned in therapy and in this book?"

The answer to this question lies in the concept of **separation, individuation, and reintegration**, which has parts of its origin in Object Relations Theory. As with the theory of Transactional Analysis, I have modified and adapted this theory to meet the demands of the concept of childhood abuse, neglect and trauma.

Separation, individuation and reintegration are the only ways you and any survivor can begin to stop reacting to your past and the people who still cause you difficulty today. It is the first step in the process. If you don't apply this concept to your life, your recovery will be much more difficult and in some cases impossible. Nothing can or will change unless you do something differently. This will become more evident as the details of this concept are unveiled.

The best way to introduce the concept of separation, individuation, and reintegration is with a diagram. Please look over the diagram carefully before reading any further.

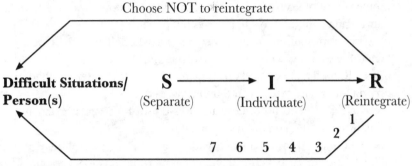

To the far left-hand side of the diagram are the **difficult situations** you find yourself in as you go through your life. These situations involve specific people, such as your parents, in-laws, bosses and spouses. They are also the people who hurt you as a child or who remind you of the people who hurt you.

You, as the survivor, have to stop and look at who the people are who hurt you in the past and who still hurt you today. You have to recognize who the people are in your everyday life who cause you to maintain an ego state other than that of the adult. You have to identify the people who still negatively influence how you feel about yourself and how you behave.

It will be important for you to make a list of the people who have hurt you in the past, who still hurt you today and who treat you like someone from your past. This list might contain your boss who constantly criticizes you just like your father did, a friend who neglects you just like your mother used to, or a boyfriend who hits you just like your uncle did. It could also include your mother who used to emotionally and physically abuse you as a child, and who continues to verbally bash you when she calls every six months or so. It might include a parent who still tries to make you think you have to be perfect in every way, even though you are now an adult.

It will be imperative for this list to include all of the people who hurt you in the past; who cause you to maintain the child ego state; who created your emotional scars; who you are still unable to stand up to; and who you are still afraid of today. The list must be thorough. It must also be made with the intent that you will be the only person who will see this list.

Making your list might be difficult. It might generate some unsettling feelings: maybe some guilt, neediness, desperation or fear. It might include people you needed to love and take care of you as a child, but who ended up hurting you instead. You may still feel as if you need them to love you today, and that's okay. Remember, this list isn't being made so you can point a blaming finger at someone or make someone else look bad. It is merely a tool to help you identify who hurt you and who you need to work out your childhood issues with so you can recover.

Let's apply the difficult situations and list of people to Regina.

As an adult, Regina found people who would treat her just like her mother had when she was a little girl. These people included her husband and employer and kept her in one difficult situation after another. Her difficult situations were also created each time her mother called or showed up at her house trying to control her. Thus, the first step in Regina changing her life begins by recognizing when she is in difficult situations and then identifying the people who keep her stuck in the child ego state: her mother, father, husband, and employer. Her mother and father were directly related to her childhood and were the ones who had hurt her, while her husband and employer treat her like her parents had and remind her of her unresolved childhood issues.

The "S" in the diagram stands for **Separate**. Once you have figured out who the people are who hurt you and who you still have issues with, then it will be necessary for you to separate yourself from them. The purpose of this separation phase is to break the habit you have developed over the years—automatically jumping into the child ego state when you are around the people who hurt you or who remind of the people who hurt you.

The separation can be an emotional or physical one. However, for most survivors the physical separation usually works best. This is true because most survivors are still locked into playing the role of the child and aren't strong enough to emotionally stand up to the people who hurt them so deeply. When they are around the people who make them feel powerless, they go into automatic response mode, automatic child mode, just like with the green light. They become the child who is incapable of taking care of themselves; the child who cannot speak their truth. Thus, I recommend you physically separate yourself from those people until you are strong enough to speak your truth and interact with them as an adult.

You might be wondering, "How am I supposed to separate myself from the difficult people in my life?"

If the person you need to separate yourself from is an active part of your life, I recommend you either call them or write them a letter explaining that you are trying to work some things out for yourself and need some time alone. Emphasize this decision has nothing to do with them, that you aren't mad at them, or upset with them about anything. It is merely your need for some private time. Also make sure you let them know you will contact them when you are ready. This means no telephone calls, letters, invitations, or any other contact from them. Because you are learning to speak your truth and play the role of the adult, no other explanation is necessary. If someone tries to push you for an explanation or to validate why you are doing this, look at why they might be pushing you for an explanation. Are they feeling threatened because you are handling things differently? Are they trying to maintain the parent role they have always played with you? Are they afraid of what would happen if you both played the role of the adult? Are they afraid of losing the control they maintain in your relationship?

By allowing yourself the invaluable opportunity of stepping back from these people, you will begin seeing them in a different way. You will start developing a different perspective about them, one that is objective. You will start seeing them for who they really are as opposed to the person you made them out to be as a small, helpless child. You will begin seeing they don't have all the power, they just think they do. You will see they can't hurt you unless you allow them to. You will begin seeing the role they assigned you and the role you both have continued playing even though you are now an adult.

Going back to Regina for a moment, while she was in therapy, she identified her mother as one of those people who kept her locked in the role of the child. Thus, it became important for her to let her mother know she needed some time away from her while she worked on herself. So Regina spoke with her mother and explained her need for a short period of time away from her; time to work on herself. In the beginning, Regina's mother didn't honor her request. She continued to call and drop by her house unexpectedly. Regina continued speaking her truth and repeated her request to her mother several times. Because Regina didn't back down and maintained the adult ego state, her mother eventually started honoring her request. After Regina had time away from her mother, she began seeing her mother for who she really was. It was separating herself from her mother that gave her the opportunity to form her own opinions about her mother and to take the time she needed to work on herself.

It is important for you to keep in mind that you cannot move on to the next step of this concept without completing the separation phase. If you cannot identify the people who hurt you and ask for what you need in the form of separation, then you won't be able to take the next step. So please take the time now to complete these steps before reading any further.

The "I" stands for **Individuate**. Individuating means you start developing a positive, constructive relationship with yourself. It is NOT about camouflaging self-destructive behaviors and making it look like you are being kind to yourself. It's not going out and treating yourself to a beer when you are an alcoholic or indulging in a piece chocolate cake when you are a compulsive overeater. You can't continue trying to protect yourself from your own feelings by covering those feelings up with alcohol or some other self-destructive behavior (adverse reaction). Instead, you have to learn how to be nice to yourself and develop a positive relationship with yourself.

Individuating starts with you learning how to be with just you in a positive a way, and one that helps you to know who you are. It is spending time with yourself in a way that allows you to answer the questions, "Who am I? What do and don't I like? What do I want my life to look like? What makes me feel good about me? What kind of a person am I? What are the positive aspects of my personality? What are the things I need to do to become the person I want to be?"

It is knowing everything there is to know about yourself and learning how to be comfortable with who you are. It is developing a relationship with yourself so you can stand up for yourself and one day be able to speak your truth with the people you separated yourself from. It is knowing what you are and are not willing to put up with in your new life. It is defining who you are as a person so other people don't shape and define who you are.

How you get to know yourself can happen in many ways. For most survivors, individuating is like dating, but the person you are dating is yourself. It is planning things you like to do and allowing yourself time to do them. It is pampering yourself and doing things, which make you feel good about you. It is going on long drives in the country, taking yourself camping, going on a trip, curling up on the couch watching a favorite movie, or sitting in the grass feeling the warmth of the sun shining on your face. It is planning picnic lunches at the lake and reading a book on the beach. It is spending quality time with just you.

Individuating is also about incorporating into your daily life the techniques you are learning in your recovery process. Every time you apply a technique and respond to a situation differently, you are growing into a new person, and that is the epitome of individuating.

It isn't enough though just to do something nice for yourself or to keep applying concepts to your daily life. These things must be accompanied with a time of reflection. So each time you do something that moves you in a direction of growth and increases your knowledge about yourself, take a moment to feel what it feels like to be doing these things and how it feels to be growing and changing. Take time to reflect on how special it makes you feel and how it changes how you feel about yourself. You might feel more confident, more deserving, proud of yourself, and so forth. The possibilities are endless.

Developing a relationship with yourself and getting to know who you are aren't the only benefits you will get out of individuating. Later, you will learn that it will give you an opportunity to determine how you really think and feel about things. It will allow you to develop your opinions and draw your own conclusions. It will allow you the space you need to change your perspective about things. It will allow you to feel like an adult and to respond to the world through the adult ego state. In essence, you will get the chance to start thinking and feeling for yourself; to know it is all right to own your thoughts and feelings; and its okay to feel good about yourself. You will soon realize how vital all of this is because there will come a time in your recovery when it will be imperative for you to look at what happened to you as a child; to decide how you felt about what happened; and to take ownership of your thoughts and feelings about it.

Once again, going back to Regina, she might decide to start developing that relationship with herself by doing one nice thing a day for herself. She might go for long walks, take long bubble baths, treat herself to movies on the weekends, or take herself out for picnic dinners under the stars. She might also get a babysitter and go away for a long weekend. Each time she does one of these nice things for herself, she then takes a moment to reflect on how good it felt to be developing a relationship with herself.

Once you have individuated, you are ready to move on to the "R" portion of this concept, which stands for **Reintegrate**. Remember though, you cannot reintegrate or pursue a relationship with the person you separated yourself from until you have first separated and individuated.

Reintegration consists of two possible courses of action. Let's continue using Regina as an example to help illustrate the reintegration process.

The first option Regina has is this: To choose NOT to reintegrate, or resume a relationship with her mother (arrows at the top part of the diagram on page 58) because her mother has not worked on herself or changed. Regina chooses not to reintegrate because she believes that if she tries to reintegrate with a mother who hasn't made any changes, she will lose herself again. She believes the reintegrating would cause her to lose the progress she has made and resort back to the helpless child. Thus, resuming a relationship with her mother would not be a healthy thing for Regina to do at this time.

Keep in mind though, the decision Regina made about not reintegrating with her mother does not have to be a permanent one. It just means she is not ready to reintegrate with her mother at this point in her recovery process. As Regina gets better at playing the role of the adult and operating out of an internal locus of control, she may get to the place where she is ready to try to re-establish a relationship with her mother, even if her mother has not made any changes. However, she can only do this when she feels she is ready to, not when her mother deems the time is right.

The second option for Regina is this: To choose to try to reintegrate with her mother; to try to develop a relationship with her that is both functional and healthy (bottom of diagram on page 58). Even though Regina has made the decision to resume her relationship with her mother, it will be important for her to remember that she can only do this one step at a time. Regina has to figure out what she can and cannot do with her mother; how she can and cannot interact with her; and how much time she can spend with her mother without it effecting how she feels about herself.

Step 1 might entail Regina calling her mother and talking with her on the phone. When Regina deems their telephone conversation went well and she feels ready, then she can proceed to step 2. Step 2 might involve Regina inviting her mother out to lunch. At lunch, her mother was on her best behavior and didn't criticize Regina at all. This made her very happy and hopeful. Because lunch went so well, Regina decides to proceed to step 3, inviting her mother over for a family dinner. During dinner, her mother stopped smiling and acting cordial. The atmosphere grew tense. Regina's mother began criticizing her about how she had cooked the roast beef and how she thought her house could be cleaner. Regina began feeling like the imperfect child again who couldn't speak her truth. She felt herself wanting to fall back into the role of the child. This was Regina's clue that she needed to stop and look at what was happening and if she could truly reintegrate with her mother in this manner.

Should Regina still wish to reintegrate with her mother, she now knows it can only be done on a very limited basis. She can only interact with her the way she did in steps 1 and 2. She could only do it by restricting their level of activity to talking on the phone and occasionally getting together for an outing. Anything else would threaten the progress Regina had made and the possibility of losing the relationship she had developed with herself.

So the two options to reintegration are:

1. Choosing NOT to reintegrate with the person you separated yourself from;
2. Trying to reintegrate with that person, but with the understanding you will have. to learn how far you can reintegrate with them without loosing yourself.

The separation, individuation and reintegration process is going to be one of the most important things you do for yourself in your recovery process. It allows you the opportunity to separate yourself from the people who hurt you long enough to figure out who you are as an individual, and long enough for you to decide if you want to reintegrate (if at all) with them. To help you better understand this process, please take the time to turn to the next page and complete Exercise F. Then allow yourself the freedom and opportunity to follow through with the separation, individuation and reintegration process and do something nice for yourself each and every day of your life.

Exercise F:

Separation, Individuation, and Reintegration

Step I: Make list of the people you feel you need to separate yourself from in order for your recovery process to begin. Write their names below and a brief description of why it is essential for you to separate from them in order to heal.

Example: My Mother: It will be hard for me to recover as long as she is in my life because she continues to treat me the same way she did when I was a child. My stomach gets tied in knots around her because I feel like I have to be perfect. I can't share how I feel with her without her telling me I don't feel that way. She doesn't listen to me. She constantly puts me down and doesn't respect the rules I have set down for my kids. When I am around her, I have nightmares about not being perfect.

Person #1:

_____

_____

_____

_____

Person #2:

_____

_____

_____

_____

Person #3:

_____

_____

_____

_____

Step II: Write out how you plan to separate yourself from each one of the people you mentioned above.

Example: My Mother: I will need to write her a letter explaining why I need to have some time away from her.

My Uncle: I will meet him for lunch and explain that I am working on some difficult issues in my life and need to spend some time with just myself for a while. I will let him know I will call him when I am ready to get together with him again.

Person #1:

_____

_____

_____

_____

Person #2:

_____

_____

_____

_____

Person #3:

_____

_____

_____

_____

Step III: Write out a list of ten nice things you can do for yourself that will help you begin the individuation process. Take 15 to 30 minutes a day and do one thing from your list. Keep track of the one nice thing a day you do for yourself.

1.
2.
3.
4.
5.
6.
7.
8.
9.
10.

Chapter 5

Cognitive Emotional Restructuring Therapy

Most therapeutic approaches are considered very limited because they only focus on one aspect of the recovery process or only one part of who you are as a person. They might only focus on what your thoughts are, what current self-destructive or maladaptive behaviors you engage in, what current difficult situations you find yourself in today or how you feel about yourself.

Approaching therapy like this is much like having tunnel vision. It only looks at what is in front of you today and your present day problems. It only deals with the distorted thoughts and feelings (misperceptions) you maintain as an adult and the adverse reactions you engage in (alcoholism, addictions, etc). For example, these therapeutic approaches only look at the fact that you have low self-esteem and believe you are incompetent, and that you cover it up with self-destructive behaviors such as gambling or over eating. They don't look at what buried deep inside you or in your past that is causing you to think, feel and behave the way you do; causing you to have low self-esteem, to feel incompetent, to gamble and to overeat. They don't address the underlying core issues that caused the distorted thoughts and feelings or the adverse reactions in the first place. They don't go back to the things that happened to you in your childhood, which might have caused the low self-esteem, such as the physical abuse, sexual abuse, neglect, divorce or rape.

Many therapists and therapeutic approaches just treat the symptoms and not the underlying cause of the symptoms. It's like a doctor who treats a patient for weakness and nausea with medication, but he doesn't stop long enough to find out what is causing the weakness and nausea. If he had stopped to explore the possible underlying causes, he would have discovered they were being caused by cancer. He also would have realized the cancer could not have been eradicated with the medications he had prescribed. Thus, the cancer would have continued to spread and would have eventually killed the patient.

This is what is happening to abuse survivors as well. Many physicians and therapists are merely treating their symptoms without addressing the underlying issue of childhood abuse, neglect and/or trauma. Thus they are condemning survivors to a type of death—an emotional death.

In my professional and personal counseling experience, I have come to understand that childhood abuse, neglect and trauma cannot be healed with anything less than a holistic therapeutic approach. An approach, which deals with the past, the present and the future. An approach which goes all the way back to the abuse itself; back to the core issues; and back to the things that made you, the survivor, feel bad about yourself.

Like cancer, childhood abuse, neglect and trauma don't just effect one area of your life or one part of your being. It affects your thoughts and how you feel about yourself, how you interact with others, how you perform on your job, how you view the things that happened to you, your spiritual relationship with God, and so forth. So the recovery process must be a holistic one as well, and one that addresses each part of you as a human being. Thus, I have developed a new holistic therapeutic approach called **Cognitive Emotional Restructuring Therapy (CERT)**.

Cognitive Emotional Restructuring Therapy is an integration of many therapeutic approaches as well as my own personal approach to recovery. For example, the cognitive, or thinking, part of this therapy is based on a system of psychology called cognitive retraining. It was first developed and used by Aaron Beck and then many other therapists such as Donald Michenbaum, M.J. Mahoney, and Albert Ellis. Their theories of cognitive retraining are incorporated into Cognitive Emotional Restructuring Therapy. However, the specific techniques outlined in my theory reflect what worked in my recovery process and what I have seen to be effective in the healing of other abuse survivors in the therapeutic setting.

In Cognitive Emotional Restructuring Therapy, there are two main components—the first one being a cognitive, which deals with one's thoughts, and the second, an emotional one.

The goal of the cognitive retraining is to take the messages you were given and developed as a child, and still give yourself as an adult, and change them through conscious repetitious input, or practice, if you will. As your thoughts change so will your perception about how you think and feel about yourself and the world around you. This change in perception will help you develop an internal locus of control, which in turn will strengthen your ability to operate out of the adult ego state. The cognitive retraining will also provide you with immediate relief from your overwhelming feelings and will help you to be able to cope with your daily life. It will reduce the degree to which your inner child bleeds over into your adult self. The cognitive retraining will be explained in more detail in the next chapter.

The goal of the emotional restructuring is to allow your inner child the opportunity to go back and acknowledge and then experience the painful events of his/her past. This will allow you to embrace what happened to your inner child, to see it in a different light and to then heal from it. After you have resolved those emotional issues and have faced the feelings left over from the abuse, you will then learn how to meet the needs of your inner child; to re-parent your inner child; and to help your inner child grow up in a healthy and nurturing way. Ultimately, this will allow you the opportunity to alter your misperceptions (distorted thoughts and feelings) about what happened to you as a child and how you feel about your inner child. It will allow your inner child to grow up and become the well-adjusted adult who operates out of an internal locus of control rather than self-destructing through adverse reactions.

The ultimate goal of Cognitive Emotional Restructuring Therapy is to teach you a new way of life; to help you develop the ability to deal with the world and its problems as a well-adjusted adult; to interact with others in a way that is healthy and fulfilling; to feel good about yourself again; and to become the person you were meant to be despite the abuse.

Keep in mind though that this approach to recovery is not a quick fix. It will not work unless you make a personal commitment to do whatever it takes to heal and to practice everything you know on a daily basis. It will be necessary for you to eat, drink, sleep, and be consumed with your own recovery; to ponder it and think about it every spare moment of your day. Then, once you have gotten to a place where you feel that you have mastered the recovery techniques and have overcome your childhood, it will be imperative for you to continue using the tools you've learned on a daily basis. Without maintaining the tools, you won't be able to maintain your progress. You could very well slip back into your old thoughts, feelings, and behaviors, and become the helpless child again. This is true because no matter what you do your inner child will always be a part of who you are. However, the degree to which your inner child impacts your life is up to you. Your inner child can be a part of you in a good way or in a destructive way.

Right now, you might want to believe it would be easier for you to get rid of your inner child completely, to ignore he/she even exists, or to separate from this part of yourself. Unfortunately, recovery doesn't work this way. The Chinese also found this to be true. They developed a proverb which stated, "that which we resist, persists."

Let's look at an example of how this might be true for you. Pretend you are locked away in a room with nothing but the chair you are sitting in. You look over to your right and see a wounded dog lying next to the wall. You see he needs help and maybe even some bandages, but you do nothing because you're afraid of dogs. Your heart beats fast. You tremble out of fear of getting bitten by the dog. He wants you to help him, but you think to yourself, "If I just ignore the dog long enough he'll just go away." So you look to the other side of the room hoping you can distract yourself.

Days pass by as you stare at the other wall, trying to ignore the wounded dog. However, the dog is still hurting. He is now getting restless and hungry. He knows you are still sitting there trying to ignore him. Tired of hurting and being hungry, the dog decides to crawl toward you. He wants to see if you'll help him, or maybe even feed him. You notice his movement but you keep trying to ignore him by staring at the other wall. Then it happens, the dog becomes frustrated. He gets tired of being ignored and not taken care of, so he bites you. You look startled and act surprised. You scream and cry as you ask the dog, "Why have you bitten me"?

He answers, "Just because you chose to ignore me didn't make me disappear. It didn't make my pain or hunger go away. It only made me more aware of my pain and how hungry I was".

This analogy applies to childhood abuse, neglect and trauma. The wounded dog represents your past and the pain your inner child still carries around; the emotional hunger you have for someone to love you. The person sitting in the chair is your adult self who is trying to ignore what happened to you as a child and the feelings that resulted from it. No matter how much you try to ignore the abuse or your hurt inner child, they will continue nipping at your heels until you look at them, clean their wounds, and feed their emotional needs. It will interfere with your daily life until you learn the necessary skills to embrace them, take responsibility for your own recovery and feed your emotional needs. So resisting your inner child will only delay what you will ultimately have to do: Face the abuse, embrace the pain and integrate your inner child into your life. For you to give your inner child what he/she has always needed from your parents: love, attention and nurturing.

Another reason why you don't want to completely ignore or lose your inner child is this: It is your inner child who reminds you of where you came from and the lessons you learned along the way. Your inner child also holds onto the lessons you are learning in your recovery process. Thus, if your inner child completely disappeared, he/she would take the lessons you learned with him/her. This would cause you to be doomed to repeat the same mistakes over and over again until you relearned all of your life's lessons. None of this means that your inner child has to run your life or be the dominating force in it. It only means that you have to hold on to enough of your inner child to keep the lessons you have learned available for continued growth. You have to use the lessons your inner child is teaching you today as a reference point for how to handle future problems.

So the question becomes. "How much of your life do you want your inner child to influence and control?"

If you are a survivor who ignores your inner child, it will cause your inner child to create situations to get your attention, much like the dog biting you. Thus, your inner child will bleed over into your adult life and could occupy as much as 95 percent of your attention. However, if you choose to embrace your inner child, resolve his/her issues and integrate him/her into your life, your inner child could occupy as little as five percent of your attention. Your inner child will only show up when you need to be reminded of a lesson you've already learned and to keep you from being doomed to repeating past mistakes. It is up to you to determine how much of your life and attention your inner child occupies, and whether it is in a positive or negative way.

Chapter 6

The Cognitive Retraining

As mentioned earlier, the first part of Cognitive Emotional Restructuring Therapy consists of cognitive retraining or changing the way you think. The cognitive retraining has to be done first before the emotional restructuring work can even be considered. The reason for this can be illustrated with the following diagram:

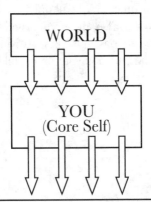

Before abuse survivors get into recovery, there seems to be something missing in how they cope with life. While others seem to possess the ability to let stress and negativity bounce off of them, abuse survivors tend to take everything to heart; they become fragile and vulnerable in difficult situations. Everything, including work, relationships, and daily life stressors tend to go directly to the core of their being. Once inside, those situations reawaken their inner child who holds onto the misperceptions (distorted thoughts and feelings about themselves) they developed as children. Those misperceptions cause them to feel overwhelmed, emotionally fragile, and eventually question their self-worth. When those distorted thoughts and feelings become too much to bear, the survivor then turns to self-destructive behaviors or acting out to relieve their pain and as a means of crying out for help.

For example, a boss yelling at them may immediately bring them to tears. A boyfriend breaking up with them may cause them to become suicidal. A friend canceling a dinner date may cause them to get depressed and then drunk. Not getting a promotion may cause them to binge and purge. A co-worker looking at them in a snide way may cause them to feel worthless, so they hide out in their home and starve themselves for the next several days.

Reading this, you may see yourself, or you may be thinking, "These people are overreacting." Considering the size of the situations, they are over reacting. So the question at hand is this, "Why do abuse survivors tend to let everything go directly to their core self, tap into their misperceptions about themselves and cause them to self-destruct?"

The answer to this question lies in the fact that abuse survivors, as children, weren't provided the necessary tools to build what I call a **protective layer**. They weren't taught how to erect this protective layer between them and the world they live in so they can feel safe.

The function of this protective layer, as most people who grew up in functional families know, is designed to protect your core self from the world. It keeps things from overwhelming you; from controlling your thoughts and feelings. It keeps the pain other people may try to inflict from penetrating the essence of who you are. It allows you to feel in control of your thoughts and feelings. It allows you to believe no one can hurt you unless you allow them to. It allows you to believe in yourself no matter what anyone else's opinions are. It allows things that don't really matter to bounce off of you.

So what constitutes this protective layer and what tools do you need to acquire to build your own protective layer?

The protective layer consists of a combination of everything you have learned so far. It is the four basic concepts that help you know you are a good person, that you can trust people, that there is order in the world and that you are not vulnerable. It is knowing how to operate out of an internal locus of control so you are the one who determines how much you let things effect you. It is you playing the role of the adult so you can interact with the world as an adult and can allow others to do the same in return. It is you stopping long enough to individuate so you can know who you are and what you want your life to be like.

These tools are just the beginning of many you will acquire. Your protective layer will continue being built as you work your way through this book and your recovery process. Each tool you add to your protective layer will make you stronger and will give you the ability to be the adult in any situation.

You might be wondering why you and other survivors weren't taught how to erect your own protective layer as a child. To answer this question, you have to look at your parents and how they were raised. The fact that you were abused, neglected and/or traumatized as a child implies that your parents likely grew up in the same type of environment. Thus, you likely had parents who couldn't provide you with the necessary tools to develop your own protective layer because they weren't provided them as a child either.

I liken this whole process of not having a protective layer to being a soldier who is fighting a battle without wearing armor or a bulletproof vest. When the enemy fires its guns, the bullets go directly to the soldier's heart and kill him. For you, the survivor, your enemy is your past and the people or difficult situations in your present day life who remind you of your past. The bullets fired are emotional ones that threaten to kill the heart of your innocent child, who has no way of protecting him/herself.

When you realize that, even as an adult, you still don't know how to protect yourself or the child who lives inside of you, you self-destruct and act out. This is why recovery is important. It is the recovery process that will help you to acquire the tools you need to erect your protective layer. And, if you can establish your protective layer, you will be able to operate out of the adult ego state so fewer things penetrate your core being. In the end, this will give you the ability to be able to deal with your present day life more effectively.

Let's look at an example of someone who didn't develop a protective layer as a child. When Judy was a little girl she grew up in a family who lived in a rundown trailer park out in the middle of the country on a dirt road. Almost every day of Judy's life her mother would get high and tell her, "You're going to get stuck here in this hell hole just like me. No one in our family has ever gotten out of here. No one has ever married a nice guy or lived happily ever after. It definitely won't happen for you. You're too ugly and too fat to get a nice looking guy. They want someone with a little less fat around their hips."

Every time Judy heard those words, she would run into her bedroom.

She would cry herself to sleep as she wondered, "Why does Mom hate me so much? What did I do wrong? What made Mom not love me anymore? Am I really that fat and ugly? Will I really be stuck here the rest of my life?"

Judy didn't want to believe what her mother was saying. She didn't want to believe she was doomed to live on this dirt road for what seemed an eternity. However, the day finally came when Judy's mother's comments broke her spirit. As a result, Judy gave up hope of ever leaving the trailer park and her mother. So she quit school and got a job at the local convenience store.

The years passed by slowly. Judy felt trapped and worthless as a human being. She began starving herself, hoping she could get thin enough so her mother or maybe someone else would love her. Then one day at work, Judy and one of her co-worker's were joking around. In the middle of a bunch of jokes her co-worker blurted out, "Your momma's right. You are too ugly for a rich, nice-looking man. You are poor and ugly just like the rest of us. There's no way you'll ever get a date with anyone."

Those comments crushed Judy. She felt like someone had just punched her in the stomach.

The laughter stopped and was replaced with nothing but silence. Judy's co-worker asked, "What's wrong. I was just joking around. I didn't mean anything by it."

Judy didn't know what to say. She wanted to cry, but was too embarrassed to cry in front of her friend. So she ran out of the room and back to her dirty trailer on the dirt road. She sat there and did nothing but cry for the next several days while cutting on her arms and starving herself.

So the question becomes, "Why did Judy allow her co-worker's comments to upset her to the point of being overwhelmed?"

Because Judy was never taught how to develop her own protective layer using the four basic concepts, she didn't believe "I am good person no matter what anyone says" or "I am not vulnerable so no one can hurt me unless I allow them to hurt me".

Because she wasn't taught how to function out of the adult ego state, she assigned her co-worker, and everyone else for that matter, the role of being the critical parent while she played the role of the wounded child. She didn't know there were other choices she could make and other ways she could respond to people.

Because she wasn't taught how to have an internal locus of control, she didn't know to question what was being said to her and to take into consideration who was saying it.

So what happened to Judy was this: She let her co-worker's comments go straight to her core being because she wasn't taught how to build her own protective layer as a little girl. Thus, her co-worker's comments reinforced the distorted thoughts and feelings (misperceptions) she already had about herself. Those old misperceptions reawakened her wounded inner child. Not knowing what to do with her child's pain, she cut and starved herself for days (adverse reactions).

If Judy had acquired the necessary tools to develop her own protective layer as a child, she could have drawn on the tools in the middle of her difficult situation. She could have remembered she was an adult, a good person and someone who was in control of her life. This would have allowed Judy to understand and believe she was a good person and could get a date no matter what anyone's opinion of her was. No one's negative thoughts or opinions would have caused her to question her self-worth or to self-destruct.

So the purpose of starting with the cognitive techniques and all of the concepts you have learned so far is to help you to acquire the tools you should have learned in childhood so you can build your own protective layer. It is the four basic concepts, loci of control, Transactional Analysis, separation/individuation/reintegration, and the tools to come in the next chapters, that will help you erect your protective layer. This will help you build a buffer between your core self and the world; and will keep your child from bleeding over into your adult. This, in turn, will reduce the likelihood of you getting overwhelmed during your recovery process and in whatever difficult situation life presents to you. It will also increase your ability to be able to handle the emotional work that is to come. There are two diagrams which best illustrate these points. Please look over them carefully and make sure you understand them before reading any further.

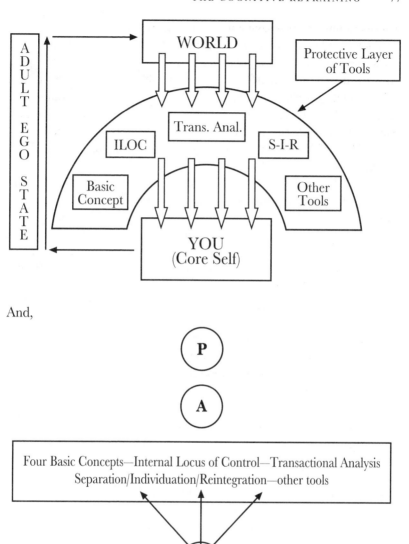

And,

COGNITIVE RETRAINING

Let's take a moment and review what has been mentioned regarding misperceptions. This will help introduce you to the importance of cognitive retraining. As a survivor who grew up being abused, neglected and/or traumatized, you developed distorted thoughts and feelings about yourself. You grew up believing you were to blame for everything bad that happened in your family and everything abusive that happened to you (egocentricity). You felt responsible for the abuse; like you deserved it because you weren't good enough. You began believing, "If I had just been a good little girl/boy, then Mommy and Daddy wouldn't have hurt me," or "I must be a bad person because people only hurt me and they don't want to love me." The distorted thoughts and beliefs you developed were called misperceptions.

As the years passed, you carried those misperceptions over from your childhood into your adulthood.

Your distorted thoughts became a habit and started whirling around inside of you like, "I am to blame for everything that goes wrong in my world. I am defective somehow. Everyone else is better than me. I can't do anything right. I can't trust anyone, and if I did, I would get hurt again. If anything bad is going to happen, it will happen to me. I can't let anyone see how I feel or know my pain. I have to be perfect. It's not safe to let anyone close to me. I have to keep the past a secret."

What you and most abuse survivors don't realize is that they unconsciously maintain these distorted thoughts. For most people, they aren't aware of their negative thoughts about themselves. Sometimes they happen so fast they aren't aware of them, much like driving a car through a green light. Even if done unconsciously, it doesn't mean the misperceptions or negative self-talk don't exist. It doesn't mean they don't effect how you feel about yourself.

The problem with the distorted thoughts you developed as a child is that they influence how you feel about yourself today. You have repeated those distorted thoughts so much in your mind that you have begun to believe what you have been saying and feel the consequences of those negative thougts. So the consequence of telling yourself, "I am defective somehow," for 20 years has left you feeling inadequate and inferior. This feeling of inadequacy and inferiority bleeds over into every aspect of your life: work, home, relationships, family and friends. In essence, you have taken on the identity of what you were told as a child. You have become what you have been telling yourself all of these years. You have become what you believed as a child.

Thus, the goal of cognitive retraining is for you to learn how to change the thoughts (misperceptions) you developed as a child and still hold onto as an adult. And, according to cognitive retraining theory, if you can change your thoughts, you will change the way you feel about yourself and ultimately the way you behave. If you can change the thought "I am inferior" to "I am a capable person who does well in everything I do," you will begin feeling capable in your abilities and will start completing projects with enthusiasm and success. Because you thought you would be successful, you felt successful. Because you felt successful, you were successful.

So cognitive retraining stated plainly says this: My thinking leads to my feelings and my feelings lead to my behaviors. The order of this cannot be rearranged or adjusted, it is a fact of life and of human behavior. Think about this for a moment. Can you genuinely cry (behavior) about your best friend's death without first feeling the sadness associated with your friend's death? No, you can't. Respectively, can you feel the sadness associated with your friend's death without knowing your friend died and without being aware of the thoughts your friend's death has generated? No, you can't. So in essence, your thinking (knowledge) of your friend's death leads to your feelings (sadness) and your feelings lead to your behaviors (crying).

To help you understand this concept a little better let's look at another person who supported the theory of cognitive retraining. Albert Ellis, another renown psychologist, developed a style of therapy based on the philosophy that thinking leads to feelings and feelings lead to behaviors. He called it Rational Emotive Behavior Therapy (REBT). In essence Ellis stated this: A situation will produce the same consequences or feelings over and over again as long as you attach the same beliefs or thoughts to that situation. Thus, the only way you can change the consequences (feelings) is by changing the thoughts you attach to that situation. It looks like this:

$$A \quad + \quad B \quad = \quad C$$

(Situation)   (Belief)   (Consequences/Feelings)

Let's look at Tony and Jan as an example to help you better understand this concept. Tony and Jan are in the same class in school (A-Situation). Every time Tony goes to class he gets anxious and has panic attacks (C-Consequence/feeling). Jan, on the other hand, thrives in class (C-Consequence/feeling) and wishes she could spend all day there. So the questions are, "What is causing Tony to have panic attacks and Jan to thrive in the same class? What is causing the difference in how they feel about the same class?"

The only difference in both of these people is the messages they are giving themselves, their self-talk (B-Beliefs) about the class. Tony's constantly tells himself, "I'm no good in school. I just know I'm going to fail this class. It is too hard for me." While Jan, on the other hand, reminds herself, " I can do anything I put my mind to. I will ace this class just like I do everything else I try." So Tony is doing the following:

A   +   B   =   C
(Situation: (Belief/Thoughts: (Consequences/Feelings:
Class)   I'm no good in school)   Anxiety & Panic Attacks)

So what does Tony need to do to be more like Jan and to become someone who thrives in school?

He must change his current negative thoughts and the messages he gives himself (D). By changing those messages, he gives himself the opportunity to believe something different about himself and his abilities (E). When he can change what he believes about himself, he can then attach his new thoughts and beliefs to the old situation (class). This will cause him to feel differently about the class he is taking. In other words:

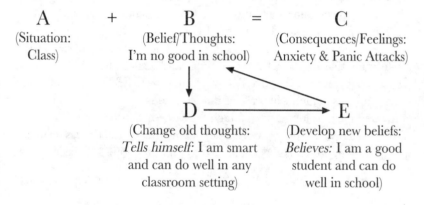

A   +   B   =   C
(Situation: (Belief/Thoughts: (Consequences/Feelings:
Class)   I'm no good in school)   Anxiety & Panic Attacks)

D ——————————→ E
(Change old thoughts: (Develop new beliefs:
Tells himself: I am smart   *Believes:* I am a good
and can do well in any   student and can do
classroom setting)   well in school)

Thus, the final equation looks like this:

A   +   E   =   C
(Situation: (New Belief/Thoughts: (Different Consequences/Feelings:
Class)   I am a good student   good grades, no panic
and can do well in any   attacks, success)
classroom setting)

So the first step in the cognitive part of recovery is learning how to change your thoughts so you can change your feelings, and thus change your behaviors.

As an example of how this applies to childhood abuse, neglect and trauma, let's look at Danny. As a little boy, Danny's father used to physically abuse him. Almost every day of Danny's life was filled with acquiring a new set of bruises and sometimes broken bones. He was terribly afraid of his father, but at the same time wanted his father to love him. As Danny's father beat him he wondered, "What did I do wrong? I must be a bad little boy. I wonder why Daddy doesn't love me? " (egocentricity).

As the beatings got worse and started happening more frequently, Danny began feeling sad and depressed. He grew lonely because he believed no one liked him and he was unworthy of anyone's love. He was afraid of everyone and believed he was just a bad kid who couldn't do anything right (misperceptions).

By the time Danny started high school, he began acting out and getting suspended from school (adverse reactions). He did this because he believed, "No matter what I do I won't ever be good enough, not for my father and not for anyone, so why try."

After Danny graduated from high school, he went to work in a steel factory. His acting out had mutated into sadness and depression. He still felt like the incapable child who couldn't do anything right. He still held onto the thoughts his father had instilled in him. After carrying around those thoughts several more years, Danny became apathetic about his life in general. He quit his job, became an alcoholic and got on welfare. He spent his days locked up in his trailer drinking himself into oblivion. Because Danny had isolated himself away from everyone, no one realized what was happening.

So, how does Danny begin the process of breaking free from his past? He has to begin with changing the thoughts he has about himself. The thoughts he learned as a child and maintain as an adult. He has to replace the old negative thoughts with new positive ones. As the new thoughts begin to take root, Danny will begin feeling better about himself. He will begin developing some positive self-esteem. The positive self-esteem will ultimately change how Danny behaves and what he does with his life. He will likely become more motivated because he no longer believes the things his father instilled in him. He will only believe what he tells himself, and as a result becomes a sober, successful and productive member of society.

Before going any further, I would like for you to take a moment and think about the negative, repetitious thoughts you developed as a result of your childhood. The negative messages you still give yourself today. What are those thoughts? How do those thoughts make you feel? How do they reinforce you remaining the small, helpless child who felt stuck? How do they reinforce your defiant teenager or wounded child ego state? How do you feel about yourself today because of the old childhood thoughts

you still maintain? Take a moment and write out the answers to these
questions here:

_____

_____

_____

_____

_____

_____

_____

_____

_____

_____

_____

_____

The goal of this chapter is to help you change the messages you give
yourself, either consciously or unconsciously, as a result of the abuse. The
way you do this is by you first determining what you want to believe about
yourself and the world. Then you take those things you want to believe
and instill them inside yourself through what is called **conscious repetitious
input**.

Conscious repetitious input is the same thing as practice or telling
yourself the same thing over and over again until you have learned it and
until you believe it. Some people might call this brainwashing, but it's not.
Brainwashing is when someone else tries to make you incorporate or
believe something that is harmful or self-defeating. Cognitive retraining
is you deciding what is healthy for you to believe and changing your
thoughts and beliefs based on that decision. Cognitive retraining will
ultimately help you replace the negative self-talk and thoughts you acquired
as an abused, neglected and/or traumatized child with positive self-talk
and thoughts you should have learned as a child.

I liken negative vs. positive thoughts to a hole in the ground. Each
time you have a negative thought or give yourself a negative message,
what you are doing is taking a shovel and scooping out one load of dirt
out of the hole. Each time you do this, it makes the hole a little deeper,
a little darker, and a little more difficult to see into. Eventually, the hole

becomes so deep you have to jump down into it to scoop out the next load of dirt; the next load of negative thoughts. Then, one day you jump down into the hole to scoop out your load of dirt, but the hole is so deep you can't get back out of it. You are trapped in the hole with nothing but yourself and your negative thoughts and beliefs. On the other hand, each time you replace a negative thought with a positive one, it is like taking one load of dirt and putting it back into the hole. After a while, the positive thoughts fill the hole and you up. Your heart becomes filled with positive thoughts and feelings about yourself; positive self-esteem and self-confidence.

COGNITIVE PHRASES

The way you go about changing your negative thoughts and self-talk is by using what is called **cognitive phrases**. Cognitive phrases are nothing more than a list of phrases of things you want to believe and you choose to tell yourself. They are the thoughts you want to believe; the messages you want to live by; and a reflection of who you want to become.

You are the only one who can decide what you want to replace your old, negative thoughts and self-talk with. No one can do this for you. However, I would like to share the cognitive phrases that helped me during my recovery process and the ones my patients have found to be helpful.

Please understand that changing your thoughts with the cognitive phrases will take a lot of work on your part. It will require dedication and a constant effort. My part will be providing you with the cognitive phrases. Your part, should you choose to accept it, is to buy a set of spiral bound index cards and write one phrase on the front of each card and its meaning on the back. Then learn those phrases through conscious repetitious input. What that means is that you carry your cards around with you every where you go and you repeat them over and over to yourself all day long until you have memorized them. Then you say the cards over and over to yourself until you understand what they mean. Then you continue repeating the phrases over and over to yourself, while meditating on their meaning, until they drop from your head into your heart and they become a normal part of who you are.

An example of how to use the cognitive phrases can be illustrated with Bill. Bill is a junior partner in a law firm. One day, he attends a meeting with the senior partner and one of his co-workers. Bill's boss is angry because client referrals are down. In the middle of the meeting Bill's boss blames him for this. Because of Bill's childhood, he instinctively begins telling himself, "He's right, I'm no good. I can't do anything right. I'll never make full partner because no one likes me. My clients don't even like me."

The moment Bill notices the negative self-talk, his new responsibility is to remind himself, "My thinking leads to my feelings and my feelings lead to my behaviors, so I have to change my thoughts right now. I am a good employee. I have the ability to find out what is wrong with client referrals and fix it. My clients really do like me."

This positive self-talk allows Bill to feel more confident about himself; to feel more in charge of what is happening in his life today; and allows him to move out of the child ego state into the adult ego state so he can handle this problem appropriately. Bill can now take action to rectify the problem and still make partner one day.

As you go through the process of learning the cognitive phrases, it will be extremely important for you to do what Bill did and to look for situations where you can use the cards. This will help make the cognitive phrases more of a habit and will increase the likelihood that you will use them on a daily basis. They are another tool in your protective layer.

Here is a list of cognitive phrases I have accumulated over the years and ones I suggest you begin with. Please put them on your index cards and learn how to apply them to your daily life situations:

1. ***Thinking leads to feelings and feelings lead to behaviors:***
   This is just a reminder card. In the midst of any difficult situation, stop and remind yourself: it is my thoughts that are determining how I feel and how I am responding to this situation. The only way I can change my feelings and the situation is by changing what I am thinking about it.

   $$T_{(thinking)} \longrightarrow F_{(feelings)} \longrightarrow B_{(behaviors)}$$

2. ***People don't do things against me, they do things to meet their own needs:*** No one ever does anything intentionally against me, they do things to make themselves feel better. So if my boss yells at me for something it is because he/she is blowing off steam, had a fight with their spouse, or feels incompetent themselves. People only behave in ways that make themselves feel better about themselves. If they didn't get something out of how they were acting they wouldn't maintain that behavior. So I don't need to take anything personally because it is never about me (as long as I am maintaining the adult ego state).

3. **How people behave tells me about them, not about me:** How someone treats me tells me about them and how they are feeling, it doesn't say anything about me. It gives me hints about what is going on with them and in their life. But, in order for me to know this I have to ask myself the question, "So what does it tell me about them?" I must try to answer this question, even if all I am doing is guessing. By asking myself this question, I am getting the focus off of myself so I can stop making everything my fault. It then helps me to see that how other people act isn't because of me or about me (as long as I am maintaining the adult ego state). It is about them and only them.

4. **Things don't bother me, it's the view I take of them that does:** My perspective about a person or situation will determine the way I respond to that person or situation. If I see a person or situation through the eyes of the child then I will respond in the child ego state. If I see a person or situation through the eyes of the well-adjusted adult then I will respond in the adult ego state.

5. **I learned to be this way, so I can learn to be different, and I am learning to be different:** This is the hope card. It helps me to understand that since I learned to be the way I am then I have the ability to learn how to be different. I have the ability to be who I want to be now, especially since I am not being abused anymore and am giving up the child ego state. I also know that I am learning to be different as a result of all the things I am learning and practicing, such as these cognitive phrases.

6. **That was then and this is now:** When something reminds me of the past or how I was treated, I can remind myself that it isn't happening to me today so I don't have to respond to it in the same way I used to. I can focus on how things are for me right this minute. I can focus on the here and now and be the adult instead of the wounded child.

7. **My name is_____, and I am ENOUGH!!!:** I have to realize I am enough just the way I am. It doesn't mean that I might not need a little tweaking, but overall I am good enough. I need to know I have positive qualities. If I don't believe I am enough and can't accept my positive characteristics, no one else will.

8. *My attitudes, values, beliefs, opinions and feelings are just as good as anyone else's:* I need to understand what my attitudes, values, beliefs, opinions and feelings are now that I am becoming a new person. If I don't believe that my attitudes, values, beliefs, opinions and feelings are just as important and just as good as everyone else's then no one will believe it either. Thus, people will have a tendency to discount me, and I won't be able to be the adult who can stand up for myself.

9. *I must allow others to pursue their own path, and in allowing them to do so, I can accept them even though I don't wish to follow them:* I have to get to the place where it is all right for other people to be who they need to be and for them to follow the paths they need to follow without feeling responsible for their behavior and wanting to make everything all right. When I can do this I will reach a place of acceptance; a place where I can focus on me and what I need to do in order to be okay. I will see that I am only responsible for my own thoughts, feelings, and behaviors.

10. *I believe in myself. I gain courage, strength, and confidence each time I stop and look fear in the face. I must do that which I think I cannot do (paraphrased from Eleanor Roosevelt):* I cannot run away from my fears any longer because each time I do I am playing the role of the child and assigning everyone else in my life the role of being my parent. When I face my fears, I am building myself up and learning that I can take care of myself. I am learning that no matter what, I have to face my fears so I can believe in myself. Each time I face my fears, I gain the confidence I need so the next time something scares me I can deal with it.

11. *I am no longer the wounded and tortured child who needs the love and affection of anyone in order to be all right:* I am now capable and responsible for loving myself. It isn't anyone else's job to be my parent and to make me feel loved and whole. I am no longer wounded but healed; no longer tortured but helped and loved by myself. I am no longer the victim who can't help myself, but a competent adult who can meet my own needs. I have the ability to give myself what I have always wanted from my parents.

12. *I don't need to defend myself, I only need to speak my truth:*
Defending myself is playing the role of the child or parent and
implies that I feel as if I have done something wrong. It causes
my body to feel tense. Speaking my truth is the adult part of me
who can say how I feel without feeling the need to convince others
of the validity behind what I think and feel. I can be relaxed and
know that because they are my thoughts and feeling it makes them
all right.

13. *Things that happen to me can change me, but I don't have
to let them reduce me:* I can allow situations in my life today
to help me grow and/or to change me, but I don't ever have to let
them take me back to the place of being the small and helpless
child I once was.

14. *How I act or react to things is based on my ability to be
objective:* If I stand in the middle of a situation and behave the
way I have always behaved (through the child or parent ego state)
then all I am doing is reacting and perpetuating my past as small
and helpless child. My goal today is to learn how to step back
from a situation long enough to remember that I am not small
and helpless, that I can take of myself if I use my tools, and I am
an adult.

15. *It's okay for me to be seen and own how I feel:* It is all right
for me to allow people to know my thoughts and to see my feelings.
It is entirely acceptable for me to allow people to get to know the
real me instead of the facade I have generated in order to protect
myself. I am a worthy person who is likeable and lovable.

16. *Things may feel the same but I don't have to let them take
me back to the same place:* Things that happen to me in my
life today may remind me of something that happened to me a
long time ago. They may create the same feelings, but I now have
the ability to stay in the present and be the adult, instead of the
helpless child.

17. *The only way I can be abandoned is if I abandon myself:*
No one in my life today has the ability to abandon me unless I
allow them to. The only person who can abandon me is me.

18. **My past does not determine my future:** I have the ability to change who I am and to become the person I want to be. I don't have to recreate my family in order for my life to feel status quo and familiar. It is okay for me to experience myself and my life in a different way and with different expectations.

19. **I am not my feelings:** Even though my childhood experiences left me with a myriad of negative feelings, such as depression, sadness, shame, ineptness, and guilt, it doesn't mean that I have to take those feelings and make them a part of who I am as a person. All it means is that I have leftover feelings from my childhood that need to be resolved and then replaced with more realistic and positive views of who I am today.

20. **Separate the distortions of your child's perspective and replace them with the insight and understanding of your adult:** I need to replace the harmful things I thought and felt as child with the insights and understandings I am gaining in my recovery process. I am the one who is responsible for changing my beliefs about being small and helpless and adopting the insight that I am lovable and capable.

21. **Watch your thoughts, for they become your words. Choose your words, for they become your actions. Understand your actions, for they become your habits. Study your habits, for they will become your character. Develop your character, for it becomes your destiny:** My destiny begins with my thoughts. If I want to change the outcome of my life, then I need to pay attention to my thoughts. My words, actions, habits, and character all follow my thoughts and determine who I become as a person.

22. **I need to do what I need to do in order to take care of me first:** My sole responsibility today is learning how to take care of me first. If I don't learn how to do this, then I will be doomed to continue playing the role of the parent or child ego state the rest of my life. I will be doomed to let everyone's needs come before my own. I must learn how to take care of me first because everyone else is doing the same for themselves.

It will be important for you not to rush through learning these cards. If you do, you may miss an important meaning or a critical way the card may tie back into your childhood. There may be an important piece of insight that may go unseen.

My suggestion is for you to learn no more than three or four cognitive phrases a week, and not move forward in this book until you can apply them to your daily life. Take the time to really learn them. To meditate on their meaning until you can feel them. To know them intimately. To allow them to be a part of who you are. To glean any hidden jewels of insight. Then and only then will you be able to use them properly and will see your life begin to change.

After you have demonstrated the ability to apply the cognitive phrases, please turn the page and complete Exercise G. This exercise will help you develop your own cognitive phrases.

Exercise G:

Cognitive Phrases

Continue using your cognitive phrases on a daily basis, saying them to yourself as many times a day as you can. As you get comfortable using them, start seeing how you can come up with your own phrases and cards. In the midst of difficult situations, try to think about what you could say to yourself to change the way you are feeling and the way you are viewing the situation. Then write out the new cognitive phrases you developed below:

Card 1:	Card 2:
Card 3:	Card 4:
Card 5:	Card 6:
Card 7:	Card 8:

Chapter 7

Pre-Cognitive Phrases

You MAY FIND that learning the cognitive phrases is much easier than applying them. As a matter of fact, you may notice you are having difficulty remembering to use your cognitive phrases, especially in the middle of difficult situations. Don't worry, this is very common. It happens to just about everyone who is first learning how to do things differently; who is learning how to think and respond to their world more appropriately; and who is acquiring a whole new set of tools to live by. Not many people have the ability to take something new, especially something as difficult as changing the way they think, and immediately be able to implement it into their lives. They lack this ability even if the situation isn't that stressful or difficult. Thus, learning and applying your cognitive phrases will take much practice, effort and time. However, when it is all said and done, you will be much more in control of your thoughts and your life in general. You will be able to handle difficult situations through the adult ego state.

So the questions become, "Why, in the beginning, will you likely forget to use your cognitive phrases in the middle of difficult situations? Why will you only remember that you should have used them when the situation has passed? "

To answer these questions, you have to go back to a concept discussed in the previous chapter. When you were a child you were taught how to think and feel, and how to respond to your world. You were taught that when your mom got drunk, the safest thing was for you to hide. You learned that when your father screamed, "You are stupid," the best thing was for you to remain silent. You were taught that when your father was hitting your mother, the only way to protect her was by getting angry and hitting him, hoping it would stop him long enough so you could help your mother escape. You learned that when your uncle came into your room at night to molest you, that you had to give into his demands so he wouldn't hurt you.

You then took those thoughts, feelings and responses you were taught as a child and practiced them for years. You practiced the art of feeling afraid and hiding; being degraded and not speaking your truth; getting angry; and giving into other peoples demands when being violated. You practiced those things until they became a habit, much like driving through the green light without having to think about it. By the time you became an adult, those thoughts, feelings and behaviors had become such a habit that they automatically came to the surface when you got into a difficult situation, especially since you didn't have a protective layer. They were the way you learned to automatically respond to your world.

Just because you are in recovery today doesn't mean those automatic responses are just going to magically disappear. So, when you get into a difficult situation you might instinctively flash back to the child you once were and might continue responding just like you used to when you were a child. You might forget to use your cognitive phrases until after the situation has passed. Remember that in the beginning this is understandable. But also remember, the one thing that is different today is you have a tool box full of tools, which include your cognitive phrases.

Your old, automatic thoughts and responses will come first until you have practiced the cognitive phrases long enough for them to replace your old thoughts and responses; until they become your new habits and new responses. Ultimately your new way of thinking will replace your old thoughts and you will be able to use the cognitive phrases in place of your old thoughts anytime you deem necessary. You will be able to use them in the midst of any difficult situation.

In the meantime, what you need to do is to recognize when you missed an opportunity to apply your cognitive phrases. At that point, you need to stop and think about what you should have done with the phrases and how you could have applied them in that difficult situation. Each time you do this it will help prepare you for the next situation that comes along, and will help you to remember to use your cognitive phrases sooner the next time. You will eventually find yourself using the cards in the middle of your difficult situations rather than afterwards.

For most people, not remembering to use their cards in the midst of a difficult situation causes them to feel a great deal of stress and disappointment in themselves. This is where you have to be gentle with yourself and allow yourself time to adjust to this new way of life. In the meantime, there is a technique that can help prevent you from getting overwhelmed in the middle of difficult situations so you don't instinctively jump back into your automatic response mode and the child ego state. It will help you until you are able to apply your cognitive phrases more automatically. This technique also involves phrases, but in a very different way. These phrases are called **pre-cognitive phrases***. Pre-cognitive phrases teach you how to prepare for and how to respond to difficult situations before they occur. For example, if you knew you were going to give a speech to a room full of people, what would you do? You would feel nervous and anxious, and therefore would prepare and practice what you were going to say to them. You would practice how it would feel to be standing if front of all those people. You would visualize yourself in the conference room giving your speech. This is exactly what the pre-cognitive phrases do: They prepare you for what you will say in difficult situations before the situations occur.

By deciding what you want to say in any difficult situation and preparing for that situation in advance, you are decreasing the likelihood of getting caught off guard and responding to that situation in an old, reactive way; in the child ego state. This is important because what commonly happens is this: Abuse survivors will find themselves in difficult situations and with people who remind them of someone from their childhood. They become nervous and fearful. They begin to feel as if they are the child they used to be when they were growing up. Thus, they automatically respond to the situation just like they did in their childhood. They either grow silent and don't speak their truth, or they respond in an instinctual, angry and defiant manner. Both of these responses are nothing more than the child ego state being tapped into. Neither of these approaches is acceptable to any survivor who is in recovery. Thus, the purpose of the pre-cognitive techniques, if applied properly, is to prevent other people from being able to provoke you into an ego state you don't want to play. It's a way of you speaking your truth in such a generic way that the other person doesn't know how to respond to you except in a generic way as well. It prevents the other person from responding to you in any other role than that of the adult. Thus, the pre-cognitive phrases prevent you from getting overwhelmed and playing the role of the child again.

The first step in the pre-cognitive phrase process is for you to think of at least three to five generic cognitive phrases you can say to someone and then write them down in your spiral bound index cards. These phrases must be so neutral that they won't give the other person any recourse whatsoever and won't give them any reason to respond back to you in a negative fashion. They are different from the cognitive phrases mentioned earlier as they are meant to neutralize a situation rather than change your thoughts about the situation. They just buy you time so you can choose how you want to respond to the difficult situation, so you can remember to use your cognitive phrases and can respond as an adult rather than a child.

The second step is to practice the generic pre-cognitive phrases in your mind until they become a habit, just like the cognitive phrases. Practicing them ahead of time will increase the chances of you remembering to use them in the midst of whatever difficult situation you might find yourself in. If you don't learn them ahead of time, you will likely resort back to your old behavior. You will likely become the wounded child or the defiant teenager all over again.

The third step is to recognize when you are in a difficult situation and when you are beginning to feel like the child again. As soon as you recognize those old, familiar feelings of panic, fear and intimidation and when you feel like your child is trying to bleed over into your adult, it is time to think about your pre-cognitive phrases. It is time to listen to what the other person is saying and to respond back to them using your pre-cognitive phrases.

When you have been able to successfully use the pre-cognitive phrases in the midst of your difficult situation, watch how the other person will momentarily pause because they don't know what to say back to you. Notice how they don't know how to respond to your neutral pre-cognitive phrases. See how they are caught off guard because you aren't automatically jumping into the child ego state and acting like a child. Thus, the fourth step is for you to capitalize on this moment of time the pre-cognitive phrases have bought you. Use this time to think about which of your cognitive phrases you can now use with this difficult situation and use them. This will help you to continue responding to the situation like an adult.

Now that you know the steps of how to develop and use the pre-cognitive phrases, let me share with you the pre-cognitive phrases I use the most often:

1. I'm sorry you feel that way.
2. I'm sorry, I have a different opinion.
3. Right or wrong, this is how I feel.

You are probably noticing the first two pre-cognitive phrases contain the words, "I'm sorry". You are not apologizing for how you feel. This part of the phrase is merely being used as a way of transitioning into your phrases and helping to neutralize what you are saying. So practice saying the pre-cognitive phrases in a nonchalant and casual way instead of in an apologetic way. If done right, you will be able to hear and feel the difference in these two ways.

An example of how the pre-cognitive phrases work can be seen with Joyce. As a little girl, Joyce had to grow up fast because both of her parents died in an automobile accident when she six years old. Joyce had loved both of her parents dearly and had always felt loved by them. However, after their death, Joyce fell apart. She felt as if a part of her had died. She did nothing but cry for months.

To make matters worse, Joyce was sent to a foster home until the authorities could figure out who would be willing to take on the responsibility of a six-year-old girl. When no one else would claim her, her paternal uncle agreed she could live with him. The only reason he wanted Joyce was so he could collect the monthly check the government would send him every month for fostering Joyce in his home.

After Joyce moved in with her uncle, she was given a bedroom the size of a closet. She was never given any love or attention. Instead, she was made to cook and do all the household chores. She was never allowed to talk or have friends. Even after Joyce started school, she was never allowed to do anything but cook and clean. She grew sad and lonely. She wondered how long she could live like this.

By the time Joyce became an adult, she didn't know how to think or feel about herself. She was confused. All she knew was that at one time she had a set of parents who had loved and cherished her. Then, she was forced to live with an uncle who hated her and treated her like a slave. She didn't know if she was capable of being loved or accepted again.

After many years of feeling lost and having one disastrous relationship after another, Joyce decided that if she was ever going to be able to function in a relationship she needed to get into counseling. While in therapy, Joyce learned a great deal about herself. She learned how she had assumed the role of the silent, wounded child who didn't know how to stand up for herself or how to take care of herself. She learned about ego states and loci of control. She was taught how to use the pre-cognitive phrases.

About three months into therapy, Joyce met a man named Tony. Her therapist tried to tell her it was too soon to begin a relationship, but Joyce didn't want to wait any longer. Not long after, Joyce and Tony moved in together.

In the beginning, Joyce thought there was nothing that could go wrong with this relationship. She was basking in the progress she had made. Then the day came when Joyce walked in the door of her home after a very long day at work. Tony stood there glaring at her with anger in his eyes. He slammed the door shut behind her and yelled, "You are a lousy girlfriend. You don't have my dinner on the table yet. I worked hard all day and don't deserve this from you. You should have dinner on the table every night and it should be something I like. Get in there and cook me something to eat!"

For a moment Joyce just stood there not knowing what to think. She began feeling anxious and fearful. Tears began welling up in her eyes as she tried to explain she was late getting home and late with dinner because of a meeting at work. Tony yelled back, "I don't care about your stupid meeting. You're my girlfriend. You're supposed to have dinner on the table for me when I get home. You aren't good for anything."

Then Joyce remembered what her therapist had taught her. She recognized she was feeling like the wounded child all over again. She remembered that when she was feeling overwhelmed she needed to use her pre-cognitive phrases. Thus, Joyce looked at Tony and said, "Well I'm sorry you feel that way."

Because Tony didn't expect Joyce to respond in such a neutral way and with such a generic comment, he just stood there for a moment thinking, "How am I supposed to respond to that?"

This gave Joyce the time she needed to remember her cognitive phrases. So she said to herself, "**People don't do things against me, they do things to meet their own needs.** So Tony is acting like this to meet his own needs. **I don't need to defend myself, I only need to speak my truth.** Thus, I will only explain I was late because of a meeting and if that isn't good enough then Tony has no one to look at but himself. **I need to do what I need to do in order to take care of myself first.** So I need to either let Tony know that I won't be his maid or I need to decide this relationship isn't healthy for me and leave."

These cognitive phrases helped Joyce to regain her ability to operate out of the adult ego state again and thus she could respond to the rest of the conversation with Tony as an adult.

The pre-cognitive phrases, like everything else will require practice and then even more practice. So please take the time now to turn to Exercise H on the next page so you can develop your own pre-cognitive phrases. You are welcome to use the ones mentioned above, but it will be important for you to practice coming up with your own as well; to come up with ones that pertain to your life.

Exercise H:

Pre-Cognitive Phrases

Step I: Take a moment and think about some difficult situations you have encountered lately. Think about what you could have said (in one sentence) to have neutralized that situation. Remember this sentence must be neutral. It cannot be worded in a way that will attack the other person or be used in defense of yourself. The pre-cognitive phrase must be generic, neutral and benign.

Listed again are the three pre-cognitive phrases I use:

    1. I'm sorry you feel that way;
    2. I'm sorry, my opinion happens to be different;
    3. Right or wrong, this is how I feel.

After you develop your own pre-cognitive phrases, write them in the space below.

Pre-Cognitive Phrase #1:	Pre-Cognitive Phrase #2:
Pre-Cognitive Phrase #3:	Pre-Cognitive Phrase #4:

Step II: Practice using the pre-cognitive phrases. As you use the pre-cognitive phrases, write out how it felt to use them and the outcome of the situation because you used them. Also write out how the situation might have turned out if you had NOT used the pre-cognitive techniques.

Situation 1:
Description of event:

_____

_____

How it felt and the outcome because you used phrases:

_____

_____

_____

_____

Possible outcome if you had NOT used pre-cognitive technique:

_____

_____

_____

_____

Situation 2:
Description of event:

_____

_____

_____

_____

How it felt and the outcome because you used phrases:

_____

_____

_____

_____

Possible outcome if you had NOT used pre-cognitive technique:

_____

_____

_____

_____

Chapter 8

Diaphragmatic Breathing and Journaling

THERE ARE two last cognitive techniques I would like to share with you before moving on to the emotional restructuring work. Both of these techniques are extremely important in the healing process as they allow room in your daily life for learning how to be with just you, and your own thoughts and feelings. They will also help you with the individuation process and developing a relationship with yourself.

An added benefit of practicing these two techniques at this point in your recovery is this: By the time you get to the emotional restructuring work you will have had plenty of practice with getting in touch with yourself. This in turn will make it easier for you to get in contact with the parts of your inner child who need healing. It will make the emotional restructuring process move more quickly.

SETTING THE STAGE

Many abuse survivors often find it very difficult to be quiet or be alone with themselves. This is usually a very scary prospect for them. It is usually a dangerous time because they have nothing but their own thoughts and feelings to be with. It is when there are no distractions that they are reminded of the abuse and how it made them feel. They remember the feelings of shame, depression, hopelessness and guilt. Unfortunately, they begin to believe that it is the act of being still that causes them to feel these unwanted thoughts and feelings. This isn't true.

What causes the painful and negative thoughts and feelings is the fact that they haven't gone back and dealt with the abuse itself. Thus, the pain and hurt lingers. So any time they stop and spend a moment of quiet time with themselves their inner child breaks through to the surface saying,

"I can't go away until you look at and deal with what happened in our childhood. Don't you remember what happened to us? You have to look at what happened so we can heal."

So being with themselves in a quiet way only makes them feel bad about themselves because it reminds them of the pain they still carry around. It results in their going to any length to stay busy and/or numb to the past. In the end, they become workaholics, alcoholics, drug addicts, overeaters, compulsive spenders, perfectionists, and so forth (adverse reactions) to quiet the voice of their inner child.

Another thing that happens to abuse survivors is that they tend to stay tense and keyed up. They are constantly on the move. They try to avoid being still for all the reasons mentioned above. This tension and constantly being on the move lives in their bodies. It shows up in the form of tense, rigid muscles, tight shoulders, and shallow breathing.

It is important to understand that this way of living goes back to their childhood and how they learned to live with the abuse. In the middle of being physically abused they learned to tighten the muscles of their body to keep the beating from hurting so badly. While they were watching their father get drunk and tear up the house, their breath grew quiet and shallow so they could hide and be safe.

They learned to stay in constant-alert-mode as a means of protecting themselves and anyone else they were given the responsibility of taking care of. They believed that if they could stay on guard long enough it would decrease the likelihood that something would catch them by surprise and hurt them again. This keyed up, constant alert-mode, called **hypervigilance**, is a common phenomenon among abuse survivors.

Even though hypervigilance serves a very distinct purpose in childhood, it is counter-productive to the abuse survivor who wants to heal and it has an adverse effect on their body. It interferes with their ability to handle difficult situations without panicking and becoming emotionally overwhelmed.

It works like this. When they are in the middle of a difficult situation, they jump into automatic response mode, just like driving through the green light without having to think about it. Their breathing becomes shallow. Their muscles become tense. Their body becomes rigid. Their brain can't get the oxygen it needs to make rational decisions because their breath is so quick and shallow. Thus, their body begins to feel just like it did when they were a small child.

When their body becomes tense and has minimal oxygen with which to operate, it results in their dealing with difficult situations just like they did when they were a child. They might panic or become frightened.

This causes them to become the wounded child again. They might even get angry or frustrated and become the critical parent.

Unfortunately, I am describing something you might struggle with as well. What you have to realize is that ignoring your inner child, staying hypervigilant and avoiding being with yourself doesn't help you to overcome your past. It doesn't give you the chance to really know who you are underneath the negative feelings. It doesn't give you an opportunity to know who you are in spite of the abuse. It doesn't allow you to deal with difficult situations outside of constant alert-mode and in the adult ego state. Consequently, you feel alone because you are the one who hasn't stopped to learn how to develop a positive and nurturing relationship with yourself.

By reading this book, you are at least considering getting to know yourself in a different way. You are entertaining the idea that there might be a better way to be with yourself and to like being with you. You are at least considering that being in constant alert-mode is counter-productive. So I would like to share two exercises that will help you to begin developing a kind and loving relationship with yourself, and that will help you to learn how to be with your own thoughts and feelings without it having to be a negative experience.

The first technique comes in the form of what is called **diaphragmatic breathing**. Diaphragmatic breathing has been done for centuries in eastern countries to aid in the art of meditation and relaxation.

There are many benefits to learning how to breathe from your diaphragm, as opposed to your lungs. The most important one is that it will help you to get in touch with yourself and your feelings. It will teach you how to be still and be with yourself in a positive manner. It will help you to get to know who you are and how you feel about things. It will help you to find your inner child so you can find inner peace. Most therapists and healers believe a person's emotions are stored in their diaphragm, so the only way to access those emotions is through your breath and breathing from your diaphragm.

Diaphragmatic breathing will also increase the amount of oxygen you have in your body so you can respond to difficult situations in a relaxed, adult manner; so you can feel calm and as if you are in control of how you handle things.

Just keep in mind it is physically impossible to feel tense and relaxed at the same time. Thus, the diaphragmatic breathing pushes away the tension and replaces it with relaxation. It pushes the child ego state aside and replaces it with the adult ego state. It pushes aside the external locus of control and replaces it with an internal locus of control.

To get started, I would like for you to sit (not lie down) in a chair or something that is comfortable. It needs to be in a quiet place. Place one hand on your chest and the other directly below on your stomach (in the middle of your abdomen). Slightly above your stomach is where your diaphragm is located. As you breathe, look at your hands and notice which one moves. This will tell you whether you are a chest breather or a diaphragmatic breather.

Now remove the hand that is on your chest and look at the hand that is remaining on your stomach, your diaphragm. Only using the muscles of your stomach, and not with your breath, I would like for you to practice pushing your stomach out and then sucking it in. Watch as your stomach moves in and out. For many people this is a difficult thing to do because they don't exercise. So be sure to take the time now to practice what it feels like to use your stomach muscles as these will be the only muscles you will be using during the diaphragmatic breathing exercise. Nothing but your stomach should move. Not your chest, not your shoulders, nothing else. Moving nothing but the muscles of your stomach is a very deliberate act and can only be mastered with practice.

After practicing this for several minutes, try adding your breath to the movement of your stomach. Each time you breathe in, breathe in through your nose. Watch your stomach as you intentionally push your stomach muscles out with each breath. Imagine you are inflating a balloon. As the air is breathed into the balloon, it inflates. This is the same thing that happens with your stomach as you breathe in.

Now, each time you exhale, exhale through your mouth. Watch your stomach as you intentionally suck your stomach muscles in. This process is like sucking all the air out of the balloon and watching it deflate.

It is important to remember to do this part of the exercise slowly so you don't end up hyperventilating. Each breath should be slow, rhythmic and relaxed. Take time now to practice this part of the exercise until you are comfortable with it.

The next step is to remove your hand from stomach and place it on your lap. Do not let your hands touch, keep them separate and relaxed. Now close your eyes and begin breathing in through your nose while pushing your stomach out. Then hold your breath for a moment. Then exhale through your mouth while sucking your stomach in. Practice this until you are comfortable with this part of the exercise.

The last step is learning how to count while you are breathing. I usually suggest people start with a 2-2-3 count. This means you breathe in for a count of 2, hold your breath for another count of 2 and then breathe out for a count of 3. It is important not to skip the "hold your breath" part of the exercise.

As you get more proficient with the diaphragmatic breathing, you can increase the count, but remember to always make the breath in and hold the same number and the breath out one count longer. For example, 3-3-4, 4-4-5, and 5-5-6.

Now, I would like for you to take the time right now to close you eyes and practice the diaphragmatic breathing with the counting. If you find your thoughts wandering, gently remind yourself to focus only on your breathing or the counting of your breaths. In the beginning, most people have to redirect themselves frequently. This is very normal. As time goes on, the frequency of this redirection will diminish and you will have learned to focus on nothing but your breath or counting of your breath.

As you incorporate all these steps together, you should experience a sense of relaxation and what a lot of survivors in my practice have called "getting in the zone". The outside world and your thoughts momentarily fade away while a sense of well being and calmness sets in. It allows your brain to turn off and your body to turn on. It allows you to relax and regenerate so you can feel good about yourself and your ability to deal with life.

Now that you have learned how to diaphragmatically breathe, I would like for you to practice it at least four times a day for a couple of minutes each session: First thing in the morning upon waking up to set the tone of your day, a couple of times during the day, and before you go to bed.

JOURNALING

The second task is for you to learn how to be with your thoughts and feelings in a positive way on a daily basis. And, for you to understand you don't have to hide what you think and feel anymore. This can be accomplished by learning how to **journal**.

Journaling is a very personal and kind thing to do for yourself. It can be very healing. It prevents you from having to feel alone anymore because you will always have someone to talk to, yourself. It will teach you that thinking or writing about things, which may have been forbidden in the past, doesn't mean bad things will happen to you today. It will show you that writing about the people who hurt you doesn't mean you are pointing a blaming finger or trying to make them look bad. It just means you are sharing your experiences, and what you think and feel about those experiences with yourself. It is you speaking your truth to yourself and it being all right.

So the first step in journaling is telling yourself, "It is okay for me to share my thoughts and feelings with myself. I am allowed to write about the things that happened to me. It is okay for me to be comfortable with myself. It is all right for me to ponder my thoughts and feelings in a healthy way. It is all right for me to look at how I feel now and how I felt in the past".

The second step is to buy a journal, which reflects who you are as a person. If you love nature, buy an earthy one. If you are a painter or artist at heart, buy an artsy one. If you are an athlete, then one with runners, basketball players, or tennis players all over it. Whatever you get is fine, just as long as it is NOT a plain white lined note pad. If what you are trying to journal in something that isn't appealing to you, you probably won't write in it.

The third step in journaling is to create a private place where you can journal in peace. For many people, it is a secluded place. It may be a spare room you decorated in your favorite colors, with scented candles and soft music. It may be sitting out on your back deck that overlooks the lake. It might be an attic you restored with over-stuffed furniture and a skylight. It is important this place is somewhere you would like to spend time and one you feel comfortable and safe in.

The fourth step is scheduling time into your day to journal. I usually recommend that most people journal in the evening before going to bed. However, I have had people share their preference for journaling first thing in the morning before they begin their day. Whatever works for you is fine. I personally prefer to journal in the evening. It gives me time to reflect on how my day went and to unload my thoughts so I don't dream about them. It provides me with a sense of closure about my day so I can start fresh in the morning.

The fifth step is to open your journal and allow your thoughts and feelings to flow freely. Anything you write is okay. You can even draw or cut out words and pictures from a magazine to put in your journal. It is all right to personalize your journal and to make it about you, no matter how that looks. There isn't anyone who can punish you for what you think or feel today, except you, so be kind to yourself. Allow it to be all right for you to put on paper how your day went, what you thought and felt that day, what those thoughts and feelings reminded you of in your childhood, and how you would like things to be different.

One thing to keep in mind is this: Journaling isn't just about writing down the negative things that happened in your past or the bad things that happen in your day. It is not just about writing out the things you want to change about yourself. It is also writing about the things you like about yourself; the things that are going well in your life; and how you are changing into the person you want to become. It is you writing about how wonderful it felt to get that long-awaited promotion. It is being able to able to write in your journal without feeling guilty. It is reminding yourself about the joy you experienced setting up your private room and how rewarding it feels each time you are able to use your cognitive phrases and respond like an adult. It is learning that it is all right to look at and write about the positive things in your life today. It will be important for you to begin focusing on those positive aspects of your life and your accomplishments, as this is the direction you are moving in. It is healthy for you to notice your days are getting better and so are you.

Now that you have learned how to diaphragmatically breathe and to journal, it will be important for you to incorporate these activities into your daily life. The diaphragmatic breathing should be done in the morning and in the afternoons as mentioned earlier. In the evening, I would like for you to do your breathing first as a way of centering yourself and preparing yourself for your journaling time. The breathing will help you to calm down and get relaxed so you will feel more comfortable and open with what you want to journal. When you have finished journaling, do one last round of breathing and then go directly to bed for a good night's rest. The last round of breathing puts space between what you journaled and your sleep time, and in turn will decrease the likelihood of you dreaming about the things you journaled. Please be kind to yourself and allow yourself a week of practicing the diaphragmatic breathing and journaling before reading any further.

Chapter 9

The Plan

THUS FAR you have been exposed to a number of concepts and techniques that have helped you become more aware of your behavior, and to better understand it. You have been exposed to things such as egocentricity and misperceptions and how they can become adverse reactions. You now understand how your behavior as an adult was shaped in your childhood. You have learned to identify what role you were assigned as a child and why you maintain that role today as an adult. You have become aware of what needs to be done to change how you see yourself and how to handle difficult situations in more of an adult ego state. You now know what tools you weren't provided as a child and how that has impacted the way you respond to the world. Not only have you acquired this knowledge and understanding, but you have also taken the time to practice your skills as they have been presented to you.

At this point, you may be wondering how all of these concepts and techniques are supposed to fit together. If you are wondering this, you are on the right track. It is one thing to have knowledge but it is something entirely different to know how to use and incorporate that knowledge into your everyday life; to know how to put all the pieces of the puzzle together so they make a complete picture. This is the next step.

It would be great if I could tell you that you have all the pieces necessary to make a complete picture of recovery, but you don't. Because we have only been dealing with the cognitive part of recovery, you only have one part of the puzzle. So the question at hand is this: How do you take the information you have learned so far and incorporate it into your life so you can use it and continue recovering?

The answer lies in what I called **The Plan**. The plan takes what you have been introduced to and have been practicing thus far and puts it all together. It gives you a vision of how the puzzle of recovery is supposed to look; a glimpse of the direction your life is moving in; and how it will ultimately look. As you are successful with using the plan, you will notice a sense of excitement growing inside of you and a new determination to finish what you started. Each time you handle a difficult situation or unwanted thoughts and feelings successfully, you will become more and more excited about the person you are becoming. You will notice that you are beginning to like who you are and the person you are evolving into. Remember though, what you are being provided is only part of the plan just like what you have learned so far is only part of the puzzle. The rest will come as you venture through the emotional restructuring process in the next section.

The purpose of the plan is to provide you with a comprehensive means of dealing with any difficult situation you come across in your daily life. It will help you change any unwanted thoughts, feelings and behaviors so you can respond to the world in a more adult fashion. It will allow you the opportunity to choose what ego state you want to operate out of rather than playing the role you were assigned as a child. It will give you a chance to be objective and see the situation through the eyes of the adult rather than the heart of the wounded child. It will give you what you didn't have as a child—a choice. You will now have the choice to choose how you want to behave, how you want to speak your truth and how you want to own what you think and feel.

An added benefit of the plan is this: Each time you handle a difficult situation through the adult ego state, you will begin experiencing and understanding what it feels like to be operating out of an internal locus of control. You will start understanding what it feels like to be in charge of yourself, your actions and ultimately your life. It is like that feeling you had the first time you were able to peddle your bicycle on your own. It's that feeling of pride you had; that feeling of "I can do anything"; and of being invincible.

THE PLAN

There are five steps to this part of the plan. You will recognize and understand each step because they have already been discussed in great detail in the previous chapters. This brief description will help you to understand how to think and use each step.

The first step of the plan is: *Notice in my body when I am becoming stressed, depressed, anxious, etc (child ego state).* You will need to replace the words stressed, depressed, and anxious with words that describe the emotions you struggle with, i.e. angry, frustrated, terrified, controlling, abandoned, cornered, defensive, paranoid, etc. Personalize it to match what you would normally feel in the middle of a difficult situation. Then sit back and imagine yourself in the middle of a difficult situation. Feel what it would feel like in your body to experience being in that difficult situation. Allow yourself to feel the physical sensations and to experience them. Notice if your body becomes tense, your breath shallow, your heart races, your limbs feel heavy, or your jaws clinch tightly together. Notice if you get migraine headaches, your blood pressure goes up, or your stomach burns.

These physical sensations are what I call the **red flag**. They are your body's way of signaling you that something is wrong; there is something you need to pay attention to; and that something emotional is working it's way to the surface. What is working its way to the surface is your inner child. It's your inner child's way of telling you he/she is in trouble and needs your help. It is you moving back down into the child ego state.

In the past, moving back down into the child ego state has been an instinctual act and one of self-preservation. It has been your way of protecting yourself and getting your needs met. However, you are now aware of how your inner child and child ego state operates. You know what purposes they serve. So today you can stop looking at these physical sensations as a problem and see them as a gift from your inner child; as a personalized message via your body that something is wrong and you need to do something different. So recognize this red flag as a distress signal and as an opportunity to work the rest of the plan so you can handle your difficult situations through the adult ego state.

Finally, know this is the most important step of the plan. If you cannot recognize the red flag, or your body's clues that something is wrong, you will be doomed to respond to any and all difficult situations just like you have in the past; just like the wounded child or defiant teenager. On the other hand, if you recognize the red flag you will be able to use the plan and everything you have learned so far.

The second step of the plan is: *Do my diaphragmatic breathing*. It will be important for you to do your diaphragmatic breathing as soon as you recognize the unwanted physical sensations. It will help your body to begin relaxing so you can use the rest of your tools mentioned in the plan.

If you become tense and remain that way, you will respond to the situation at hand just like you have always done in the past. You will respond like the scared and wounded child. However, if you do your diaphragmatic breathing and allow yourself to begin relaxing, it will help to put space between you and the situation so you can choose to do something differently; so you can work towards responding like the adult who is in control of your life.

While you are doing your breathing it will be important for you to begin step 2A: *Look at what role I am playing and what role I have assigned the other person(s).* Knowing what role you are playing will help you understand why you are feeling the way you are. It will help you to see what role the other person is playing and why they have taken on that role. As you look at what role you are playing, feel what it feels like to be playing this role. Feel what it feels like to have assigned the other person a role other than that of the adult. Take a moment and feel how this doesn't work for you anymore.

After you have figured out what role you are playing, ask yourself why you are playing that role again. What was it that caused you to resume that role, even though you are now an adult? What are you protecting yourself from? What needs are you trying to get the other person to fulfill?

After you have figured out what role you and the other person are playing and why, you will need to pursue step 3: *Choose which cards (cognitive phrases) go with the situation and repeat them to myself until I have developed a new perspective.* The cognitive phrases are the first step in you moving out of the child ego state and advancing towards the adult ego state. This is the first step where you make an effort to look at the situation more realistically and to see yourself and the situation more objectively; to see the situation for what it really is as opposed to what it reminds you of from your abusive childhood. The cards with your cognitive phrases on them will help you to develop a different perspective, a different way of thinking about the situation and the person you are dealing with. You will begin seeing the situation isn't really about you as a person and it isn't your fault. It is just a situation that needs to be resolved; a situation that is giving you an opportunity to practice the new you, the new adult. It is this new perspective, that isn't based out of old childhood traumas, that will create the opportunity for you to handle the situation like an adult.

With your new perspective in mind, you are now ready for step 4: *Choose to respond to the situation differently and do so (adult ego state).* Now that you have developed a new perspective you can choose how you want to deal with the situation and how you want to respond to it. It now becomes a choice. You can choose to put the plan aside and respond the way you have always done in the past (child ego state). Or, you can decide you are ready to deal with the situation differently and as an adult.

The choice is yours because you are aware of what is happening and why. In the past, you didn't have a choice as to how you responded to things because you didn't understand yourself or why you were behaving like you were. However, today you have an intimate knowledge of your behavior. Thus, you have a choice and are responsible for whatever choice you make today. The new you will learn how to use the cards and will choose to respond to each and every situation out of the adult ego state.

The last step is: *Afterwards: Meditate on how I handled the situation, what I learned from it, how I could have handled it differently and journal it.* Objectively looking at how you handled the situation is vital. So take the time to think about what you did right and how you could have handled things differently. What were the things you did that looked like the adult? What were the things you did that looked like the child? Look at what you learned from the situation. Was something in particular a stumbling block for you? Did you see something in a different light? Did you have insight about something you hadn't noticed before? All of these are important questions to ponder.

After you have answered these questions, write out your answers in your journal. Don't be neglectful of journaling these things. Writing out what you learned and the insights you gained will increase the probability that you will remember and will be able to apply what you learned to the next difficult situation. It will allow you to carry important insights, information and lessons you learned forward.

Let's look at Judy again. We've already examined her situation to see how she might have used the plan in the middle of her difficult situation. Her story will be reiterated here to help you remember the details of her difficult situation.

When Judy was a little girl she grew up in a family who lived in a run-down trailer park out in the middle of the country on a dirt road. Almost every day of Judy's life her mother would get high and would tell her, "You're going to get stuck here in this hell hole just like me. No one in our family has ever gotten out of here. No one has ever married a nice guy or lived happily ever after. It definitely won't happen for you. You're too ugly and too fat to get a nice looking guy. They want someone with a little less fat around their hips."

Every time Judy heard those words, she would cry herself to sleep wondering, "Why does Momma hate me so much? What did I do wrong? What made Momma not love me anymore? Am I really that fat and ugly? Will I really be stuck here the rest of my life?"

Judy didn't want to believe what her mother was saying. She didn't want to believe she was doomed to live on this dirt road for what seemed like an eternity. However, the day finally came when Judy's mother broke her spirit. Judy gave up hope of ever leaving the trailer park and her mother. So she quit school and got a job at the local convenience store.

Judy began starving herself, hoping she could get thin enough so her mother or maybe someone else would love her. Then one day at work, Judy and one of her co-workers, Suzy, were joking around. In the middle of a bunch of jokes Suzy blurted out, "Your momma's right. You are too ugly for a rich, nice-looking man. You are poor and ugly just like the rest of us. There's no way you'll ever get a date with anyone."

Those comments crushed Judy. She felt like someone had just punched her in the stomach.

The laughter stopped and was replaced with nothing but silence. Suzy asked, "What's wrong. I was just joking around. I didn't mean anything by it."

Judy didn't know what to say. She wanted to cry, but was too embarrassed to cry in front of her friend. So she ran out of the room and back to her dirty trailer on the dirt road. She sat there and did nothing but cry for the next several days while cutting on her arms and starving herself.

So the question becomes, "How could Judy have used the plan so she didn't end up spending the next several days crying, cutting her arms and starving herself?"

The first thing Judy could have done was to recognize how Suzy's comments were causing her to feel uncomfortable physical sensations in her body. She needed to have noticed when it felt like someone had punched in her in the stomach, when she felt crushed and wanted to cry. This was her red flag. It was her body's way of telling her that her wounded child was being tapped into and that something was wrong. It was her body's way of notifying her that Suzy's comments had pushed one of her emotional buttons and was causing her to move out of the adult ego state into the child ego state.

The next thing Judy should have done was to do her diaphragmatic breathing to help her calm down and to become centered. While doing her breathing, she needed to have asked herself, "What role am I playing and what role am I assigning Suzy?"

Judy needed to have seriously contemplated these questions. She needed to have looked at what she was thinking and feeling. If she had stopped long enough to do this, she would have seen she was playing the role of the wounded child and how she had assigned Suzy the role of being the critical parent. She would have realized the way she was feeling in front of Suzy was the same way she had always felt when she was dealing with her mother.

After realizing she was playing the role of the child, Judy needed to have thought about her cognitive phrases and which ones would have pertained to her situation. She could have chosen and repeated to herself, **"My name is Judy and I am enough. People don't do things against me they do things to meet their own needs.** So Suzy didn't say those things to hurt me, but to make herself feel better about herself. What she said isn't about me but about her and her concerns about being trapped, ugly and poor. **Things don't bother me, it's the way I look at them that does.** So I need to take Suzy out of the role of being my critical mother and see her for who she is, just my co-worker. **I need to do what I need to do in order to take care of myself first and that means I don't need to defend myself, I just need to speak my truth.** So I need to let Suzy know how I feel about her comments in an adult fashion. **Things can change me but I don't have to let them reduce me.** So I can hear what Suzy said and realize it is about her and not about me. I can realize her comments remind me of the things my mother has said to me but I don't have to become the wounded and helpless child again who can't stand up for myself."

Judy could have told herself all of these things until her perspective about Suzy changed. Until she no longer saw Suzy as her critical mother, but as the person she was, her co-worker.

When Judy was able to change the way she saw Suzy and the situation, it would have allowed her to start moving toward the adult ego state. It would have given her the opportunity to choose how she wanted to respond to Suzy and to do so. She could have explained to her, "I am in charge of my life and how I look, not my mother. I am not trapped here. I'm not poor or ugly. I can get a date anytime I want one. So I would appreciate it if you wouldn't joke around with me like that anymore."

Because Judy would have been operating out of the adult ego state it would have allowed Suzy the opportunity to do the same in return. If may have even allowed Suzy to apologize for her inappropriate comments.

Then, after Judy had spoken her truth, she could have gone home to her trailer and completed the rest of the plan. She could have gone to her quiet place and meditated on how she had handled the situation, looked at what she had learned from it, how she could have handled it differently and then journaled it. This would have helped Judy to see how well she had done, to feel the joy that came from stepping out of the child ego state and to have handled a difficult situation like an adult. She could have felt the tremendous pride that comes from being the winner; from being the one who saw her past trying to sneak up on her again and doing what it took not to allow that to happen. It would have given her the opportunity to look at the areas in which she could have done better. It also would have given her the chance to evaluate what she had learned from this experience so she could apply it to the next similar situation that comes along.

I suggest you do the same thing with the plan as you did with the cognitive phrases. Write them down in your spiral bound index cards. This will give you easy access to the plan when a difficult situation occurs. Having the plan written down as a card may end up being the difference between you handling a difficult situation through the child ego state as opposed to adult ego state.

If you get into a difficult situation, panic and forget the steps of the plan, you will end up playing the role of the child one more time. However, if you panic and go to a quiet place where you can pull out your cards with the plan on it, you will likely be able to develop a more healthy perspective about the situation and be able to respond to it as an adult. Writing the plan down on your cards is you doing everything possible to ensure your own success; it's your setting yourself up with a safety net.

Please take several weeks and practice using the plan as often as you can. Practice it until you thoroughly understand how to use it and feel comfortable using it in the middle of any difficult situation. Please do this before moving on to the emotional restructuring work in Section II.

Once you feel you have mastered all of the tools and exercises mentioned so far in Section I, it will be time for you to move on to the next chapter and to begin the emotional restructuring work. Please do not move forward until you have made sure of your mastery of these skills and techniques.

If you are beginning to experience difficulty with anything, or if overwhelming thoughts and feelings are being triggered, please make sure you seek professional help now. Do whatever it takes to ensure your safety and you being able to continue your journey of healing.

Finally, as mentioned earlier, you will start feeling better about yourself as you work the plan. But remember all the techniques you have learned so far are merely stepping stones to where you want to be, healed and recovered. The stepping stones you have acquired so far get you only part of the way across the creek of recovery. If you stop now, you have no option but to either stand still in the middle of the creek or to turn around and go back to where you came from.

Don't let the fact that you are feeling a little better cause you to stop or make you think everything is fine and resolved because it's not. It is only a temporary illusion, a temporary fix. You have only looked at the ripples on the pond. You haven't found the rock lying at the bottom of the pond. You still haven't looked at the original abuse, neglect and/or trauma you endured. You haven't dealt with the feelings associated with what happened to you as a child. Unless you go back and face what happened to your inner child and how it felt, your inner child will be like the dog that keeps nipping at your heels until you stop and help bandage his/her wounds.

Remember though, you have made progress, so continue keeping up the good work and continue being kind to yourself. Honor your desire to be healed, once and for all. Continue working your way through this book and the recovery process, so the emotional stepping stones can be laid in their proper place in the creek and so you can cross all the way over to the other side.

SECTION II

EMOTIONAL RESTRUCTURING

Chapter 10

Emotional Healing
through Emotional Restructuring

Look around you and you will see many people who have started the recovery process but stopped half way through it. They gathered a little bit of information and made a few changes. They used their tools and began feeling a little better about themselves and their ability to handle difficult situations. Then, when they realized that part of the healing process would involve experiencing their feelings and that sooner or later they would have to face their emotional pain, they quit. For them, the easier thing to do was to settle for the little bit of happiness they had acquired from the cognitive work and then leave well enough alone. This wasn't necessarily a conscious decision on their part. It was just their way of protecting themselves from having to feel the pain of their childhood again. They didn't realize this so-called easier path wouldn't last and it would ultimately rob them of the happiness they could have had. If they had just kept going and had been willing to look at the heart of their inner, wounded child and at what had happened to that child, they would have found what they were looking for. They could have found healing and wholeness; a life filled with new meaning and new feelings.

You, on the other hand, haven't quit. So I would like to congratulate you for choosing to honor yourself; for choosing to complete the recovery process rather than settling for a temporary fix. You have worked hard and deserve a pat on the back for the progress you have made, and for the courage it has taken for you to embark on this journey. For the effort you have put into saving yourself and your inner child.

I know it hasn't been easy, but you are doing it, so keep up the good work. In the end, you will be pleasantly surprised at how resolved everything feels and how free you feel for the first time in your life. You will have a new lease on life and a new sense of self. You will know the freedom that comes from living in the present moment and having a meaningful relationship with yourself. You will know the pride that comes from being able to take care of yourself and being able to meet your own needs. Not to be afraid anymore, but to be happy to be alive. In the meantime, there is a lot of work left to do, but work you now have the ability to do. So let's continue what you've started.

WHY EMOTIONAL RESTRUCTURING

Until now, you have been dealing with the cognitive, or thinking part of the recovery process. You have been learning how to change your thoughts about yourself and the world around you. You have been learning important tools and concepts to enhance your every day life and to improve your ability to handle difficult situations. You have also learned that the cognitive part of recovery is only half of the equation; it is only half of what you need in order to recover from the abuse, neglect and/or trauma you sustained as a child.

Coming to terms with the idea that what you have learned so far is only half of the healing equation might seem puzzling to you, especially since you have begun feeling better about yourself and your abilities. You might be wondering, "Why can't the recovery process just entail changing my thoughts and why aren't the cognitive techniques and phrases enough for me to heal from the abuse?"

To answer these questions, you must first understand how the conscious and unconscious mind work and what roles they play in the recovery process. This concept is very similar to Freud's Iceberg Theory. Here is an illustration of the conscious and unconscious mind so you can refer to it as they are being explained:

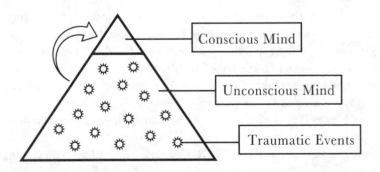

The **conscious mind** only makes up about ten percent of your total mind and primarily operates out of the present moment. It is basically a processing facility for things that are happening in your life today. It is aware of everything that is going on in your world: what you are seeing, the sounds you are hearing, the smells in the air, the temperature of the environment and anything your senses can sense. It processes information in a linear, chronological and ordered fashion. It deals with the here and now, and resolves situations as they occur, as long as those situations are not traumatic. It processes everything in the order in which it happens. Thus, your conscious mind doesn't store anything for future thought or analysis.

The conscious mind is also the place where you think freely in the present moment. It is very aware of what you are thinking at all times. The conscious mind is the place you go to solve problems and to remember what you are supposed to be doing at any given moment. It tells you when you are doing a good job, helps you to remember what appointments you have and tells you how you think and feel about things in your world. It also reminds you of your cognitive phrases and which tools to use and when.

There is one problem with the conscious mind though: It is the place where the negative thoughts you have about yourself manifest themselves. The place where you criticize yourself, put yourself down, and maintain your negative self-talk. This might sound like a bad thing to have happening but it really is a blessing in disguise. Because your conscious mind is aware of the negative things you are saying to yourself, you can change them. You can use the cognitive phrases and techniques you already learned in Section I to convert those negative thoughts into positive self-talk. You can only do this because those thoughts are living in your conscious mind and thus you are aware of them. It is your awareness of those negative thoughts that make it possible for you to change those negative thoughts into positive self-talk.

The other part of your mind is called the **unconscious mind** and it is very different from the conscious mind. It makes up the other ninety percent of your mind and is the exact opposite of the conscious mind in several ways. The first difference is that the unconscious mind is a storage facility rather than a processing facility. It stores traumatic events that happen to you today and that have happened in your past. It is the place where your abuse, neglect and/or trauma got tucked away for safekeeping. The place where difficult situations you encounter get stored if you don't handle them immediately and out of the adult ego state. The place where any and all traumatic events are kept until they can be dealt with in a safer, less traumatic environment.

The second difference is that the unconscious mind isn't linear and ordered and it doesn't store things chronologically. This tends to make the unconscious mind a very chaotic and disorganized place, and one most people don't understand. This part of the mind is like a huge filing cabinet with several sheets of paper stored in the bottom drawer. Each one of those pieces of paper represents one traumatic event from your childhood. However, each time one of those pieces of paper was put in the bottom drawer of your unconscious mind's filing cabinet, it was just randomly dumped in there. No time was taken to neatly categorize it by date, time or event. By the time you became an adult, you may have ended up with a hundred pieces of paper in the bottom drawer of your filing cabinet that were randomly dumped in there without any chronological order. This has created a problem for you in your recovery process. It has made it difficult for you to make sense out of the chaos in your unconscious mind. It has made it difficult for you to figure out where you got emotionally stuck as a child because you can't find the one piece of paper that contains the one traumatic event where you got stuck. It has made it almost impossible for you to find that one piece of paper from your past, which will allow your recovery to be possible.

You might be wondering, "Why doesn't the unconscious mind take the time to order what it stores?"

The answer may seem oversimplified, but the truth is this: There isn't time. Let's look at why this is true.

As you go through your day, your conscious mind is processing everything as it happens. It is keeping you and your day organized. Then when the conscious mind perceives there is danger, it dumps the information about the dangerous event and the emotions associated with that event into your unconscious mind. Your unconscious mind's job is to hide that information so you don't get overwhelmed and so you can do whatever is necessary to ensure your survival. Your unconscious mind continues holding onto that information, even after the traumatic event is over. It holds onto it until you decide you are in a safe enough place physically and emotionally to deal with that event. Then, and only then, will your unconscious mind allow that traumatic event to drift back up into your conscious mind so you can look at it and resolve what happened to you. In essence, this is your mind's way of protecting you and providing you with a safety net.

Let's look an example. One day you and a friend are hanging out in a coffee shop, enjoying each other's company and conversation. At this point, your conscious mind is processing everything: The taste of the coffee you are sipping, the jokes your friend is telling, the smell of the pastries you are eating, and the sound of the music that is playing softly in the background. Moments later, an armed robber runs into the coffee shop and holds a gun to your head. Your conscious mind recognizes there is imminent danger, so it pushes the severity of this event and the fear of losing your life deep inside your unconscious mind. This gives you the opportunity to focus only on what you need to do to save your life, and maybe the lives of everyone else in the coffee shop. If your unconscious mind had taken the time to neatly and chronologically store the traumatic event it would have been using up precious mental energy and time needed to put you into self-preservation mode so you could physically survive the event.

After surviving the traumatic event in the coffee shop, there is still work left for you to do. You still have to find a safe place to process what happened to you. You have to allow your unconscious mind to let the event drift back up into your conscious mind so you can resolve what happened, how you felt during the event, and how it changed you as a person. If you don't do this, the overwhelming, fearful thoughts and feelings from the traumatic event will hover in your unconscious mind and will affect you the rest of your life. As a result, you may become fearful of going out in public, develop a mistrust of men, become afraid of guns, avoid coffee shops, develop a fear that something bad will happen if you relax, and so forth. Thus, in order for you to set yourself free of the traumatic event, you have to stop long enough to find a safe place where you can face and resolve that traumatic event.

The third difference between the conscious and unconscious mind is the information stored in the unconscious mind isn't easily accessible, so most people *aren't aware* of what is actually stored in their unconscious mind. For most abuse survivors, the abuse, neglect and/or trauma they sustained was so emotionally overwhelming that it got buried deep within their unconscious minds. Not only was the abuse itself stored there but also the thoughts and feelings the abuse generated, such as fear, shame, guilt, and anger. In the many years I have been a therapist, I have come to believe that the severity of the abuse determines how deeply it gets buried in the unconscious mind. The more severe the abuse, the deeper it gets buried.

Let's look at an example at how the unconscious mind stores the events and feelings of a traumatic situation and keeps the survivor unaware of what is being stored.

When Dan was a little boy, he grew up in a family where domestic violence was rampant. His father was an alcoholic and got drunk almost every day. Dan's childhood was filled with endless days of watching his father get drunk and physically abusing his mother. Each time Dan saw his father get drunk and beat up his mother he stood there crying and screaming, "Please stop hurting my mom. Please stop before you really hurt her."

When Dan realized he couldn't make his father stop, he became frightened and wondered, "Is Dad going to end up killing Mom this time? Is she going to end up in the hospital again? Is he going to start hitting me, too?"

Every day Dan got home from school, he was terrified of what he might find. He lived with nothing but fear.

As Dan got older, it became harder and harder for him to see his father hitting his mother. Each time it happened, Dan became more afraid that his father would end up killing her or he would start hitting him. He wanted to run and hide and to make all of this disappear.

By the time Dan became a teenager, he felt as if he was always on guard for what might happen next (hypervigilance). In order to emotionally survive living like this, he started staying away from his house. Dan's unconscious mind also helped him out with this task by taking the traumatic beatings of his mother and tucking them away deep inside his unconscious mind. This helped Dan not to fall apart emotionally. It helped him to continue surviving in an environment filled with constant fear and danger.

His unconscious mind also helped Dan out in another way. It took what he thought and felt about those traumatic events and how powerless he felt and stored them away as well. His unconscious mind tucked away for safe keeping the messages, "I am worthless and powerless because I can't make Dad stop hitting Mom," "Dad is hurting Mom because I am a bad little boy" (egocentricity), and "He is going to end up killing me or Mom one day."

By the time Dan became an adult, he made the decision that he didn't ever want to get married or have children. Instead, he became a reclusive alcoholic (adverse reaction). What Dan didn't realize was he was isolating himself and drinking himself to death because of the traumatic events that were stored in his unconscious mind; because of the negative thoughts and feelings (misperceptions) that had gotten buried in his unconscious mind years ago. He didn't know that his unconscious mind had stored every one of those traumatic events and everything he had said to himself. Thus, Dan unconsciously carried over into his adult life the negative messages, "I am worthless. I can't do anything right. Only bad things happen to me. People can't be trusted because they will end up hurting me some how," but without realizing he had done this. He didn't understand these messages were being generated by his unconscious mind. He didn't understand he couldn't get rid of the negative self-talk, even with the cognitive phrases, until he opened the bottom drawer of his unconscious mind's filing cabinet and looked at the traumatic events that got stored in there.

So the question becomes, "How does this discussion about the conscious and unconscious mind support why the cognitive techniques aren't enough to recover from childhood abuse, neglect and/or trauma?"

The answer lies in the following explanations. The cognitive part of recovery says you can recover from childhood abuse by merely changing the way you think about the abuse. It focuses only on the thoughts you developed as a result of the abuse. This implies the memories and thoughts about the abuse are already accessible to your conscious mind and that you are aware of what those memories and thoughts are.

Now think about this: What if your childhood abuse was so traumatic that it got buried deep in your unconscious mind; in a place where your awareness is limited? What if those events and feelings are still being tucked away for safekeeping? How then can the cognitive techniques be applied to the abuse, neglect and/or traumatic events? How can you deal with them if they are stored in your unconscious mind? How can you change your thoughts about something you're not aware? How can you heal from what you thought and felt as a child if you don't have access to those old traumatic events? The answer is, you can't.

The second problem with using cognitive retraining as a sole means of recovery is that it ignores the emotional side of the abuse. It doesn't take into account the feelings the abuse generated and how they might still be locked away in your unconscious mind. It doesn't look at the abuse itself and what happened that caused the feelings in the first place. It doesn't look at the feelings the abuse left you with. It goes back to treating the symptoms, or the ripples on the pond, rather than the cause of the symptoms, or the rock lying at the bottom of the pond. Thus, the cognitive work is only half of the equation.

The emotional restructuring work is the second half of the recovery process. It is vital because it picks up where the cognitive work logically ends. It says you have to look at the abuse itself because the abuse is what caused the distorted thoughts, feelings and behaviors (misperceptions) in the first place and the ones you still maintain today as an adult. It says you, the survivor, must be willing to go back and acknowledge where your pain began and to look at the abuse face to face, and heart to heart. You have to be willing to feel what happened to you; to know what you thought and felt as the child who was being hurt and wounded; and to remember your vulnerability. This will tell you what unresolved thoughts and feelings you are still holding onto in your unconscious mind and where you got emotionally stuck as a child. It will allow the traumatic events and how you thought and felt about those events to drift back up into your conscious mind so you can resolve them and heal from them.

This may sound like an overwhelming or maybe even daunting task, but it isn't something you have to do by yourself. You will be supported throughout this book with encouragement and guidance. You won't have to figure this process out by yourself either because you will be provided with specific instructions on how to face your abusive past and in a way that leads to resolution and healing. And, if you feel the need, you can share with a friend or therapist your need for support as you embark on your journey of facing the abuse, neglect and/or trauma you sustained.

Once those childhood issues are emotionally resolved, you will then be able to incorporate the cognitive techniques you've already learned. They will help you change what you think about the abuse now that the hidden details about the abuse are available to your conscious mind. You will start seeing what happened to you through the eyes of the adult rather than just the heart of the child. As your perceptions change so will your ability to help your inner child heal and grow up. You will be able to take care of the little girl or boy who lives inside of you. You, the adult, will be able to protect your child and meet his/her needs. Then, the best gift of all will happen. You, the adult, will be the one who responds to the world in place of your child. The pain of your child will grow dim while the wonderful feeling of being able to take care of your child will grow more and more each day with a sense of pride. You will no longer be controlled by your emotions because the adult who possesses the cognitive skills will take control. It will look much like this:

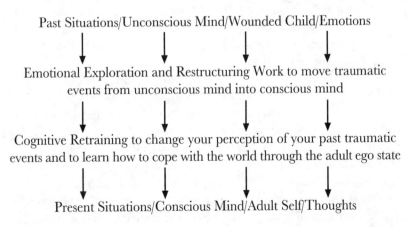

Past Situations/Unconscious Mind/Wounded Child/Emotions

Emotional Exploration and Restructuring Work to move traumatic events from unconscious mind into conscious mind

Cognitive Retraining to change your perception of your past traumatic events and to learn how to cope with the world through the adult ego state

Present Situations/Conscious Mind/Adult Self/Thoughts

What I would like for you to take away from all of this is that the cognitive retraining work cannot be done without the emotional restructuring work and vice versa. Recovery is not possible unless you have both components and address both the cognitive and emotional aspects of the abuse, neglect and/or trauma that happened to you as a child. Both are vital and necessary pieces of the recovery process. Neither can stand alone.

So let's look at an example of why the emotional restructuring component is necessary to recovery and how the cognitive retraining component logically follows the emotional restructuring work.

Sarah is a 30-year-old woman who lives alone in an apartment in a secluded part of town. As a little girl, her father sexually abused her almost every day for seven years. He also threatened to hurt her if she ever told anyone their secret. So Sarah was the good little girl who tolerated her father's molestation and then smiled when she was around her mother and friends.

By the time Sarah became a teenager she couldn't stand how dirty and ashamed she felt, how helpless and worthless. She didn't date boys, but instead began isolating herself away from everyone. She began drinking as a way of tolerating her feelings about herself and her father (adverse reaction).

By the time Sarah became an adult, she remained in her cubicle of isolation even though she didn't completely understand why. She knew her father had hurt her, but she kept telling herself, "That was a long time ago so it can't still be bothering me now."

Sarah was also constantly contemplating death and suicide (adverse reaction). Anything unpleasant that happened in her life upset her terribly. She didn't know how to handle people or difficult situations without becoming upset or crying; without wanting to hurt herself; without wanting to drink herself into oblivion (no protective layer).

Then one day after a horrible drinking binge, which sent her to the hospital, Sarah got into therapy. She was fortunate to have found a therapist who knew how to do Cognitive Emotional Restructuring Therapy. Thus, her therapist started the counseling process with teaching Sarah the basic cognitive tools, such as the four basic concepts, the ego states, loci of control, diaphragmatic breathing, journaling, the plan, etc.

In a very short period of time Sarah started demonstrating the ability to handle things in her present day life more appropriately. She began feeling better about herself and her ability to handle difficult situations. She stopped drinking and contemplating suicide. She felt so much better that she decided she wanted to stop her counseling sessions. Her therapist tried to explain to Sarah that they had just begun therapy. She tried to help her understand that what she was experiencing was only temporary because she hadn't gone back and looked at the abuse. However, Sarah didn't believe what her therapist was saying, so she opted to discontinue her sessions.

About three months later, Sarah started noticing she was feeling a little depressed and sad even though nothing bad was happening in her life. She didn't understand why she was feeling this way. To cope with the depression and sadness that was growing more intense by the day, Sarah began having a few drinks after work. About three more months later, Sarah was drinking alone in her home and was contemplating suicide again. Not knowing what else to do, she called her therapist.

Once Sarah was safely back in her therapist's office, she learned why she began feeling depressed and sad again. It was because her hurt and wounded child was bleeding over into her adult. Because her inner child was still living with the sexual abuse and all the things her father had done to her even though she had temporarily felt better as an adult. It was her inner child's way of telling her that she had not visited her unconscious mind to see what was bothering her; that she had not gone back and looked at the sexual abuse by her father, how it made her feel as a little girl; and how it caused her to self-destruct as an adult.

Once Sarah realized her inner child was crying out for help, she agreed to the emotional restructuring work that needed to be done. She allowed her therapist to take her back to the abuse and back to the little girl who was stilling hurting inside of her. She opened up the events, thoughts and feelings that were buried in her unconscious mind and allowed them to drift back up into her conscious mind so she could feel her inner child's pain. She then learned how to comfort her inner child through that pain. She resolved the things her father had done to her and how she *felt* about her father and what he had done.

Because Sarah was able to go back and uncover the things her father had done to her and then embrace her inner child's pain, she was then ready to apply her cognitive tools so she could change how she *thought* about the abuse and the world she now lived in.

From that day forward, it wasn't Sarah's little girl who came to the surface when she was dealing with a difficult person or situation, it was her adult. It was her adult who was now capable of taking care of her inner child and who could meet all of her needs. It was her adult who dealt with anything that came along in her life that was overwhelming or reminded her of her childhood. Her inner child was free to be the child she had always wanted to be. The child who felt loved, taken care of and important. Because her little girl was finally getting these things she could let go of her past and grow up.

Lets look at one more example. Steve has been an alcoholic for almost 25 years. He has gone through one treatment center after another. He has tried several support groups and has seen several therapists who believe in cognitive retraining as a sole means of therapy. Steve does what his therapists have asked of him and keeps telling himself, "I will never drink again. I am in control of what I do. I am capable of remaining alcohol free. I am a good person who can do whatever I set my mind to do." However, about every six months or so Steve relapses and gets drunk for about a week. Based on what you have learned, why is this happening to Steve? Why can't he stay sober for more than six months at a time?

The reason Steve can't stay sober is this: He hasn't gone back and uncovered why he drinks, what he is running from, and what he is trying to anesthetize himself from. He hasn't learned why he is self-medicating. If he had done the emotional restructuring work, he would have realized he is drinking himself to death as a means of covering up the feelings he had as a little boy when his father was getting drunk and beating him and his mother. He would have realized he was still running from the feelings of terror, hurt, and guilt because he couldn't make his dad stop hurting him or his mother. He would have realized he was trying to conquer his feelings of inadequacy. He would have realized he was feeling like a bad little boy because he believed his father didn't like him.

Once Steve realized where his pain was coming from, he could then address that pain, and heal from it. Once the emotional wounds were resolved, Steve could then successfully apply his cognitive retraining techniques and cognitive phrases to keep him sober. Because he had resolved why he drank, he could use his cognitive phrases and they would work.

THE INNER CHILD AND THE UNCONSCIOUS MIND

There is a direct link between your inner child and your unconscious mind and that link is your emotions. As you already know from previous chapters, your inner child lives in your heart and in your emotions. But what hasn't been discussed is that your inner child possesses, on an emotional level, an awareness of everything that is locked away in your unconscious mind. However, because your inner child is just a child, he/she can't tell you in words what is locked away in your unconscious mind, so he/she acts those things out, hoping you will understand what he/she is trying to say.

Even though it was your unconscious mind that stored the events of what happened to you as a child, it was your inner child who made some very important emotional decisions based on those events. Thus, it is your inner child who maintains how you feel about yourself and how you see the world based on those experiences stored in your unconscious mind.

In a way your unconscious mind and your inner child are like the lens in a pair of glasses. They determine how clearly you see yourself and the world, and how you look at difficult situations. If you grew up in a home where you were loved and were provided everything you needed in order to be healthy and happy, then as an adult you likely see yourself and the world through a pair of glasses with clear lenses in them. On the other hand, if you were raised in a family where abuse, neglect and/or trauma were prevalent, then you likely see yourself and the world through a pair of glasses with colored or jaded lenses. Your clarity about yourself, the world and other people are probably colored and skewed. Everything is tainted through the eyes of the angry and/or wounded child, causing you to respond in the child ego state.

Thus, one of your tasks is to figure out what is stored in your unconscious mind and how those things have effected your view of yourself and your world. So take a moment and go to your quiet place. Close your eyes and do your diaphragmatic breathing. As you breathe, see yourself as a child and think about the things that happened to you. Think about the decisions, thoughts, agreements and opinions you made as a traumatized child. Think about what lessons you learned. Feel what it felt like to learn those things. What conclusions did you come to about yourself and the world? Then, write out what you discover in the space below.

_____

_____

_____

_____

_____

_____

_____

_____

This task may have proven to be a very difficult task for you. That's all right, it's to be expected. You have spent years hiding from the painful events and feelings that are stored in your unconscious mind. Thus, it will take more than a few minutes to break this habit and to become proficient with uncovering the hurt and pain of your inner child who still resides in your heart.

In the meantime, I would like to help you change some of the decisions, thoughts, agreements and opinions you might have developed as a traumatized child and still maintain today as an adult. These are important because the first step in the emotional restructuring process begins with you, the adult, taking charge of your own recovery; taking charge of your own thoughts, feelings and behaviors. You have to change the agreements you made with yourself a long time ago. One of you is going to be in charge of your recovery process: either your child or your adult. If you decide you are ready for your adult to help your inner child to recover, then here are some new agreements I would like for you to make with yourself and then abide by them the remainder of your recovery process.

1. *I am where I am because of the choices I made as an adult. I will start taking responsibility for where I am today*: Even though being abused as a child wasn't something you chose, the way you have dealt with it and continue dealing with it is your choice. Even after you left home and were no longer being abused, you continued abusing yourself as a means of coping with what happened to you. This self-abuse is what was described earlier as an adverse reaction. It is you being an alcoholic, drug addict, chronically depressed, suicidal and so forth. It is necessary for you today to accept responsibility for where you are and to make the conscious decision to stop abusing yourself. You cannot recover until you do this.

2. *I will give up all of my addictions and escapes*: As long as you are hiding behind an addiction or any means of escape, even negative thoughts, you will never be able to face your childhood and how it changed you as a person. The addictions and escapes put a barrier between you and the things you need to work on. It is only by giving up your addictions and escapes that you will be able to face your past and recover from it. It's the only way your inner child will be able to get what he/she needs so he/she can grow up into a well-adjusted adult. Giving up your addictions and escapes will allow you the invaluable opportunity to embrace what happened to you and to heal.

3. *I will become an observer and stop being a victim*: Abuse survivors

tend to get caught up in their own thoughts and feelings. This is detrimental to you being able to cope with life as an adult. You spend time emotionally reacting from one crisis to another, and feeling like the helpless victim. The goal is to learn how to become the observer who can emotionally sit back and observe the situation or crisis from a distance. To observe the situation without becoming emotionally tangled up in it gives you the ability to act, not react, out of the adult ego state.

4. *I will stop giving people the job of taking care of me. I will assume responsibility for myself and my recovery*: As a child, you may have wished someone would rescue you from the terrible things that were happening to you. You may have tried over and over again to get someone, like a schoolteacher or minister, to make the abuse stop. But because no one came to your rescue, you continued the search and still do. Because your inner child runs your life, you maintain the pursuit of someone rescuing you and making everything inside and outside of you okay. The truth is, no one is coming and will never come. The only person who can come to your rescue is you. This leaves the responsibility for yourself and your recovery in your own hands.

5. *I will redirect the energy of my anger and rage into my recovery*: It is important to take the energy of the negative and explosive feelings you were left with as a result of the abuse and convert that energy into something constructive; to take the destructive and make it constructive. Instead of using your anger, rage and disappointment to fuel your self-destructive behaviors or adverse reactions, put that energy and effort into your recovery, and into your inner child growing up.

6. *I know I wasn't responsible for the things the adults in my life did to me, so I give them the responsibility for what they did*: It is time for you to stop blaming yourself for what happened to you. You were only a child when the abuse happened, so there was no way you could have caused it. You need to allow the adults, who inflicted the abuse to take responsibility for what they did, so you can stop punishing yourself for other people's actions. The only thing you are responsible for is what you do with the abuse today. You can choose to remain the victim or become the survivor.

7. *I am now responsible for how I respond to the past*: Because you are learning about the recovery process, you can now look at what happened to you differently. It is now up to you to choose how you perceive what happened to you and the people who violated

you. You can, at any time, let those people go and focus only on your recovery.

8. *I will stop modeling myself after others and will start discovering who I am*: Children who were abused tend to focus only on surviving. They don't have the luxury or encouragement from their parents to think about their future, who they are or what they want to be. However, just because your parents didn't encourage you doesn't mean you can't start dreaming now. Just because they expected you to play a certain role doesn't mean you have to maintain that role. You can now choose to become the person you know you are inside and have always dreamed of being.

9. *I will start focusing only on the positive aspects of things*: Your whole life has been filled with negativity and some of it you brought on yourself with the adverse reactions. It is now time to focus on the positive aspects of your life so you can continue cultivating positive things in your life. Remember: Things don't bother me it's the view I take of them that does.

10. *Be kind and gentle to yourself*: Childhood abuse is filled with nothing but hate, anger, hurt, and destruction. Today you are no longer being abused, so make a commitment to yourself to learn how to be kind and gentle with you and your child self. Don't try to push the inner child away, but learn how to embrace him/her as a parent would a child. Loving yourself is the only path to the healing and resolution of many old wounds.

It will be important for you to become intimately acquainted with these new agreements. So your assignment is this: Write down the agreements in your spiral bound index cards. You need only to write down what is underlined. Then, every morning, go to your quiet place, sit in your comfortable chair and do your diaphragmatic breathing. While doing your breathing, say these agreements out loud to yourself and meditate on what they mean. As you meditate on them, focus on feeling them in your heart and what it would feel like to be the person who lives by these agreements. Every day you do this, you are increasing your chances of recovery. You are giving yourself permission to change and to take responsibility for your own healing. This will be extremely important in the chapters to come, so do this process for at least two weeks before moving on to the next chapter.

Chapter 11

Back to Basics

As you think about the messages and emotional decisions you made as a child and reflect on the things that might be stored in your unconscious mind, you may notice something starting to happen to you. You may notice some feelings from your childhood are beginning to make their way to the surface. Feelings of hurt, sadness, betrayal, anger or even despair may have started whispering around inside of you. You may be feeling a little uncomfortable with these feelings. It is all right. At this point in your healing process, it is normal. Your inner child is waking up and letting you know he/she is ready for your help, ready to face the past, and ready for you to take care of him/her as you go through the rest of this process. Your inner child is ready to let go of the hurt and pain, and is ready to stop suffering.

While your inner child is getting used to what it feels like to feel all of these feelings again, there are some fundamental concepts and additional tools you need to be exposed to. These concepts and tools will help you to understand what those feelings are about. They are a must before you can fully embark on the journey of emotionally restructuring your childhood. They will help you to understand what is needed in order for change to occur in your life; to learn what splitting is and how it is detrimental to recovery; and how to recognize when things in your present day life are tapping into things from your past.

THREE THINGS NEEDED FOR CHANGE TO OCCUR

The first set of tools you need to acquire in the emotional restructuring process is an understanding that there are **three things needed in order for change to occur***. These may seem a bit over simplified, but they lay at the core of what is needed to overcome the abuse, neglect and/or trauma you endured. They are the foundation your emotional recovery will be built on one brick at a time.

The first thing you need in order for change to occur is **the desire to change**. Without this desire, recovery is impossible. And, your desire must be a personal one. It can't be based on a fantasy that you can change for someone else or to make them happy. You cannot obtain recovery if you are doing it to keep your job, your wife or to stay out of jail. You cannot do it to get your family or friends off your back. You have to do it because your recovery is the most important thing in your life. Because you want to be happy and free of the pain you carry around inside of you. Because you want to like yourself and be comfortable with your life. You have to want to recover because you are worth it and because you deserve to be happy. You have to be the one who makes the conscious decision to get better, to recover and to look at your pain. You have to be the survivor who makes the commitment to yourself to follow through with your recovery no matter what it takes.

The second thing you need is **the knowledge of how to change**. If you don't know how to change, what steps you need to take or how to take those steps then you can't get from "abused and miserable" to "healed and happy." It is like trying to drive from Florida to California without a map. You can guess what roads you will need to take to get to California, but chances are you will end up somewhere you didn't plan. Or, you may not get anywhere at all.

In many ways, knowing how to change is like needing a blueprint and the right set of tools to do a job. If you want to build a wooden box, you need to buy a carpentry book. In this book you will learn what tools it will take to build the box and the step by step instructions. You will then have to gather the proper tools together and follow the instructions provided. Without the proper tools and instructions you will likely end up with something other than a wooden box.

Recovery works much the same way. You have to know what you want and then have the tools and instructions to get there. This book will give you both the tools and the knowledge you need to heal.

The third thing needed in order for change to occur is **an environment where you can practice your new behaviors**. Without an environment where you can practice your new behaviors and what you have learned, you won't be able to maintain your new behaviors or the new you. Without practice, you will revert back to the person you used to be prior to your recovery.

This isn't only true for recovery but for everything in life. Let's look at what seems like a silly example to help illustrate this point. Let's say all of your life you have been tying your shoelaces using the cross-and-pull-through method. Then one day on television you see someone tying their shoelaces using a new-fangled method called braiding. Because it is the latest fad you decide you want to start tying your shoelaces this way. You are sure this will cause all of your friends to envy you. So you go the bookstore and buy a book called, *How to Braid Your Shoelaces and Anything Else You Want to Look Fashionable*. To your surprise, you learn how to braid your shoelaces in a matter of minutes. However, you don't get a chance to practice your new braiding method very often because the shoes you wear every day to work don't have shoelaces.

About a month later, you get a call from one of your friends who wants to play tennis with you. You smile and accept the invitation. You think to yourself, "This will be my moment where everyone will see me as fashionable. They will see my new braided tennis shoelaces and think I am on the cutting edge of fashion."

So you run up to your room, get your tennis shoes out and spend several minutes trying to braid them, but become frustrated because you can't remember how. You can't remember how to braid your shoelaces because it has been a month since you practiced. Your excitement quickly turns into disappointment when you realize you will have to resort to being just like everyone else who will show up with their shoes laced up in the old, traditional cross-and-pull-through method.

This may sound like a trivial analogy, but it is exactly what happens in life and the recovery process. New behaviors that aren't practiced will slowly fade away. When this happens, there isn't anything left but for you to resort back to your old behavior, back to the old you, and back to playing the role of the child.

Another reason why it is important to provide yourself with an environment where you can practice the new you and your new behaviors is this: It will give you the invaluable opportunity to see which of your new behaviors work and which ones don't work. It will show you what areas you are doing well in and what areas you still need to work on.

Finding these new environments will also give you a chance to be around a different set of people and maybe even those who interact with their world through the adult ego state. It will be vital for you to find these people who are well-adjusted and who are emotionally stable so they can respond to the new you in a positive way. These new positive people with their positive responses will reinforce who you are becoming and will motivate you to continue growing. You will then notice that you won't have to seek these people out, but they will naturally begin gravitating toward you. Instead of attracting people who are like your dysfunctional family, you will attract people who represent who you are becoming.

In many ways the three things needed in order for change to occur can be compared to a little girl who has known no other way of riding her pink bicycle except with training wheels. For the past six months, she has been cruising up and down the neighborhood streets on her pink bike with training wheels. She has felt really good about herself, like she is a big girl now because she isn't riding a tricycle anymore. Then, one day she decides she wants to learn how to ride her bicycle without the training wheels (the desire). She runs into her house and announces to her mom and dad her newfound desire to be even a bigger girl than she already is by learning how to ride her bike without training wheels. So her parents take her outside and show her how to balance the bicycle and explain how to ride it without the training wheels (the knowledge). Then, they put her on the seat, push her off, and shout encouraging words as she peddles hard and tries to stay upright. Because this is her first time trying to ride her bicycle without the training wheels, she falls over. However, her parents pick her up and tell her how good she is doing (the environment). Their encouraging words give her the desire and courage to get back on her bicycle again, hoping this time she will be successful. Then, lo and behold, after several attempts the little girl is cruising up and down the streets once again, but this time without her training wheels. She is so proud of herself and knows she doesn't ever want to go back to riding her bicycle with training wheels ever again.

In this story learning to ride the bicycle is a lot like recovery. You have to have what the little girl with the pink bicycle had: The desire to change, the knowledge to know how to change and then a supportive and encouraging environment where new behaviors can be practiced.

There is one thing to keep in mind though as you move through your recovery process. When you are dealing with the three things needed in order for change to occur, you are rarely working on one thing or on one particular step at any given time. This means you will find yourself working on different traumatic situations at the same time and you will be on different steps with each situation. For example, let's say you have identified that you need to work on the results of the physical abuse you endured from your mother and the neglect you sustained from your father. For you, the physical abuse from your mother is a lot more painful than the neglect from your father. So with your mother you might only be on step one, gaining a desire to change, and with your father you may have been able to advance to step two, gaining the knowledge to know how to change.

This is how it is for everyone in recovery. You will work on different things at different times. You cannot force yourself or your inner child to work on something you are not ready to work on or to face something you are not ready to face. You have to be patient and allow yourself to move through your issues and the three things needed for change to occur at your own pace.

It is now your turn to look at the issues you need to work on from your childhood and to see where you are in your recovery process with each one of them. So please look to the next page and complete Exercise I that has been provided to help you with this.

Exercise I:

Three Things Need for Change to Occur

Step I: Take a moment and think about the issues and events you need to work on in relation to the abuse, neglect and/or trauma you sustained as a child. Make a list of those issues in the space provided:

Example: My mother was an alcoholic who constantly pushed me around when she got drunk.

1.

2.

3.

4.

5.

6.

7.

8.

9.

10.

Step II: Review the list and circle which step you are at in relation to the three things needed in order for change to occur.

Example: Desire   Knowledge   Environment (I have the desire to change and am in the process of learning how to change my thoughts and feelings about my mother.)

1.   Desire   Knowledge   Environment

2.   Desire   Knowledge   Environment

3.   Desire   Knowledge   Environment

4.   Desire   Knowledge   Environment

5.   Desire   Knowledge   Environment

6.   Desire   Knowledge   Environment

7.   Desire   Knowledge   Environment

8.   Desire   Knowledge   Environment

9.   Desire   Knowledge   Environment

10.   Desire   Knowledge   Environment

SPLITTING

Have you ever met someone who sees everything as black or white; good or bad; all or nothing; healthy or unhealthy; safe or unsafe, and so on? Have you ever met anyone who demands things to be one way and one way only, and there is no room for considering anything else? What about someone who is overly opinionated and who believes everyone else's opinions are wrong? What about someone who believes the way they experience things is the only way to experience them? What about a friend who goes to the extreme with everything? How about someone who takes everything personally or makes everything about them? If you know someone who does these things, or even if you yourself engage in these behaviors, you are doing what is called **splitting***.

Splitting is when you see everything as polar opposites: good or bad, black or white, acceptable or unacceptable and so forth. It is also you reacting to situations in the extreme: getting angry with someone and refusing to speak to them ever again, taking everything personally, becoming suicidal when someone doesn't listen to you, isolating yourself from your best friend because he/she hurt your feelings, getting drunk every time you and your spouse have an argument and etc. It is also when you believe your way is the only correct way and you refuse to take anyone else's opinions into consideration. It is when you think in all or nothing terms and judge yourself and everyone else in those same terms. For example, believing you are good and everyone else is bad. Believing you are right and everyone else is wrong. Believing everyone is happy and you are the only one who is sad. Believing everyone else is doing well in their life and you won't ever be able to accomplish anything. Believing everyone else had a good childhood and yours was the worst.

Splitting is a very common pattern of behavior and isn't something that is done just by people who were abused, neglected and/or traumatized as children. Many people engage in splitting, but are unaware they are doing so. It's a defense mechanism people develop as a means of protecting themselves. However, for the sake of this book we will focus on splitting only as it pertains to abuse survivors.

Splitting is like a wall. It isn't built out of concrete or stone, but out of rigid thoughts, opinions and beliefs. Like all walls its purpose is to keep things in or out. For most survivors, their wall of rigid thoughts, opinions and beliefs is maintained to keep people out. They believe this will reduce the risk of them getting hurt again. They believe it will keep everything and everyone from being able to seep through their defenses so they don't end up questioning themselves or feel like they did when they were a child.

They also believe it will keep the feelings of their wounded child safely tucked away so no one can know how vulnerable they feel. What these survivors don't realize is this wall of splitting doesn't work and it doesn't protect them long term; it only causes a physical and emotional separation that eventually leads to isolation and loneliness.

Let's look at a short example of how splitting might happen and how someone might try to protect themselves with it.

When Mary was six years old her father died. This left Mary's mother raising her alone and in the only way she knew how. She worked two jobs and attended night school. Mary tried her best to help out around the house with the chores. She tried to do well in school so her mother wouldn't have to worry about her. When her mother would get home late at night, Mary could tell she was frustrated and sad. She did everything she knew how to do as a little girl to make her mother feel better. She tried telling her jokes, turning down the sheets of her bed, drawing her pictures, making her cards, doing well in school, and telling her mother how proud she was of her. However, the only response Mary ever got back from her mother was, "What do you know? If it weren't for you I wouldn't be in this mess. You have no idea how hard it is being a single mother and raising you. You don't know anything about anything. You can't do enough to make up for how hard I have to work. Just leave me alone."

Every time Mary's mother spoke to her in this manner, it crushed her little spirit.

Each year that passed with her mother's degrading comments, Mary began questioning her self-worth and how she felt about things. She began believing that no matter what she did nothing was good enough. She began believing she was a burden and that no one wanted her. Not only this, but she was learning that in difficult situations the way a person protects themselves is by being rude and pushing people away. This was the lesson she was learning from her mother.

By the time Mary became an adult, she was very rigid and stoic. She wouldn't let anyone get close to her. She emotionally isolated herself from everyone. She wouldn't allow herself to develop anything but superficial friendships. She believed other people would hurt her if she allowed them to get close. So she began telling herself, "I am better than everyone else and no one's opinions matter but my own. If I become better than everyone else, then no one can hurt me (overcompensating and splitting)."

Mary became so proficient in this way of thinking and behaving that no one, not even the people at her job wanted to be around her. No one liked the fact that she had an extremely narrow point of view and she believed everyone else's opinions were faulty and useless. The only person she listened to and who she believed was right was herself.

So the question becomes, "How did Mary's splitting affect her life and how did it protect her?"

Mary learned from her mother that being rude would push people away and it would keep her from getting hurt. So Mary, even though done unconsciously, repeated her mother's pattern of protection. She developed such a rigid set of thoughts and opinions, and became so rude that no one wanted to be around her. In the end, this left Mary alone and isolated. It left her without the possibility of anyone getting close enough to hurt her.

Mary's splitting also reduced the possibility of other people treating her like her mother had done and making her feel the same way she had as a child. It kept her from feeling the pain of not being good enough and from reliving how it felt being abandoned as a little girl when her mother had pushed her away. But, this was only temporary. Mary eventually had to relive the abandonment she felt as a little when she realized that as an adult she had no friends and no one to spend time with because she had pushed everyone away with her splitting.

In addition, Mary's belief that everyone was wrong allowed her to focus only on their inadequacies and faults. Because she was so busy looking at them, she had no time to look at her own emotional pain and what was causing her to behave the way she was. So Mary's form of splitting kept her from having to face herself and how she was treated as a child.

Mary's ultimate fear was this: "If I allow myself to feel, even if for just a moment, that someone else is right or might have a valid opinion then I might hear my mother's voice again telling me, 'What do you know? You don't know anything about anything. You can't do anything right. You're just worthless'."

This would have left Mary feeling inadequate and worthless just like she did when she was a little girl. So her splitting and extreme opinions helped her to reduce the possibility of feeling like the wounded child and being hurt again in her adult life. However, it also prevented her from being able to face her past and recover from it.

Another problem with splitting is it tends to alienate you from people. It doesn't allow for compromise or flexibility. For example, let's say Barbara, who is an abuse survivor, works out at the gym three days a week. On one of her workout days, she meets a woman named Cindy.

For the next several months Barbara and Cindy try to cultivate a friendship and work out at the gym together. Because Barbara is an abuse survivor who hasn't dealt with her emotional issues, she really struggles with her new friendship. She struggles with feeling needy all the time and wanting Cindy to make her feel good about herself (external locus of control). Cindy is also struggling with the friendship because Barbara demands a lot of her time and attention.

Then one day, Barbara calls Cindy and asks her to go to the movies. However, Cindy already has plans for the evening and tries to gently explain this to Barbara, hoping it won't hurt her feelings. However, Barbara feels rejected by Cindy and takes her "already having plans" as a personal affront. She becomes the wounded child and gets extremely angry with her friend. As the perceived rejection stirs around inside of Barbara, she comes to the conclusion that Cindy doesn't want to spend time with her because she isn't good enough. She takes this conclusion and begins splitting. She becomes inflexible and makes the decision, "If Cindy won't go to the movies with me tonight then I won't ever spend time with her again."

So Barbara stops calling and working out with Cindy at the gym. She won't return any of Cindy's phone calls, and yet she won't tell Cindy why she is angry and hurt. She just abruptly cuts the friendship off. In the end, Barbara has completely alienated herself from yet another friend because her splitting didn't allow for compromise or flexibility, and because she wouldn't tell Cindy that her feelings had gotten hurt.

SPLITTING AND THE CHILD EGO STATE/ EXTERNAL LOCUS OF CONTROL

As you can see with the example with Barbara and Cindy, splitting can be tied back into the ego states and locus' of control. For most abuse survivors, and maybe even for you, telling other people how you feel is a very difficult task. You avoid it at all costs. You avoid it because you don't want to feel the fear that comes with speaking your truth. You don't want to feel the fear of getting in trouble again, hurting someone else's feelings, being abandoned if someone disagrees with you, or being told your feelings don't matter.

To protect yourself, you jump back into the child ego state and don't speak your truth. However, this only makes you feel like the wounded child all over again who doesn't have the ability to protect or stand up for yourself. Because you don't feel safe enough to speak your truth, you act it out. You split and then punish people before they have the chance to hurt you or penetrate your wall. This is what happened with Barbara. She was too afraid to admit to her friend Cindy that her feelings had gotten hurt. When Barbara didn't feel as if she could speak her truth and felt abandoned, she fell back into the child ego state. She fell back into the pattern of needing to protect herself. She did this by making sure Cindy wouldn't ever be able to hurt her again. She did this by pushing Cindy away with her silence.

Splitting is also nothing but an external locus of control. In Section I, we discussed what happens when you take what other people are doing or saying personally and become the wounded child. You are operating out of an external locus of control. When you try to control how other people think and feel so you can keep your focus on them and off of your yourself, you are operating out of an external locus of control.

Barbara operated out of an external locus of control when she took personally the fact that Cindy couldn't go to the movies. She allowed it to make her angry and for her to then act out that anger. Barbara allowed a person and an event outside of herself to determine how she felt about herself and how she acted.

STOP JUDGING AND RECOVER

As you go through the recovery process it will be important for you to remember things aren't necessarily good or bad, or black or white, when it comes to your childhood or the recovery process. Your thoughts, feelings, behaviors, and life experiences are neither good nor bad; they are what they are and nothing more. If you believe this, then you will also understand it is all right for you to change how you see the things that happened to you and how you feel and felt about those things. It will be permissible for your perspective about your past and the abuse to change so it can enhance and not detract from who you are becoming as a person. It is time to stop judging the abuse, neglect and/or trauma in black and white terms. It keeps you isolated and locked away in the role of the child. Replace the judgement with a willingness to look at your past and how it affected you in a different way. Look at it in a healing way.

Last but not least, until you can get to the place where you can identify when you are splitting, it will be difficult for you to play the role of the adult in difficult situations and for you to recover from your childhood. You are probably asking yourself, "How am I supposed to catch myself when I am splitting? And if I can catch myself, how am I supposed to change what I am doing and how I am responding to that situation?"

The answer can be found in the plan. You start off with step 1, which is recognizing in your body when you are splitting (red flag). Do you feel anxious or nervous? Do your muscles get tight or your breath grow shallow? Do you feel defensive or superior to everyone else? Do you feel threatened or get a nervous stomach? Does your blood pressure go up?

Once you recognize when you are splitting, then all you have to do is work the rest of the plan so you can choose a behavior other than splitting; so you can respond to the difficult situation out of the adult ego state.

It is now time for you to practice identifying when you are splitting and to practice changing it. Exercise J, located on the next page, will help you with this. Please do not read any further until you have had an opportunity to work this exercise at least three times.

Exercise J:

Splitting

For seven days, notice in what situations you are splitting. Write out a brief description of each situation, how your splitting behavior was manifested, the consequences of your splitting and how you felt afterwards. Then write out how the situation might have turned out differently if you had not split. Then write out how you could have worked the plan to keep from splitting. For example (using the Barbara and Cindy example):

Description of event: I asked Cindy to go to the movies this evening but she couldn't go because of a previous engagement.

Feelings the situation evoked: Anger; abandonment; hurt; took everything personally; frustrated I couldn't get my needs met.

How my splitting behavior was manifested: I made the decision that if she wouldn't go to the movies with me tonight then I wouldn't ever spend time with her again.

Consequences of my splitting: I lost a friend and am alone again.

How I felt afterwards: I felt mad at myself for acting like a desperate child who needed someone to love and spend time with me. I hated myself for still being needy.

What would have happened if I had not split: I would still have a friend. Cindy and I could have gone to the movies tomorrow night.

How could I have worked the plan: I could have recognized that my stomach got tied into knots and my heart hurt when Cindy told me she couldn't go to the movies. I could have done my breathing and seen that I was playing the role of the child and assigning Cindy the role of the parent. I could have used my cards, "People don't do things against me, they do things to meet their own needs." Thus, Cindy was doing what she needed to do to take care of herself. Things don't bother me, it's the view I take of them that does. So my view that Cindy isn't going to the movies because she is rejecting me is a distorted view. I need to understand that she just had other plans. After realizing these things and allowing them to change my perspective about this situation, I could have gone back to Cindy and apologized for how I had treated her. I could have explained what happened to me. After I reconciled my friendship with Cindy I could have journaled what I learned.

Description of event:

_____

_____

_____

_____

The feelings the situation evoked:

_____

_____

_____

_____

How splitting behavior was manifested:

_____

_____

_____

_____

Consequences of my splitting:

_____

_____

_____

_____

How I felt afterwards:

_____

_____

_____

_____

If I had not split:

_____

_____

_____

_____

How could I have worked the plan:

_____

_____

_____

_____

_____

_____

_____

_____

_____

_____

_____

PARALLEL PROCESSING

Mark is a 47-year-old man who is the marketing director of a large corporation. He has worked hard for many years to obtain this level of success and is eager to make it to the top of his company. His dream is to one day be the president of the company.

One morning Mark goes into work and finds a memo lying on his desk announcing that the vice president of the company is retiring. Excited, Mark revises his resume and submits it for the vice president's position. While at lunch, Mark and his co-workers sit around cracking a few jokes about the vice president who is retiring and how the company will be better off without him. Mark then takes a deep breath and announces, "I have applied for the vice president's position."

Everyone starts laughing even harder because they think he is kidding. Then one of his co-workers jokingly makes the statement, "Now why would they want you Mark? You're just one of us ordinary people down here in the trenches working for a living and having too much fun."

Mark's face turns bright red. Furious, he stands up. He reaches over, picks his co-worker up by the collar and starts shouting, "Who in the hell do you think you are telling me I'm a nobody? If I wasn't at work right now, I would beat you into a pulp and then throw you away!"

When Mark realized what he was doing, he put his co-worker back down and flew out of the room. He ran down the hall and into his office. He sat behind his desk with his face hidden in his hands. He was embarrassed and wondered, "Why did I get so angry? What caused me to get so out of control?"

Mark was confused. He didn't understand why he had responded so strongly to his co-worker's comments. He sat there for a long time just asking himself over and over again, "What's wrong with me?"

As Mark sat behind his desk pondering what had happened at lunch, his thoughts quickly turned back to the time when his father had teased him about running for class treasurer in junior high school. His father laughed at him as he said, "You'll never amount to anything. No one will vote for you because you're nothing but a worthless, scrawny kid who can't do anything right. You're just poor white trash like the rest of us."

Mark reflected back on this memory for quite some time. As he did, he realized his father's demeaning words and his co-workers' comments made him feel the same way: angry, trapped, hurt, worthless, and unworthy.

What happened to Mark is called **parallel processing***. It is a very common phenomenon that happens to survivors. Parallel processing is when an event you are experiencing today taps back into something painful that happened to you in your childhood. You then take the painful emotions of what happened to you as a child and bring them forward and mix them with the situation you are experiencing today. This, in turn, causes you to overreact to the situation in front of you. So, instead of responding to the situation like an adult, you mix it with your old childhood wounds and respond to it like a child. It looks much like this:

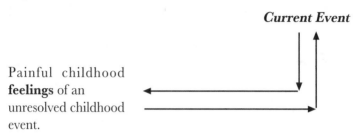

Current Event

Painful childhood **feelings** of an unresolved childhood event.

Let's go back to Mark for a moment and look at how he fell into the trap of parallel processing. Mark had 35 or so years worth of anger stored up about the way his father had demeaned him in junior high school when he was running for class treasurer. This anger got stored inside of Mark because, as a teenager, he didn't feel safe enough to tell his father how those comments had made him feel.

As Mark grew into a man, he continued carrying around that anger he had about his father. Then, when his co-worker made his joke about Mark applying for the vice-president's position, it tapped back into his father's degrading him in junior high school when he was running for class treasurer. He then took all of this anger and unknowingly unleashed it on his co-worker. He overreacted to the situation. He became the defiant teenager. His angry inner child bled over into his adult and took control. Mark became the angry child in junior high school all over again, even though he was now an adult.

It is important to understand that parallel processing can be triggered by any emotion and that emotion can be unleashed on anyone in your life, including yourself. In addition, parallel processing doesn't only involve feelings of anger like it did with Mark. However, when anger is the emotion that is being parallel processed it usually results in what Mark did, and that is acting the anger out or taking it out on someone else.

On the other hand, when a person is parallel processing other emotions, such as sadness, worthlessness, hopelessness, frustration, inadequacy, and depression something very different tends to happen. These types of emotions usually result in the person who is feeling them becoming so overwhelmed that they take what they are feeling out on themselves rather than the person who is standing in front of them.

Mark could have done the same thing. He could have heard his co-worker's remarks and let them hurt his feelings, instead of making him angry. He could have become the wounded, little boy all over again who was afraid to speak his truth; who swallowed his sadness and became quiet during the rest of lunch. After lunch, he could have then thought about nothing but what his co-worker had said and could have wondered, "Is he right? Am I really just a peon?"

These thoughts would have done nothing but continue fueling Mark's feelings of unworthiness and inadequacy. Then, not knowing what else to do, Mark could have ended up hurting himself or falling prey to any number of self-destructive behaviors (adverse reaction,) such as getting drunk, gambling or overeating.

This scenario with Mark is one that is all too familiar for most people who were abused, neglected and/or traumatized as children. They tend to parallel process anything and everything anyone says or does to them. This keeps them in the child ego state. It keeps their inner child on constant alert mode (hypervigilance,) wondering whether to defend themselves or to hide. It makes working, having relationships and anything else extremely difficult because they are too busy taking everything personally and allowing their inner child to interfere with things only the adult should be handling.

For you, the survivor, who is working your way through the healing process, it will be important for you to learn how to identify when you are parallel processing. For you to acknowledge and understand what you are paralleling processing back to in your childhood. This will help you to change the way you are responding to things in your adult life. It will also help you to identify what unresolved issues your inner child is still carrying around.

Let's take a moment and walk through the process of how you can identify when you are parallel processing and how you can identify what you are parallel processing back to in your childhood.

Like everything else mentioned so far, the first thing you need to do is to recognize in your body when you are starting to parallel process (red flag). You need to recognize when you are becoming angry, tense, sad, frightened, or nervous. For most people parallel processing is linked to feeling overwhelmed. Notice if your stomach is feeling queasy or like it's tied in knots; if your breath becomes rapid or shallow; if you want to scream or cry; or if you become afraid and feel wounded.

After your body has told you that you are parallel processing, then you need to go to a quiet place where you can sit down and be still. Begin doing your diaphragmatic breathing. It will help you to calm down and become centered. It will help you open yourself up emotionally so you can discover why you are feeling the way you are.

Once you have calmed down, then allow yourself to feel what you were feeling in the middle of your difficult situation. Feel what it felt like to play the role you were playing; to become the child all over again. Then ask yourself this question, "When do I first remember feeling this way as a child."

The key to parallel processing is to process the feeling, NOT the event. You are looking for a time in your childhood when you felt the same way as you did in your difficult situation, not to find an event that is similar to your difficult situation.

Once you remember when you first had that same feeling, then try to remember what caused you to feel that way. What was happening? Who was there? What was the circumstance that was causing you to have those feelings?

Once you have answered these questions, take a moment to write your answers in your journal.

Once you have been able to identify what you are parallel processing back to, you will need to work the rest of the plan. You will need to choose which cognitive phrases and cards go with the situation, repeat them to yourself until your perspective about the situation changes, choose to respond to the situation as an adult, and then journal what you learned from it.

Let's go back to Mark for a moment to see how he could have worked the plan. Mark's first step was to recognize in his body when his face had turned red, his breath had grown shallow and he stood up and grabbed his co-worker by the shirt in anger. This was his clue that his inner child was being tapped into (red flag).

His next step was to politely remove himself from this situation so he could find a quiet place where he could sit down and do his diaphragmatic breathing. As he did his breathing exercise, he would need to think about how he felt during that conversation with his co-worker, how his co-worker's comment made him feel and how it felt to become overly angry. Mark then needed to ask himself, "When do I first remember feeling this way as a child."

For Mark, he quickly remembered that he first felt this kind of anger when his father had degraded and teased him about running for class treasurer in junior high school. This would help him to know why he became so angry and what he had parallel processed back to. It looks like this:

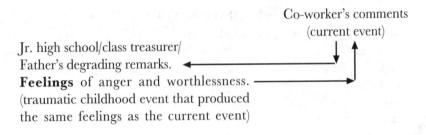

Co-worker's comments
(current event)

Jr. high school/class treasurer/
Father's degrading remarks.
Feelings of anger and worthlessness.
(traumatic childhood event that produced
the same feelings as the current event)

Now that Mark understands he overreacted to his co-worker's comments because they reminded him of how his father had treated him, he can now do something different. He can now use his cognitive phrases: **"My name is Mark and I am enough!!!** I am good enough to be the vice-president of this company. **My attitudes, values, beliefs, opinions and feelings are just as good as anyone else's.** I believe I have what it takes to be the vice-president and to do a good job no matter what anyone else thinks or believes. **The way I act or react in any situation is based on my ability to be objective.** So I can step back and see that my friends were only joking. **People don't do things against me, they do things to meet their own needs**, thus it is all right for me to meet my needs by applying for this position."

These phrases and new thoughts will help move Mark out of the child ego state and back into the adult ego state. They will help him to decide what course of action he needs to take as the adult and to then pursue that course of action. For example, he could apologize to his co-worker and everyone else who was at the lunch table. Or, he could meet privately with his co-worker and explain why he responded they way he did. Or, he could apologize and then treat everyone to lunch. The possibilities are endless. The important thing is Mark needs to recognize that he parallel processed back to an earlier time in his childhood, what he parallel processed back to, why he parallel processed and then rectify it as an adult.

One thing to keep in mind is that Mark's apologies and gestures of reconciliation may not be received by his co-workers in a way he wishes. They may be angry with him, make fun of his inappropriate behavior or refuse to allow him back in their group. If this is the case, Mark's only responsibility at this point is to maintain the adult ego state and to do what he needs to do to take care of himself first in a healthy, adult manner.

Mark's last task is to reflect on what happened that day and to then journal what he learned from this difficult situation and how he handled it. It will be important for him to do this so he can apply what he learned from this difficult situation to the next similar one that comes along.

THE FISHING TRIP

Analogies seem to be helpful for most people, so I would like to provide you with one about parallel processing. I call it **the fishing trip**.

Imagine you are sitting on a bank, fishing in a pond. The pond represents your life and the world you interact with. You bait your hook and toss it out into the pond of life. Wherever your hook lands in the pond represents a difficult situation you are encountering in your life today. When you realize you have snagged a difficult situation on your hook, you instinctively pull back on your pole. However, you pull back on it so hard that it flies behind you and lands in the bushes. The bushes that lie behind you represent your past, your painful childhood events and traumas.

You look behind you and notice your hook has landed in one of those painful childhood events (parallel processing). It is at this point that you have a choice to make. You can recognize your difficult situation has landed in your childhood, ignore it, snatch the pole out of the bushes, throw the line back into the pond of life again and respond to the difficult situation the way you always have. Or, you can recognize the difficult situation has landed in your past and choose to identify what it has tapped back into from your childhood (parallel processing). You can then change what is on your hook (your perspective about the difficult situation) by working the plan (doing your breathing and looking at what role you are playing, using your cognitive phrases, journaling, etc). Once you have changed your perspective and the bait on your hook, you can throw your new perspective and hook back into the pond of life. This will give you the opportunity to respond to your difficult situation differently and through the adult ego state.

You can only heal from your past if you are willing to recognize when you are parallel processing and what you are parallel processing back to; when you are willing to see how situations in your present day life are tapping back into your wounded or angry child. Once you understand this, you can then change how you react to your present day life's difficult situations and respond to them like an adult. Exercise K, located on the next page, can help you with this task. Please allow yourself to work this exercise for one week before moving onto the next chapter.

Exercise K:

Parallel Processing

Each time you find yourself in a situation that is uncomfortable and/or find yourself overreacting, complete the following:

Describe the event:

_____

_____

_____

_____

_____

Describe the feelings the situation evoked:

_____

_____

_____

_____

_____

Describe how you reacted or overreacted:

_____

_____

_____

_____

_____

Describe what this situation reminded you of from your childhood:

_____

_____

_____

_____

_____

*What can you do now to change how you view what happened to me as
a child, i.e. journaling, phrases, the plan, etc:*

_____

_____

_____

_____

_____

*What can you do now to change how you respond to the current situation,
i.e. use cognitive phrases and then apologize, journal and then re-address
the situation, etc.:*

_____

_____

_____

_____

_____

Chapter 12

Self-Perpetuating Rage Regenerator

It is amazing how many children grow up day after day in homes where they are abused, neglected and/or traumatized, and aren't valued as people, but seen only as burdens. So many live in homes where a portion of their spirits are ripped away every time someone withholds love from them and gives them hurt and pain instead. They grow up in families where their hearts and spirits are being broken because they can't get the one thing in life they need the most, love.

Just as striking are the multitudes of adults who have survived and yet blame themselves for the things the adults in their childhoods did to them. Not only that, but they punish themselves because they believe they caused the abuse; they believe they must have been a bad little boy or girl. They believe they must have done something to cause the important people in their childhoods to hurt them.

These same people then carry all of these distorted thoughts and beliefs (misperceptions) into their adult lives. They self-destruct and hurt themselves over and over again trying to justify what happened to them and trying to figure out why the people they loved chose to hurt them rather than love them. They act out to get someone to see their pain. They hope someone will be able to make their pain go away and make them feel loved. They try to find someone who will rescue them from their past and from who they are today.

As a survivor, you may have felt the same way and could still be doing the same thing in your life today. You may have spent the last 10, 20 or maybe even 30 years drinking yourself to death, overeating, self-mutilating, gambling, throwing up, working excessive hours, people-pleasing or engaging in a an array of other adverse reactions, hoping someone would notice your pain and rescue you. If this is true, then you are one of those many abuse survivors who have fallen victim to a vicious cycle and one you don't know how to escape.

As a survivor it will help if you understand the cycle(s) you have fallen into and what a cycle is. A cycle is a set of behaviors you engage in over and over again hoping they will help you to get your needs met or will protect you somehow. There are many cycles you can get caught up in. Unfortunately, most cycles are well hidden from your conscious mind, thus you are likely unaware of what cycle you are up caught in.

Most cycles are unconscious because they began at a time in your life when you were the most vulnerable, i.e. in your childhood. In order for you to have protected yourself during those times of vulnerability, your unconscious mind began developing ways for you to survive. Hence, your unconscious mind generated cycles of behavior so you could protect yourself from what was going on around you, to help you make sense out of what was happening and to help you find a way to get your emotional needs met. It is also your unconscious mind that still maintains those cycles today.

The problem with the cycles you created in your childhood is that you have carried them into your adult life. You continue maintaining those cycles as a means of getting your needs met. But, these cycles are unhealthy and don't lead to healing.

Because you have been unaware of what cycles you have created for yourself, you are unaware of the impact they have had on your life. Thus, you keep doing the same things over and over again, wondering why nothing seems to change. This goes back to the concept that you can't change something you aren't aware of. Therefore, part of your recovery process is going to entail you identifying the cycles you have created and learning how to break those cycles.

Let's look at an example of how a survivor unconsciously created a certain cycle for himself and why he did so.

Marty is a young man who grew up in a poverty-stricken family where there was never enough food to eat or clothes to wear. Because both of his parents were usually working two jobs, they didn't have much time to spend with him. Because Marty was too young to understand why his parents were working all the time, he felt unloved. What his parents didn't realize was they were providing for Marty's physical needs but not his emotional ones.

As a teenager, Marty discovered alcohol. He noticed that when he drank, the hole inside of him that felt unlovable would magically disappear. From that time forward, every time those feelings of being unlovable would resurface, he would get drunk.

By the time Marty became an adult he was a binge drinker and an alcoholic. In order to keep his job and be successful in life, he learned how to hide his alcoholism quite well.

When Marty turned 30 years old, he met a wonderful woman, married her and had two great children. Overall, Marty and his wife had a pretty good marriage.

Several years into their marriage, Marty's wife began noticing that he would get drunk every two months or so. She didn't really know what to do, so every time Marty went on a binge, she made sure he got to bed safely, threw out his liquor bottles and called his boss to ask for a sick day. His wife tried to drop hints to Marty about going into a rehabilitation program, but he refused to acknowledge the hints.

By their 10th wedding anniversary, Marty was still binge drinking. Somewhere inside of himself he wanted to quit. He knew he was hurting his wife and his children, but he didn't know how to deal with the feelings that always came back when he was sober; the feelings of being unlovable.

Marty's wife began growing weary of his drinking. She knew she couldn't keep taking care of him, so she started considering a divorce.

When Marty realized his wife was on the verge of divorcing him, those feelings of being unlovable began resurfacing again. He didn't understand why his wife didn't want to continue taking care of him. He didn't understand what had changed and what had caused her to stop rescuing him. This didn't stop Marty from drinking though. Instead, he started getting drunk almost every day, but not to make his wife take care of him but to punish himself for being the "bad little boy" who was unlovable all over again.

So the question becomes, "What cycle has Marty created and what unconscious needs is he trying to get met"?

The cycle Marty created centered around his alcoholism. He learned from past experience that when he got drunk, his wife would go into protection mode. She would take care of him, spend time with him and would make sure he was safe. Not only would she protect him at home but she would also protect him from getting fired from his job. Thus, Marty's cycle served its purpose: It put his wife in the role of being his caretaker so he would feel loved and lovable.

His cycle told him that if he began feeling unlovable then all he had to do was get drunk and his wife would be there to love and rescue him from himself. This was Marty's unconscious mind's way of getting Marty the love and attention he had needed as a little boy and that his inner child still needed today, even though he was now an adult.

Unfortunately for Marty though, his cycle consumed every ounce of his wife's energy. It eventually caused her to grow tired of taking care of him. In the end, it ultimately created the opposite effect of what he had wanted. Instead of his cycle allowing him to get his needs met it pushed his wife away and resulted in him feeling unlovable and abandoned all over again.

HOW CYCLES BEGIN AND CONTINUE

All cycles are created pretty much in the same way, have similar underlying emotions and serve the same purposes. Homes where children are being abused, neglected and/or traumatized tend to be fertile grounds for creating these cycles. Over time, these children begin feeling responsible for the bad things that are happening in their family and to them (egocentricity). They want the bad things to stop but because they are only children they can't make anything stop. This causes them to feel frustrated and inadequate. They also feel abandoned because no one is coming to their rescue. They believe no one cares enough to make the craziness in their home stop, that no one loves them, and that they can't get their emotional needs met in a way that makes sense to them. They believe they can't get anyone to love and protect them like a parent should love and protect a child (misperceptions).

As time goes by, their frustration evolves into anger. They don't know how to tell anyone how they feel. They are too afraid to tell anyone what is happening to them, so they begin acting out (adverse reactions). They act out as a means of venting their frustration and anger. They hope someone will notice and will rescue them. They hope someone will come along and meet their unmet needs. They act out to get someone to love them, to see what is happening in their home, and to make someone care (external locus of control).

As this child's needs go unmet and they grow into an adult, their anger mutates into rage. The rage they carry around greatly influences every aspect of their life. It keeps the abuse they sustained as child alive, but deep inside their heart and unconscious mind.

They continue acting out the rage over and over again hoping someone will help them (wounded child). When no one comes, the rage grows bigger and more intolerable. They begin trying to find ways to bury the rage. They begin self-destructing. Unconsciously, they hope someone will notice they are drinking themselves to death, over eating, are depressed and/or having suicidal thoughts. They hope their self-destructing will cause someone to care enough to rescue them. When no one notices and no one does anything to help them, they become even more enraged and dependent. They are angry because no one is rescuing them and yet feel dependent and needy for someone to love them. So they act out more and more trying to get what they need. When they realize no one is coming, they are reminded of how they felt when they were a child who was unlovable. Thus, the cycle starts all over again.

I call this cycle the **Self-Perpetuating Rage Regenerator**. In essence, what this means is you, the survivor takes the anger and rage of your past and turns it against yourself rather than directing at the people who hurt you. You regenerate and perpetuate your own anger, rage, and self-destructive behaviors, even after the abuse has stopped. You do this because you feel like you can't speak your truth to the people who hurt you, so you take it out on yourself. You continue hurting yourself just like your perpetrators or parents had done. You also keep hurting yourself because you unconsciously hope someone will notice you are self-destructing and will rescue you.

Let's look at Susan as an example of someone who is caught up in the Self-Perpetuating Rage Regenerator.

Susan is a 35-year-old woman who grew up in a home where she loved her mother more than life itself. She wanted nothing more than for her mother to love her back. However, Susan's mother couldn't return her love because she was too wrapped up in a relationship with an alcoholic who beat her regularly. Susan felt helpless as she watched her mother being beaten. She also felt abandoned and unlovable because she couldn't get her mother to spend time with her.

Because Susan loved her mother, she began feeling the need to take care of her and to rescue her from her terrible boyfriend. No matter how hard Susan tried to rescue her mother from the beatings, she wasn't successful because she was merely a child. This left Susan feeling frustrated, helpless, and worthless.

As time went on, Susan continued trying to earn her mother's love and to rescue her. No matter what she did, her mother didn't recognize what Susan was doing or what her needs were.

Some years later Susan's mother started doing to Susan what the men in her life had been doing to her, she started beating her. With each beating Susan endured, she felt more helpless and worthless. She couldn't understand why her mother would rather beat her than love her.

By the time Susan became a teenager, her frustration turned into anger. She began acting out. She started drinking and drugging. She hoped, unconsciously, that her schoolteachers would see her cry for help and would rescue her. However, no one came to Susan's rescue. No one asked why she was acting out. No one wanted to get involved. This didn't stop Susan, though. She continued acting out hoping someone would eventually recognize her cry for help.

The years passed slowly by as Susan turned into an adult addicted to alcohol and drugs. She hated how she felt about herself. She began equating who she is with how she felt. She was still angry at her mother for not loving her and for beating her. In Susan's mind, her anger and self-destructive behaviors made her a bad person, but she still wanted her mother to love her. She wanted to beg her mother to tell her what she needed to do to earn her love. She wanted her mother to see and feel her pain. At the same time though, Susan knew her mother wouldn't listen and would never understand how she felt. This put Susan in a double bind: One of wanting her mother's love but also wanting to strike out against her for hurting her. This made Susan feel even more hurt, frustrated and angry, but now at herself.

Since Susan couldn't express her hurt and frustration to her mother, she turned those feelings in on herself. The anger eventually turned into rage and depression and fueled her addictions (adverse reactions). The rage reinforced how Susan already felt about herself; like a worthless failure who was unlovable. Not recognizing the cycle she was in, Susan continued acting out, unconsciously hoping someone would recognize her cry for love and attention. But now, when no one came, Susan made the assumption it was because she was worthless and was a failure; because she was someone who wasn't worthy of anyone's love. This reinforced what she had learned from her mother.

Because no one still came, Susan felt even more enraged. It sent her spiraling down into a pit of depression. As she got depressed, she realized she was alone and had no one to talk to. However, she didn't stop to think that the reason why she was alone was because she had pushed everyone away with her acting-out, and by assigning everyone in her life the role of being her parent. She couldn't see that no one understood she had assigned them this role. This, in turn, created another double bind for Susan: One of being dependent on people for love and yet hating them for not meeting her needs. This only fueled Susan's confusion and desperation for someone to help her understand what was happening, to rescue her and to love her. When she realized there wasn't anyone who was coming to her rescue, it reminded her of the old feelings she had about her mother when she was a child. How she had felt unlovable and unworthy of anyone's attention. How her mother had never loved her and didn't care enough to help her. Thus, the cycle of the Self-Perpetuating Rage Regenerator started all over again.

As you can see, it was the anger and rage Susan kept recycling and regenerating over and over again that kept her locked into this cycle. It was her acting out as a means of trying to get people to love her that resulted in her feeling angry and rageful. It was her giving everyone around her the responsibility of rescuing her that kept her from being able to rescue herself. It looked like this:

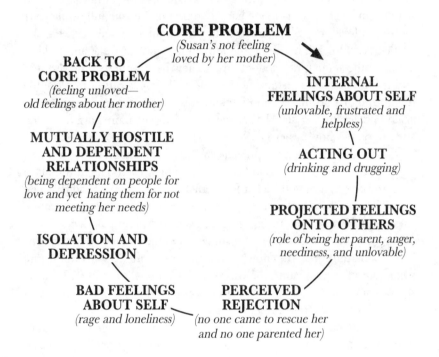

Thus, Susan kept repeating the same behavior over and over again with everyone in her life, expecting something different to happen. She expected someone to magically understand why she was acting the way she was, to feel sorry for her, and to take on the role of her loving mother. She expected someone to fulfill the needs she had when she was a little girl. Unfortunately, the only way Susan was ever going to be able to recover was by learning how to meet her own needs and rescue herself.

The Self-Perpetuating Rage Regenerator is a very common cycle abuse survivors get stuck in. They allow their anger and rage to run their life. They believe that if they can hold onto their anger then they can protect themselves and everything will be all right. This is a misperception.

Let me explain this. Imagine an anthill. On the outside, the anthill looks smooth and calm, almost beautiful in some aspects However, if you were to knock the top layer of dirt off of the anthill, you would expose hundreds of little ants running around in chaos, trying to protect themselves.

Anger is like the top layer of the anthill. Its purpose is to protect you from all of the unwanted painful emotions, such as depression, sadness, anxiety, and feeling unlovable running around inside you and inside your anthill.

Anger is an emotion many people use to protect themselves. When they experience anger, it puts a barrier up between them and everyone else, much like the outer layer of the anthill. They believe this barrier of anger keeps people from seeing their fragile and emotional insides and protects them from getting hurt again, but what it ultimately does is to push people away. They are also afraid that if they let their barrier of anger down then it will open them up to the feelings that are scrambling around beneath the surface or in the middle of their anthill.

As an abuse survivor, healing can be accomplished only when you are willing to knock the top layer of dirt off your anthill, to open yourself up to feel your inner child's pain and to let people get close to you again.

So the question becomes, "How does Susan or anyone else break free from their anger/rage and from their Self-Perpetuating Rage Regenerator?"

To answer this question you have to first look at who is holding onto your anger, who is regenerating it, and who has been the only one there during your entire life? Who was the one who survived the abuse and has carried your pain all of these years?

It is your inner child. So, in order to break the Self-Perpetuating Rage Regenerator, or any other cycle, you have to look at your inner child and help him/her resolve what happened in your childhood. You have to face the feelings the abuse, neglect and/or trauma left you with and the misperceptions your inner child has carried over into your adult life. You have to allow your inner child to go back and address the abuse and how it felt. You have to face the people who hurt you and learn to speak your truth to them. You have to help your child get his/her needs met. This is the only way your childhood experiences and emotional traumas can be embraced and then set free, no longer to ruin the life you have as an adult. This is the goal of the emotional restructuring part of recovery and the chapters to come.

I would like for you to take some time to think about what you have learned so far in this section of the book, especially this chapter, which deals with the Self-Perpetuating Rage Regenerator. Then turn the page and complete Exercise L. This exercise will help you to identify the concerns you might have about facing your childhood and your inner child. It will also help you to determine if you are ready to proceed to the next chapter.

Exercise L:

Readiness Exercise

Go to your quiet place and begin doing your diaphragmatic breathing. As you breathe, search deep within yourself to see how you are feeling about the material you have read in this section of the book. Contemplate your thoughts and feelings about your inner child and if you are ready to face the pain your inner child carries around. Then answer the following questions:

1. *My thoughts and feelings about what I have read in this section of the book are:*

_____

_____

_____

_____

_____

2. *The memories that are beginning to resurface inside of me are:*

_____

_____

_____

_____

_____

3. *When I think about the things I will need to look at from my childhood I feel:*

_____

_____

_____

_____

_____

4. *When I think about facing my childhood and feeling the pain I had as a child I feel:*

_____

_____

_____

_____

_____

5. *Am I ready to face my childhood and the pain I felt as a child: yes or no*

Please explain:

_____

_____

_____

_____

_____

_____

_____

If you have decided you are NOT ready to face your childhood or your inner child who carries your pain, it is all right. There is no shame in this. It doesn't make you a bad or weak person. It doesn't mean you won't ever recover. It just means you may need a little more time. It could also mean you need to consider finding a therapist who can help you become ready for the next step in your recovery process. You might even want to go through these last few steps of the recovery process with your therapist. This, too, is all right.

On the other hand, if you have decided you are ready to face what happened to you as a child, please turn to the next chapter.

Chapter 13

The Secret Place

IF YOU ARE READING THIS CHAPTER, you have made a conscious decision to start looking at what happened to you as a child, the people who hurt you and how those things affected you as a little boy or girl. You have made the decision to feel the pain of your past and the feelings your inner child still carries around so you can stop getting caught up in the Self-Perpetuating Rage Regenerator. You have decided you are ready to help your inner child heal, to re-parent the little boy or girl who lives inside of you and to begin living a life where you have embraced what happened to you. You have decided to take responsibility for your own healing; to open yourself up to a future that can be filled with happiness; and to find a love for yourself you may never have thought possible.

Before delving into this aspect of the emotional restructuring process, a few things need to be explained. Beginning with this chapter and continuing through the next two chapters, the process of how things will be done and how they will be presented to you will be very different. It won't be a matter of you reading a chapter, completing an exercise and then practicing what you've learned. Instead, you will read a short introduction and will then be instructed to listen to a certain track from the CD provided in the back of this book. On that CD, you will find several experiential exercises. These exercises were designed to be emotionally experienced rather than completed on a piece of paper, as in previous chapters. The exercises are being done this way to help your inner child *feel* whatever he/she needs to feel from your childhood; to teach your inner child how to allow things to be different from when you were growing up; and to allow your inner child to restructure what he/she experienced and felt in a way that leads to healing.

You won't be told in advance what you will be doing in each of the exercises, but will be provided instructions on how to complete the experiential exercises. Please follow the instructions as they are presented and as accurately as you can. Please note that at the end of each track, you will be asked to reflect on what you experienced and how it felt. After you have done this, you will need to go back to this book and finish reading the rest of the chapter.

These three chapters are being presented in a non-disclosing and non-descriptive way for a reason. All of my years as a therapist have revealed this to be the most effective method of helping people deal with the emotional aspects of their childhood abuse. It has also revealed that if I were to go into detail with you about what you were going to be doing in the experiential exercises, your unconscious mind would start working overtime. It would unintentionally sabotage what you were about to do. It would try to prepare you for the pain it thinks might be coming so it could protect you and your inner child from having to relive the overwhelming things that happened in your past. As you might remember from the first chapter in this section, it is the job of your unconscious mind to protect you from anything it deems as *potentially* harmful. Thus, your unconscious mind would think it is just doing its job when in fact what it would be doing is preventing you from being able to finish the recovery process.

At this point what your unconscious mind doesn't realize is you have acquired a great number of tools since you began venturing down this road of recovery. It doesn't fully understand you are at a place now where you are coping more efficiently with your daily life and things you feel. It doesn't realize you have the ability to protect yourself and are taking responsibility for your own recovery. It doesn't understand that the pain you might experience during the next three chapters, and with the experiential exercises, won't be the same pain you experienced as a child. It doesn't understand that the pain you might experience now won't overwhelm you as it might have when you were a child.

Because your unconscious mind is linked to your inner child, it still thinks you are small and helpless. It needs you to teach and show it you are now an adult who is learning how to take care of yourself without escaping into your unconscious mind, indulging in adverse reactions or giving into the overwhelming feelings of your child. Your unconscious mind needs you to give it permission to open up so the memories and emotions of your childhood can drift back up into your conscious mind so you can deal with them and recover. One way you can do this is by trusting the process that is being laid out before you so your unconscious mind can sit back and relax, and so you can heal.

You might be asking yourself, "What am I supposed to get out of the exercises and how will I know if I have done them correctly?"

The answer to both of these questions is this: You are looking for an emotional release that leads to resolution. You will undoubtedly know when the release happens. It will feel like whatever aspect of your childhood you are working on has been resolved. Somehow the emotional pain will dissipate and it will feel as if it has drifted away. You may feel tired and emotionally drained, but refreshed and relieved all at the same time. You will intuitively know when this happens. No one will have to tell you. Your inner child will be the one feeling it and will be telling you when things are resolved, so rely on the voice of your inner child.

Don't be surprised though if you have to do the exercises on the CD several times before you get the emotional release you are looking for. This could happen for a number of reasons. The first being you have spent years and maybe even decades covering up and/or running from what happened to you as a child. Thus, it will likely take you more than a few sessions to obtain the resolution you are looking for. This is perfectly normal.

The second reason is that you are dealing with childhood memories and emotions that have been tucked away in your unconscious mind. Thus, it may take a little more time and effort to get those memories and emotions back to the surface again, and back to the conscious mind. Notice that I said it may take more time and effort but I didn't say it would be impossible.

Third, if you are afraid of the exercises and what might happen with them, then it will affect how open you will be to them. It will be your fear that will keep your inner child locked away in your unconscious mind and your heart closed for healing. It will keep you from truly being able to look at yourself, your past and your inner child. Hopefully, you have learned to trust what is in this book by now and know that nothing would be suggested that would intentionally hurt you. Hopefully, the information that has been provided in this chapter will help lesson your fears so you can relax and allow your unconscious mind and inner child to do the work they need to do.

Just keep in mind though that it is perfectly all right if you have to do one or more of the exercises several times. It is usually this way for most people. So be kind and gentle with yourself and your inner child and allow your recovery to move at it's own pace.

Something for you to keep in mind while working your way through the experiential exercises is the need for you to EVENTUALLY be able to complete each of the exercises on the CD without using the CD. Just like everything else presented to you thus far, this can only be accomplished with practice. Practice will help you be able to use the exercises any time you need to, even in the middle of emergencies and difficult situations. You don't want the fact that you might not have access to a CD player or the CD itself to keep you from being able to take care of yourself in the middle of any situation.

Finally, you need to know the exercises on the CD are only a template, an example of what happens in a therapeutic setting or in a counselor's office. It is a compilation of what I have found to work best with the abuse survivors I have worked with in my practices. This is important for you to keep in mind because there is no way any one person can come up with one exercise that can meet the needs of every person who is in recovery. Each and every abuse survivor has experienced different things with different people in their childhood. They felt those experiences and those people in different ways. This doesn't mean the exercises won't provide you with what you need to heal. It just means you may have to adapt them to meet your own needs and base them on what happened to you as a child. Thus, what is being offered to you is a carefully designed compilation of what has worked well with other abuse survivors in a counseling setting, but in a broad, generalized way.

My preference would be that every abuse survivor would have access to a therapist who knows how to do the emotional restructuring work and who knows how to do the experiential exercises on the CD. This would by far be the best scenario. In this way a therapist could take and mold the experiential exercises to match the details of what happened to you in your childhood. This could make it easier for you to access your emotions and to heal. However, not everyone has access to a therapist and not everyone wants it. This is the reason for this book and CD.

If you have decided you want to do the emotional restructuring exercises yourself and are ready to do so, then let's get started.

INSTRUCTIONS

In order to complete these exercises, you will need a quiet room with a comfortable chair or couch in it. You will also need a CD player. I recommend you use a portable CD player so you can have easy access to a pause button. Or, a tabletop stereo CD player will work fine as long as you have a remote control with a pause button.

After you have acquired these items, go to your quiet place, sit on your comfortable couch or in your chair, read the introduction and then play the desired track of the CD. When you have finished listening to the track, it will be extremely important for you to reflect on your experience and then journal it. Please do NOT rush through any part of this program, but allow yourself to move at your own pace.

If, at any point during these exercises you begin to experience strong emotional reactions, such as anger, violence, suicidal feelings and/or a need for retaliation, *stop the CD*. Sit in your quiet place and do your diaphragmatic breathing. Consciously focus on comforting yourself and calming down until the strong reactions and emotions have past. Remind yourself you are no longer the wounded and helpless child who is being hurt. Instead, you are a person who is recovering from a horrible past; a person who is allowing their anger to be replaced with healing; and a person who is allowing things to be different from the way they were when you were growing up. If doing these things helps you to defuse those strong feelings, then resume the CD when you are ready. If you can NOT resolve the strong emotions and do NOT feel as if you can keep yourself safe, then seek the assistance of a hospital or therapist immediately.

I would also like for you to be aware that throughout these exercises I will be asking you to tell me things, to answer questions, to verbalize what you need and to describe things to me in detail. I will momentarily pause and will wait for your verbal response. You will get the most benefit out of these exercises if you will allow yourself to express your answers *verbally* and to speak your truth *out loud*. Answer the questions in an audible voice. Don't allow shame or embarrassment to step in your way. See this as an opportunity for you to finally have your voice and to speak your truth.

FIRST EXPERIENTIAL EXERCISE—THE SECRET PLACE

The first step in unlocking your unconscious mind and helping your inner child to reconnect is you finding a place where your inner child can feel safe. I call this **the secret place**. It is something you will have to find and experience on your own. It isn't something you can borrow from someone else or something you can push aside as unnecessary. If your inner child doesn't feel safe and can't find a place where change is allowed without negative consequences, then the emotional side of the abuse cannot be addressed or resolved. Thus, your emotional journey begins with finding your secret place.

To help you find your secret place, you will need to go to your quiet room where your comfortable couch or chair is and play track 1 of the CD. When you have finished this track, be sure to complete anything asked of you and then finish reading the rest of this chapter. Be sure you don't listen to any of the other tracks until instructed to do so.

Listen to track 1 now.........................

AFTER FINISHING TRACK 1

Congratulations on finding your secret place and for being kind enough to yourself to find a place where you and your inner child can feel safe; a place where you can heal. I hope what you found was everything you wanted it to be, and everything you imagined it could be.

Now that you have found your secret place, please journal the wonderful place you found. Describe what it looks like. Reflect on the beauty that surrounded you. Write out how it felt to find your special place.

After journaling your secret place thoroughly, practice going to your secret place every day for at least a week using the CD. Please remember to journal after each experience. Then, for another week, practice going to your secret place WITHOUT using the CD. It will take time and practice to get used to going to your secret place on your own, but it will be imperative for you to learn how to do this.

Please don't rush through this exercise or what you experience each time you go to your secret place. Allow it to flow through you and to become an everyday part of your life; a stabilizing force; a safe place you can retreat to for rest and relaxation. A place you can go to in the middle of difficult situations.

If you don't take the time now to really establish your secret place and practice it daily, it will keep you from being able to do the work you need to do in the next two chapters. Imagine your secret place as the foundation for a new house you want to build for yourself. If you haphazardly lay the foundation and then build the house on it, the foundation will eventually crack and the house will fall apart. However, if you take the time to carefully lay the foundation and make sure it is firmly in place, then it will support the house you are building for years to come and through all kinds of inclement weather. Your secret place is the foundation you will build the rest of your recovery on one exercise and one experience at a time. So make sure you do a good job with your secret place and build a solid foundation now.

Chapter 14

Introductions

B<small>Y NOW</small> you have found your secret place and are practicing it on a daily basis. You understand how important this place is and look forward to spending time there with yourself. You now understand what freedom your secret place can hold for you. This might be the first time in your life that you have found a place where you belong; a place that is all your own; and a place where you can feel safe. This is a place no one can ever take away from you.

It's now time to introduce you to the person who holds the key to your recovery. If you are ready, go to your quiet place, sit in your comfortable couch or chair, and listen to track 2 of the CD called The Introductions Exercise. When you have finished this track, be sure to complete anything asked of you and then finish reading the rest of this chapter. Be sure you don't listen to any of the other tracks until instructed to do so.

Listen to track 2 now..........................

AFTER FINISHING TRACK 2

You have just finished being introduced to your inner child. This was either a very positive experience or one that was very emotional. In my years of practice as a therapist, I have noticed that the child each survivor brings forward during this exercise reveals where they are in the recovery process and how ready they are to really look at the pain their inner child carries around. Let's look at an example of how this might be true.

Rick is 28-year-old man who is single and lives by himself. As a little boy, his watched his mother drink herself into a stupor almost every night of his life. He tried to be a good little boy by cleaning up after his mother when she would get drunk and vomit all over the bathroom. He would make sure she got into bed without falling down and hurting herself. He would make sure she wouldn't make any telephone calls to anyone when she was in a black-out. Most importantly, he would wake up each morning and act as if nothing had happened the night before so his mother wouldn't be embarrassed. However, no matter what Rick did, it was never enough. Each time his mother got drunk, she would physically push him around and would yell, "Just get out of my way. You can't do anything right. You're worthless. Leave me alone. I don't want to be stuck looking at you."

Rick didn't understand why his mother treated him this way when all he tried to do was to take care of her.

As a teenager, Rick began isolating himself. He stayed away from the other kids because they would tease him about his mother being a drunk. They would laugh at the clothes he wore because his mother drank up all the money. They would never invite him over to their houses because everyone's parents knew about his mother's drinking. All of this made Rick feel rejected and it reinforced what his mother had taught him his entire childhood: It's not safe to be around anyone because they will always hurt you and you are not likeable. As a result, Rick felt terribly alone and unworthy.

As an adult, Rick swore he would never do what his mother had done to him. As a matter of fact, he decided he would just forget his mother and would never talk or think about her again.

Several years later Rick met a woman he liked, began dating her and eventually married her. He also became a successful businessman who worked a lot of hours. Then, one day after work, Rick's wife sat him down and explained, "We don't have enough money to pay our bills. You might have to get another job if we are going to maintain our lifestyle."

Even though this was what Rick's wife had said, what Rick heard was the voice of his mother saying, "You're not working hard enough and aren't doing what you need to do to take care of your family."

His face turned bright red. He got angry and, without thinking, he slapped his wife across the face. After he hit her, he stood there astonished at what he had done. He was filled with guilt as he watched the tears roll down his wife's face. He didn't know what had just happened. His wife just stood there for a moment and then said, "Either you get into counseling or I will divorce you."

Because Rick loved his wife and didn't want to lose her, he went to see a therapist. Fortunately, he chose a therapist who knew how to do Cognitive Emotional Restructuring Therapy. He was taught all of the cognitive tools and the cognitive phrases. He learned how to diaphragmatically breathe and journal. He was then guided through the secret place exercise to find his secret place. He was introduced to his inner child. However, instead of Rick seeing himself as the little boy who took care of his alcoholic mother, he saw himself as a small boy who was happy and having fun. This was the time in his childhood before his mother had started drinking.

So the question becomes, "Why did Rick bring forward his inner child who was happy rather than the one who was hurt and who took care of his alcoholic mother?"

There are several reasons. The first being that Rick probably wasn't ready to remember how he had tried to take care of his mother and how she had only hurt him in return. He wasn't ready to feel the painful things he had endured with his mother. He wasn't ready to embrace how the kids at school hated him because of his mother's alcoholism. He wasn't ready to remember how his childhood had been taken away because he was his mother's caregiver.

The second reason Rick brought this happy child forward was: As an adult, he had made an agreement with himself that he was never going to think or talk about his mother again. This was his way of protecting himself and his inner child from having to feel what he felt as a child.

Rick bringing forward his happy child also served a positive purpose as well. It reminded him of the little boy he liked being and the positive feelings that little boy had once felt. It gave him an image of the part of himself he wanted to recapture in his healing process. For him this happy child was who he believed he was always supposed to become. He believed this was his natural internal state and who he would have become if he had not been abused. It was the part of himself he needed to recapture as an adult.

On the other hand, let's say Rick had pulled forward his little boy who was hurt and devastated by the things his mother had done to him. The little boy who was sad and felt unlovable because his mother had physically pushed him around and didn't appreciate the help he tried to give her. This would have shown that Rick was ready to face the pain of what had happened to him; that he was ready to meet his inner child who had held onto his pain all of those years, and who caused him to hit his wife.

You, too, may have felt a great deal of pain with meeting your inner child. If you did, it is all right. It is very normal. You have spent many years trying to hide from the pain your inner child experienced while you were being abused, neglected and/or traumatized. So in the beginning, connecting with your child may be a bit overwhelming or sad. Just allow yourself to be with it, to feel it and to know that you, the adult is now capable of taking care of your child.

The questions you need to ask yourself now are these, "Which child did I bring forward and why did I bring him/her forward? What is it I'm supposed to learn from this child? What memories and feelings is my child holding on to?"

Please take a moment and think about these questions. They are very important questions for you to answer. It will help you to know where you are at this point in your recovery. Please write your answers in the space below:

_____

_____

_____

_____

_____

_____

_____

_____

_____

_____

_____

CAUTION!!!

Occasionally, survivors who meet their inner child will feel very emotionally overwhelmed by the experience. This may be true for you as well. You may feel like you can't stop crying. You may feel very vulnerable and emotionally exposed. You may feel as if you have become who you were as a child all over again and you don't know how to get back to the adult part of yourself. If this is true, try to go back and work the plan in chapter 9 to see if this will help ground you and will allow your adult self to resurface and take control again. If you find that you still can't control the overwhelming feelings or if you begin feeling as if you want to hurt yourself, then stop what you are doing right now and call someone for help. Call a friend to talk to, go to the emergency room and ask for the psychiatrist on call or make an appointment with a therapist. The main thing is for you to do whatever you need to do to make sure you are safe.

It is all right if you need a therapist to help you work through the remaining steps of the emotional restructuring process. It is not an easy task, but one that tends to be emotionally challenging for just about everyone. If you decide to find a therapist, share this book with him/her so they can accurately walk you through the rest of the emotional restructuring steps.

ASSIGNMENT

After you have spent time looking at the inner child you brought forward in the Introductions Exercise, please take the time to reflect on your experience and journal it. Describe your inner child. What did he/she look like? How old was he/she? What was he/she wearing? How did it feel meeting him/her? What emotions did you experience? What did those childhood emotions remind you of? What was going on in your life at that time? How did it feel having your child in your secret place with you? Did you like meeting your inner child?

Once you have completed your journaling, please take the time for the next week or so to practice going to your secret place and spending time with your inner child using the CD. Then, for another week or so practice going to your secret place and spending time with your inner child WITHOUT using the CD. Please make sure you journal each experience you have with your inner child, what happened and how it felt.

Should you decide that you can continue with the emotional restructuring work on your own, then turn to the next chapter where you will work on resolving your child's pain.

Chapter 15

Resolution Exercise

Finding your secret place and getting to know the little boy/girl who got emotionally stuck along time ago is just the beginning. Now comes the time when it is necessary to allow your inner child to resolve the issues he/she had with the people who hurt him/her. It is time to allow your inner child to tell the people who hurt you how it felt, what you had needed from them, and to finally get your needs met. It is time to give your inner child the opportunity to own what happened, to say everything that wasn't allowed to be said, and to reveal the family secrets. It is time to stand up and allow your inner child to have a voice and to speak his/her truth.

Instead of being the hurt child who can't speak your truth, it is time for you to become the survivor who can say anything you need to say. Instead of being the child who was never heard, it is time for you to become the survivor who knows your words are important and can now be heard. Instead of being the child who believed no one cared about you, it is time for you to become the survivor who knows you are worthy of love and affection. Instead of being the child who feared people because everyone eventually hurt you, it is time for you to become the survivor who wants to trust people again.

Giving your inner child permission to have a voice and to resolve the abuse will allow him/her to let go of the emotions associated with the abuse. It will allow him/her to let go of the hurtful feelings he/she has carried around all of these years. Afterwards, your small child will feel free and will be able to become the person he/she has always wanted to become. From that day forward, your inner child will look to you, and you only for ongoing comfort and support so he/she can emotionally grow up.

In order for this to happen, there is one extremely important thing you will have to be able to accomplish throughout this next exercise. You will have to remember that it is your present-day heart and mind where you will be doing your emotional restructuring work, not in the past where things are frozen and rigid. This means you will need to open your heart and mind so you can allow things can be different. You will have to allow the people who hurt you to see what they did to you, understand your pain and how the things they did impacted you. You have to give them the opportunity to do things differently. This doesn't mean you are lying to yourself about what happened. It doesn't mean you are denying what they did or didn't do. It just means you are willing to allow things to be different so you can heal and let go of the past.

In other words, instead of being the child who can only see hate and anger in the face of the person who hurt you, you become the survivor who can see the sorrow they feel because of the things they did to you. You see how things were back then for them. You see how they wish they could go back and do things differently and how they wish they could have been a better parent, teacher or guardian. You see how they wish you would forgive them because they really didn't mean to hurt you. You see how they were so messed up themselves that they didn't know how to do things any better. So instead of being the child who carries around a bunch of anger and pain, you become the survivor who can see the people who hurt you for who they really were. You become the survivor who can forgive them and let them go. This is the only way recovery is possible. The only way healing can take place.

If you are still so angry and hurt that you aren't ready to see things differently or you still want the people who hurt you to pay for the pain they caused you, then you won't be able to complete this exercise. You won't be able to heal. This exercise will work only if you are ready to let go of your pain and to forgive the people who hurt you. You don't have to forget what they did, you just have to see them in a different light, forgive them and then let them go. This may sound strange now, and maybe even impossible, but you will understand it more intimately as you do the next exercise. So let's get started.

The first step in this part of the emotional restructuring process is for you to go to your quiet place and sit in your comfortable couch or chair. Close your eyes and do your diaphragmatic breathing. While doing your breathing, picture the inner child you brought forward in the last exercise. See that child standing before of you. Notice what age he/she is. Notice the expression on his/her face. Feel whatever he/she is feeling.

Then, ask your inner child this question, "Who are the people who hurt you?"

As your child gives you the names of these people, write them down in your journal. Don't be surprised though if this list of people closely matches the list you made in Exercise F when you were thinking about the people you need to separate yourself from. You may even want to go back and compare these two lists because they usually are one in the same. The people who hurt you are usually the same people you need to separate yourself from in order to begin your healing process.

After you have made your list, ask your child, "Which person hurt you the most?"

When your child gives you that person's name, write it down in your journal as well.

Then close your eyes one last time and see the person who hurt you. Feel what it felt like to be the child who was being hurt by that person, who was in pain, and who was crying. Breathe into those feelings. Remember how that person had hurt you. Remember the events surrounding your pain.

Once your inner child is fully present with those memories and feelings, I want you to open your eyes and allow your inner child to write a letter to that person in your journal. Please know you must allow the child who lives inside you to write the letter, NOT your adult self. The letter is to contain anything and everything your inner child has ever wanted to say to that person, but was too afraid to say. It should spell out in great detail the pain your child felt and the secrets he/she has been holding on to. It is to be an exhaustive letter, and one that allows your inner child to speak all of his/her truth to that person.

Beware though, sometimes a survivor has carried around their hurt and pain for so long that it has turned into anger. This may be true for you as well. So look at what you have just written and notice if your child has written a letter filled with nothing but anger. If that's what you did, it's all right. This letter was a much needed letter, but it is not the right one for this exercise. So allow yourself to close your eyes once again and see the person who hurt you. Allow your inner child to feel his/her pain and to remember the events surrounding your pain once again. Then turn to the next page in journal and allow your inner child to write another letter to the person who hurt you. Let this letter be the one that is filled with the hurt, pain, fear, and despair you felt as a child. Once your child self has finished writing the letter, do NOT mail it but place an empty chair in front of you and complete the Resolution Exercise on track 3 of the CD. When you have completed this track, be sure to finish reading the rest of this chapter and do not listen to any of the other tracks until instructed to do so.

Listen to track 3 now...........................

AFTER FINISHING TRACK 3

Hopefully what you are about to read will describe what you experienced as a result of doing the Resolution Exercise. Hopefully you felt like you got the opportunity to tell the person who hurt you, let's say it was your mother, how you felt. You got to tell her everything you had ever wanted to say to her: How it felt being her child; how it felt growing up in your home; how the abuse, neglect and/or trauma you endured felt; what you had needed from her as a child but didn't get; and how alone and hurt you felt. After you spoke your truth, you looked into your mother's eyes and saw that she had no idea how badly she had hurt you. She had never understood until this very moment the impact her behavior had on you. And, most importantly, if she could go back and do it all again, knowing what she knows today, she would do it differently. You could see how sorry she was for what she did to you. Then, you saw your mother wanting to make things right with you; to resolve the hurt and pain that stands in the way of you being mother and child. You, too, decided you were ready to let go of the pain. You became ready to accept her apology and to forgive her. So you handed your boxes of pain to your mother. You both threw them up in the air and saw them disappear because neither one of you wanted to hold on to them anymore. You felt your heart grow lighter. You saw your mother reaching out to you and you went to her, fell into her arms and cried. You heard your mother tell you all the things you had wanted to hear. You soaked up the feeling of being loved and accepted, and how it felt to forgive her. Because you forgave her, you became ready to let her and this part of your life go, knowing you could see her anytime you wanted in your secret place. You watched her walk away until you couldn't see her anymore.

You then turned around to find your adult self was waiting for you. You went over to your adult and told him/her everything that had just happened with your mother and how good it felt to speak your truth and to forgive her. Because it is your adult who takes care of you now, you felt your adult wrap his/her arms around you and ask what you needed to feel comforted and safe. You sank into your adult's arms and could hear the words you needed to hear. Maybe you heard, "I love you. I will always be here for you. I will never leave you. You can always come to me if you need something. You are special."

After feeling the safety and warmth of being with your adult, and believing he/she would always be there, you both sat in your secret place for a while, soaking up how good it felt to be loved and supported. You then became ready to find the path that leads away from your secret place and your past. As you walked down the path, you could feel your inner child merging inside your adult. You could feel how safe it felt living in your adult's heart and how it made you feel more whole somehow. Then, when you, the adult, opened your eyes, you knew in the core of your being you had made peace with your mother and this part of your childhood.

This is exactly what the emotional restructuring work and Resolution Exercise is all about. It is being able to feel the freedom that comes from embracing your past, forgiving it and letting it go. It is about knowing you have someone who will always be there to take of you, and that person is your adult self. It is about knowing that you can never be abandoned again unless you abandon yourself. You can never be rejected unless you reject yourself. You can never be emotionally overwhelmed unless you stop taking care of yourself. You can never feel unloved unless you stop loving yourself. You know no one can ever have power or control over you unless you relinquish it to them. And, most importantly, you are the one who can create whatever you want your life to look like as long as you allow your adult to take care of your child and to help your child grow up.

It is now your turn to process what you got out of doing the Resolution Exercise. So please turn to Exercise M located on the next page and answer the questions designed to help you look at your experience. When you have finished the exercise, please journal your experience with the Resolution Exercise thoroughly and finish reading the rest of the chapter.

Exercise M:

Resolution Exercise

Please take a moment and answer the following questions to help you process what you got out of the Resolution Exercise:

1. *What did you get out of the experience?*

_____

_____

_____

_____

_____

2. *What did you learn about yourself and the person you wrote the letter to?*

_____

_____

_____

_____

_____

3. *How did your child feel about the person you were dealing with?*

_____

_____

_____

_____

_____

4. *What issues did you resolve with yourself and the other person?*

_____

_____

_____

_____

_____

5. *Were you able to forgive the person who hurt you?*

_____

_____

_____

_____

_____

6. *Were you able to let go of your pain?*

_____

_____

_____

_____

_____

7. *Could your child let the person who hurt you go?*

_____

_____

_____

_____

_____

8. *Was your child able to turn to your adult for comforting?*

_____

_____

_____

_____

_____

9. Does your child believe the things your adult told you?

_____

_____

_____

_____

10. Does your adult feel capable of taking care of your child now?

_____

_____

_____

_____

_____

11. How did the overall experience feel to you?

_____

_____

_____

_____

_____

If you didn't have the emotional release you were looking for or realized after answering these questions that your work with the person in your letter isn't finished, then please go back and repeat the Resolution Exercise again when you are ready. Do it as many times as it takes, but remember the key is allowing things to be different. You have to allow the person who hurt you to hear your pain. You have to see how he/she is sorry for what they did to you, hear their apology and then forgive them.

One thing that might help is for you to remember a time in your life, even as an adult, when you caught a glimpse of how the person who hurt you might regret how they behaved when you were a child. They might not have come out and said it but you could see the guilt and pain in their eyes. Maybe it conveyed to you that they were young back then (in your childhood), emotionally immature and didn't know how to deal with the pain they were carrying around from their own childhood. Maybe you saw them feel bad about themselves because they had hurt you just like their parents had hurt them. Maybe you saw their guilt because they believed they had been a bad parent. Maybe you saw them cry as they tried to convince themselves that they did the best they could.

Remember how it felt to see that person's pain, sorrow and guilt. Then try to imagine how that person must have felt back then (in your childhood). How they had brought a child into the world while still battling their own pain from their own childhood. See how they were carrying around the same feelings of hurt and vulnerability you have been carrying around, and how they didn't know what to do with those feelings back then. Then, carry this understanding, memories and feelings into the Resolution Exercise with you. See how the person who hurt you might have felt about themselves back then. Allow yourself to see that they were so vulnerable themselves they didn't truly understand how they were hurting you until it was too late. Then allow yourself to see that if this person could go back and do it all again, knowing what they know now, they would do it differently.

Even though this wasn't how things were when you were a child, it doesn't mean they can't be that way now. You are the one who is in control. You are the one who can allow things to turn out differently in your life today with the Resolution Exercise.

Chapter 16

Trauma and the Resolution Exercise

WHAT IS CONTAINED in this chapter usually pertains to survivors who experienced and survived a trauma, such as a rape or an assault when they were growing up. Even if this isn't you, please read this chapter anyway. There may be something contained in these few pages that might help you with your own recovery or maybe even someone else's.

All trauma survivors, including you, need to do the Resolution Exercise with each person who traumatized you. However, it will require that you take the Resolution Exercise one step further.

After writing your letter and addressing the person who traumatized you through the Resolution Exercise, you will have to allow your inner child to write an additional letter. This letter is written to the one person you trust and need help from the most: your adult self. You must allow your inner child to write a letter to your adult about how the trauma felt, how it changed you and how you need your adult to rescue you. You then must allow your adult self to rescue your inner child from that trauma using the Resolution Exercise. It is your adult self who your inner child reads the letter to and your adult who you allow to rescue your inner child.

You might be asking yourself why this would be true. In all of the previous examples where the Resolution Exercise was completed, it was with people the trauma survivor was intimately acquainted with; people they had an emotional connection with, such as a parent, schoolteacher, neighbor or other relative. However, for the survivor who was traumatized in such a horrid manner as rape or an assault, they likely didn't know their perpetrator. The trauma was likely committed by a stranger or someone they only knew superficially. Because this survivor doesn't have an emotional connection to their perpetrator, it makes it much more difficult for them to get emotionally connected enough during the Resolution Exercise to resolve their feelings about the trauma and to forgive the person who hurt them. So what they have to do is to find out who they can emotionally connect with and who they believe can rescue them from this horrible trauma, and that usually only leaves one person, their adult self.

Let's look at Rachel as an example of why this is true and how this might happen.

Rachel was a woman who had grown up in a rather sheltered environment. She had been protected from the realities of life and the fact that bad things can happen to good people. Even though she didn't have a close relationship with either of her parents, she was protected from the potential cruelties of the world.

By the time Rachel became 17 years old, she left home and went off to college. In one of her classes, she met a young man named Brad. She thought he was cute and was impressed with his pledging to a fraternity. Brad liked Rachel as well, so he invited her to a party his fraternity house was hosting.

At the party, Rachel and Brad were sitting on the couch. They were talking, playing cards and getting to know each other. As the evening progressed, they were having trouble hearing each other over the music and dancing. So Brad invited Rachel up to his room so they could talk and hang out without all of the disruptions. Because of her sheltered life, Rachel didn't think twice about Brad's offer and agreed to go up to his room. Once in Brad's room, he locked the door, threw her on the bed and proceeded to rape her. She cried out for someone to help her but no one came to her rescue.

When he was finished raping her, he tied her up and left her in the room naked and scared. He then sent 31 of his fraternity buddies into the room to rape her as well. This was how they were proving they were worthy of being accepted into the fraternity as a fraternity brother. It was their version of a hazing.

When they finished raping Rachel in the early morning hours, they threw her out the front door of the fraternity house. She was crying and didn't know what to do. So she ran to the football stadium and up to the top of the bleachers. She peered over the side praying she had the courage to jump and end her life. She wanted to make the thoughts and feelings of that terrible night disappear forever.

After hours of crying and contemplating taking her life, Rachel eventually came down off the bleachers. What she didn't know was she had emotionally left her raped and traumatized 17 year old self up there.

The days passed as Rachel didn't tell the police or anyone else about the rapes. Instead, she kept the horrible secret to herself.

By the time Rachel turned 45 years old she had been married for 20 years. She didn't know how to be close to her husband, didn't like being intimate and was very disconnected from him. As a matter of fact, she didn't know how to have a relationship or friendship with anyone because she didn't trust anyone, especially men. When her marriage was about to end in divorce, she got into counseling.

Rachel found a therapist who knew how to do Cognitive Emotional Restructuring Therapy. They spent several sessions working on the rape using the Resolution Exercise. However, Rachel kept reporting that she couldn't seem to get the emotional release she was looking for because her inner child was still standing at the top of the bleachers wanting to kill herself. Thus, it became obvious that Rachel needed to take the Resolution Exercise one step further. It became clear that there was only one person who she trusted and who could rescue her: her adult self. She needed to go to the top of the bleachers and rescue her inner child who wanted to make all of the pain disappear by killing herself. She needed to go back and rescue her traumatized 17-year-old self from all the young men who had raped her.

In order for Rachel to do this, she went to her quiet place. She visualized her inner child in the fraternity house lying in the bed tied up and being raped, and then standing at the top of the bleachers, crying and wanting to kill herself. She allowed her child who had been carrying around all of those memories and feelings to write a letter to her adult self. She told her adult how she had been feeling, how the rape had changed her and how she needed someone to love her enough to make the pain go away. She then told her adult she needed her to be the one who would rescue her and make things better.

After Rachel wrote the letter, she allowed her inner child to read the letter to her adult. She told her everything she needed to say about the rape, going to the bleachers to kill herself and what she needed from her. She then envisioned her adult self going to the top of the bleachers with the intent of rescuing her inner child. She saw her adult put her arms around her child and telling her that it was over and that she was there to love her, protect her and to take her down from this place. She saw her adult take her 17-year-old by the hand and escort her down from the bleachers. She then gave little Rachel everything she had needed. She held onto her while she cried and talked about the rape. She loved her and spent time with her in their secret place while she healed.

For Rachel, the Resolution Exercise could only be successful with her adult going back and rescuing her child. She had to go back and get little Rachel off the bleachers so she could stop wanting to end her life and so she could heal. She had to rescue herself so she could learn that it was okay to start trusting someone again, even if it was only herself.

Of interesting note is that this extra step in the Resolution Exercise also has to be done in another instance. It has to be done with any and all accidents or injuries that left you with emotional scars and ones you still carry around today. The accident or injury is just another type of trauma. Thus, you have to allow your adult self to go back and rescue your inner child in that accident or injury. You have to allow your adult to do this since there wasn't any one who was hurting you intentionally. There weren't any perpetrators or abusers. There was just an accident or an injury that left you with emotional scars.

Doing this extra step with the Resolution Exercise might be something you need to do as well. You might need to allow your adult to rescue your child. If this is what you need to do, then modify the Resolution Exercise so you can accomplish this task. Allow yourself to sit in your quiet place and visualize yourself rescuing your child wherever he/she has gotten emotionally stuck. You have had enough exposure and practice with the Resolution Exercise to know how to do this for yourself. Just believe in yourself and your ability and then follow through with practicing this new skill.

Chapter 17

Beyond Resolution

YOUR JOB NOW is to do the Resolution Exercise and Exercise M with each person on your list until you obtain the emotional release you are looking for; the forgiveness that will set your inner child free from the pain of his/her childhood. As you do this, don't be surprised if you end up with several different inner children who are resolving several different issues with several different people. There could be several places in your childhood where your inner child got emotionally stuck and needs to be freed. This is perfectly normal.

To help illustrate this for you let's look at a woman named Becky. As a child she was terribly abused by her mother, father, and step-father. She had been physically, emotionally, and sexually abused as well as neglected. She also sustained a traumatic injury at the age of 6. As a result of everything Becky had been through, she tried to destroy herself for many years with alcohol and drugs. She tried to kill herself over and over again, but only ended up physically harming her body. After her last suicide attempt, she knew she couldn't keep running from the things that had happened in her childhood. She knew she had to resolve them with a therapist or she would end up killing herself one day. So she found a therapist she liked and delved back into the pain of her childhood. She worked hard for many months learning the cognitive retraining techniques and then finding her secret place and inner children. She then began working with her inner children to resolve what had happened to her. By the time she had finished the Resolution Exercise with each person who had hurt her, Becky had discovered she had five inner children at the ages of 18 months, 6 years, 8 years, 11 years, and 15 years living inside of her. As she worked with each one of her inner children, she found that the pain she had been carrying around all of those years began dissipating. Her life wasn't filled with depression or the feelings that she was a bad little girl who couldn't make the people in her life stop hurting her.

After hearing the number of people who had hurt Becky, you might be thinking that was an awful lot of people with whom to do the Resolution Exercise. She thought the same thing, too. However, in the end it proved to a positive thing for Becky. Instead of feeling alone like she had for the past 35 years, Becky now had five children to keep her company. This made her happy because she could now take care of herself and her children, and she knew she would never be alone again.

Now that you are aware that you need to do the Resolution Exercise with each person who hurt you, I would like to add a word of caution for those of you who have spent your entire lives intellectualizing what happened to you. I would like to explain something that might happen if you are one those people who strictly operates out of your mind and who rarely allows yourself to feel anything. If this is you, then you may find that doing the Resolution Exercise is very difficult. It might even be frustrating since you are NOT used to allowing yourself to feel things. Don't get discouraged though. The Resolution Exercise can work for you, too. You just have to remind yourself, "It is all right for me to feel the things that happened to me as a little boy/girl. I give myself permission to feel my inner child's pain."

You also have to be willing to do the exercise as many times as it takes for you to get the emotional release and healing you are looking for. It will definitely take practice on your part to move out of your intellectual mind and into your emotions, but it is something you are very capable of doing at this point in your recovery.

RESOLUTION AND INDIVIDUATION

As you find each one of your inner children, resolve your emotional pain and forgive the people who hurt you, it will be necessary for you to cultivate a relationship with each one of your inner children. The only way you can do this is by allowing your adult self to spend time with each one of them. You need to do this even if you only found one inner child. You need to do special things together. You need to do all the things your inner child has always ever wanted to do but couldn't. You might go on a picnic lunch at the beach together, go to the fair and ride the roller coaster, go to the movies and eat popcorn and Milk Duds, go for a walk on the beach barefooted, or go play miniature golf. Whatever you do, it will help bring you and your inner child together.

Another thing that works well is spending time with each other in your secret place or some other special place. To help you better understand this, let's look at Tonya as an example. She was a 50-year-old woman who decided she needed to go through therapy because she had been terribly abused by just about everyone in her life. She had felt alone for years and didn't believe she could ever have a relationship with anyone without getting hurt. After she finished doing the Resolution Exercise several times, she discovered she had five inner children who had been living inside of her for years. One of Tonya's most favorite ways to spend time with them was going to her quiet place, doing her diaphragmatic breathing and then drifting off into her secret place, which was on a lake. In her mind's eye, she could see the bathing suits each one of her children wore and how they played in the sand together, building sandcastles. She could see how she and each one of her children had their own lounge chairs, beach towels, sunglasses and sun tan oil. As Tonya sat back in her lounge chair watching her children smiling and having fun, it made her feel happy inside. Not only that, but her children were feeling happy as well. Somehow this made her feel more whole and more fulfilled as an adult. It made her realize she could finally let her defenses down and she was finally free of her past. She felt safe again.

Spending this needed time with your inner child will help give your child all the things he/she couldn't get growing up. It will help your inner child to feel loved, special and attended to. It will give your child a reason to want to live, to grow up and to thrive. In the end, your child will look to you, the adult, for whatever he/she needs. He/she will begin to believe you will always be there to take care of him/her. This sense of safety will let your child feel free enough to start growing up and to emotionally mature so the age gap between your child and you, the adult, will begin to grow smaller.

In many ways, what is being talked about here reinforces something that has already been discussed in an earlier chapter (Chapter 4). It goes back to the concept of individuating. It is only by developing a relationship with your child self and your adult self that you will begin to know who you are and can become the person you want to become.

On the other hand, if you ignore your inner child who has resolved his/her childhood issues, then your emotional growth will go back to being stunted once again. You will likely go back to being the person you were before beginning your recovery.

In order to continue growing, you have to develop a relationship with yourself, both child and adult, that is nurturing. You have to know who your child is and spend time with him/her so you, the adult, can get to know who both of you are apart from the abuse, neglect and/or trauma.

Once you have resolved the issues with the people who hurt you and have gotten to know your inner child, you will be ready for the next step.

RESOLUTION AND REINTEGRATION

If you will think back once again to Chapter 4, you will remember the step after individuating is deciding if you want to reintegrate with the people who hurt you. Now that you have completed the Resolution Exercise with each person on your list, you now have a choice to make. Who, if anyone, do you want to re-establish a relationship with?

You might decide you don't want to reintegrate with anyone from your childhood. If you don't, that is all right. Many people choose not to reintegrate. They don't want to run the risk of losing the progress they've made. They might decide they cannot re-establish a relationship with the people who had hurt them without losing the new person they have become. This is perfectly acceptable.

On the other hand, if you choose to re-establish a relationship with any of the people on your list, please take it very slowly; take it one step at a time. Also, go back to the illustration in Chapter 4 to refresh your memory about how to reintegrate in a healthy way. Make sure you figure out what you can and cannot do with those people; how you can and cannot interact with them; and how much time you can spend with them without it affecting how you feel about yourself.

Take it one step and one activity at a time. And remember, if at any time you feel as if you are resorting back to the wounded child or can't maintain the new person you have become around these people, you are allowed to limit or discontinue your interaction with them. The choice is yours. You are no longer the wounded or tortured child who cannot stand up for yourself or speak your truth. You are the adult who has individuated, who knows who you are and what you want. Whatever you choose is all right.

RESOLUTION AND DAILY LIFE

As you practice everything you have learned in Sections I and II and continue working the Resolution Exercise, you will notice your life and emotions will begin to even out. Your bad days won't seem as bad. Situations you might find yourself in won't seem as overwhelming. Getting upset won't always lead you to becoming emotionally debilitated. Your ability to handle difficult situations will improve. You won't be as emotional. The number of crises in your life will drastically decrease. You will feel yourself beginning to evolve into that emotionally stable person you have always wanted to become.

Despite the fact that all of these wonderful things are beginning to manifest in your life and you are handling difficult situations more appropriately, it doesn't mean that you will be forever immune to anything reminding you of your past. There will be occasions, even though few and far between, where a situation will trigger your inner child and will tap back into your old childhood traumas. These situations will remind you of the things that happened to you when you were little and will momentarily awaken your wounded child.

Finding yourself in a situation where your inner child is being tapped back into is your clue that something wasn't completely resolved with the Resolution Exercise. Maybe you left someone off your list or had forgotten about a painful incident. Maybe you just didn't work the Resolution Exercise as many times as you needed with a particular person or incident. In many ways, this goes back to something mentioned in an earlier chapter.

In Chapter 11 you were taught that when an event you are experiencing today taps back into something painful that happened to you in your childhood that is called parallel processing. You also learned parallel processing causes you to bring those painful childhood emotions forward and to mix them with your present day situation. You then respond to the person in your present day situation as if they were the person who had hurt you as a child. So, instead of responding to the current situation like an adult, you mix it with your old childhood wounds and respond to it like a wounded child.

No matter how many times you do the Resolution Exercise or use the techniques in this book, the day will come when you realize you are in the middle of a difficult situation and are parallel processing back to an earlier time in your childhood. You will realize you are feeling and behaving like the wounded child all over again because the person standing in front of you reminds you of someone or something painful from your childhood. At this point, you will have a very important decision to make. Are you going to handle this situation like you did in the past or are you going to do something differently?

If you choose to handle the situation the way you used to in the past, you will end up treating the person in your present day situation as if they are the person who hurt you in your past. You will treat them like the person who hurt you instead of the person they are. You will assign them the role of being your critical parent while you play the role of the wounded child.

On the other hand, if you choose to continue practicing the new you, you will choose to do the Resolution Exercise so you can resolve what you are parallel processing back to; so you will be able to deal with the person in your present day situation as the person they are instead of the person they remind you of. You will respond to them in the adult ego state instead of the child ego state.

The first step in this process is to figure out who the person in your present day situation is reminding you of from your past. For example, is your female co-worker, who is constantly criticizing you reminding you of your mother who told you nothing you ever did was good enough? Is your wife who doesn't work and constantly nags you about money reminding you of your father who was drunk all the time and never supported his family? Is your girlfriend who is constantly on the go reminding you of your mother who didn't care how it made you feel when she didn't spend time with you?

When you know who you are parallel processing back to in your past, you will then be able to go to your quiet place, write your letter to that person and do the Resolution Exercise with them. This will allow you to resolve the childhood situation you are parallel processing back to. It will help you to let go of it so you can then deal with the person in your present day situation as the person they are instead of the person they remind you of; so you can deal with them through the adult ego state rather than the child ego state.

What has been covered in this chapter may seem like a lot of information, and it is. The fact remains though that this information will help you to continue resolving what happened to you as a child.

Once you have worked your way through all the people who hurt you, have spent time with your inner child individuating, and have decided who you want to reintegrate with, it will be important for you to maintain what you have learned in Sections I and II. Practice is the only thing that will allow you to maintain the progress you have made and will keep you from resorting back to the child you once were.

Chapter 18

The New Plan

Before proceeding any further, allow yourself to stop for just a few moments to reflect on the tremendous amount of work you have done thus far. You have done extremely well and should be proud of yourself. You have been on an incredible emotional journey and have accomplished what most people deem to be unobtainable. You have truly made a lot of progress. You have been true to yourself and your desire to recover. You have done what it takes to look at yourself and the pain you have carried around for so many years. You have been faithful in your desire to heal no matter what it has taken to do so. You have given your best and your best is now paying off.

Allow yourself to feel the pride that comes from being committed enough to yourself, and the little boy/girl who lives inside of you, to have overcome the things that happened in your childhood. Feel the empowerment that comes from knowing you can take care of yourself and your inner child. Feel the joy that comes from knowing in your heart that you are all right and it is more than acceptable to like who you have become. Feel how wonderful it is to have the ability to be still and to be comfortable with who you are. Marvel at the person you are becoming.

Despite the remarkable progress you have made, there is one last step that needs to be taken, one last thing left for you to learn and to then incorporate into your daily life. It will be the last tool you need to acquire before you will have all the necessary tools in your recovery toolbox. It will be the tool that will meld together everything you have learned so far and will help you to maintain your progress. If you are ready, let's begin.

THE NEW PLAN

Have you ever gone to a workshop or seminar where a lot of information was presented to you in a very short period of time? Did you leave that workshop or seminar wondering how you were going to be able to synthesize all the information you were provided? Did you wonder what it would take for you to be able to use the information in your daily life, on your job, or in your marriage? Did you wonder what it would take for the information to become an intimate part of who you are so you could use it without having to think about it?

If so, you have asked yourself the same questions many people have asked. As a matter of fact, you may be asking yourself the same questions at this point in your recovery and now that you have resolved your childhood issues. You may be wondering, "How am I supposed to use all the tools I have been provided in this book? How do I know when to use what tool? How do I make sure I don't lose the progress I've made? How do I keep from resorting back to the person I was when I started my recovery? How do I use my tools in my daily life?"

There are two very important answers to these questions. Neither of them will be a surprise to you because both of them have already been partially discussed.

The first answer lies in something you were introduced to in Chapter 9 and something you should have been practicing for a while now, The Plan. The Plan took what you had been introduced to and had been practicing in Section I and put it all together. It was a compilation of the cognitive techniques you had learned up to that point. It provided you with a comprehensive way of dealing with any difficult situations you came across in your daily life, as long as those situations didn't cause you to parallel process back to a traumatic event in your childhood. It gave you a way of dealing with your life so you wouldn't become emotionally overwhelmed while working your way through the emotional side of the abuse, neglect and/or trauma you sustained.

In that chapter you also learned that the plan would be revised at some point because it only incorporated the cognitive retraining techniques and the cognitive tools of recovery. At that point you had not been introduced to the emotional restructuring techniques or emotional tools of recovery, thus they couldn't be incorporated into the plan at that time.

Now that you have been introduced to the emotional restructuring techniques and have been practicing the emotional restructuring tools, the goal is to merge the cognitive plan you learned in Chapter 9 with the emotional restructuring techniques. This will provide you with a comprehensive plan that will work in any difficult situation you might encounter today, even ones that cause you to parallel process back to your childhood. In order to ensure that the new plan will work, please make sure you write it down in your spiral bound index cards so you will have easy access to it in difficult situations. Having this new plan written down as a part of your cards may end up being the difference between you handling a difficult situation through the child ego state or the adult ego state. If you get into a difficult situation, panic and forget the steps of the new plan, you will end up playing the role of the child once again. However, if you panic and go to a quiet place where you can pull out your cards with the new, comprehensive plan on it, you will likely be able to develop a more healthy perspective about the situation and be able to respond to it as an adult. By writing the new plan down on your cards, you will be doing everything possible to ensure your own success.

Before delving into the details of the new plan, I would like for you to turn the page and look over the following diagram. It represents how the new plan should work.

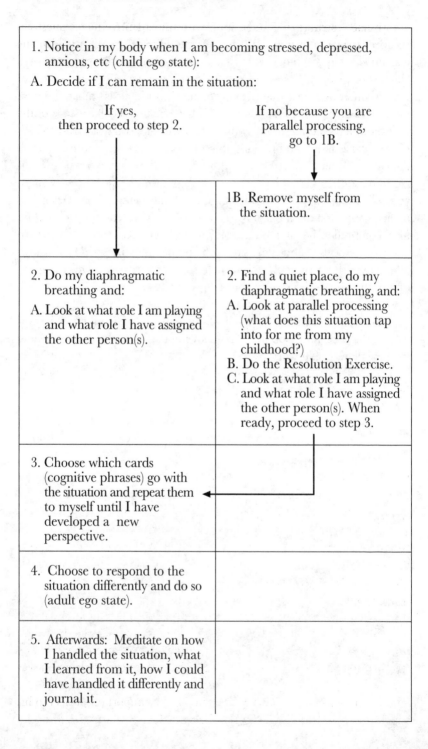

1. Notice in my body when I am becoming stressed, depressed, anxious, etc (child ego state):

A. Decide if I can remain in the situation:

If yes, then proceed to step 2.	If no because you are parallel processing, go to 1B.
	1B. Remove myself from the situation.
2. Do my diaphragmatic breathing and: A. Look at what role I am playing and what role I have assigned the other person(s).	2. Find a quiet place, do my diaphragmatic breathing, and: A. Look at parallel processing (what does this situation tap into for me from my childhood?) B. Do the Resolution Exercise. C. Look at what role I am playing and what role I have assigned the other person(s). When ready, proceed to step 3.
3. Choose which cards (cognitive phrases) go with the situation and repeat them to myself until I have developed a new perspective.	
4. Choose to respond to the situation differently and do so (adult ego state).	
5. Afterwards: Meditate on how I handled the situation, what I learned from it, how I could have handled it differently and journal it.	

Notice that the diagram begins with the cognitive techniques and then shifts into the emotional techniques and then shifts back to the cognitive techniques once again. This new plan supports the way recovery should take place so no part of any survivor is left out. Both the mind and the emotions are addressed so nothing is left unresolved. Anytime you ignore either of these parts of yourself, you will fall out of the role of the adult and into the role of the child. In turn, this will only lead to self-destructive behaviors and adverse reactions.

Let's take a moment and look at an example of how this new plan works in a difficult situation for someone who has already been through therapy and the Resolution Exercise. This will help illustrate how even after you have done the Resolution Exercise there will be those situations that come along in your life, even though few and far between, where your inner child and old traumas will be tapped back into.

Shane is a 45-year-old man who grew up with a father who ignored and neglected him. He wasn't abused in any other way, just emotionally starved for love and attention. Shane spent almost every waking moment of his childhood trying to earn his father's love. He would bring him surprises, make sure he made straight A's in school, and did everything asked of him. Shane even went as far as to copy his father's behaviors and everything he did so his father would be proud of him. But, nothing Shane did was good enough. He could never get his father to say, "I love you, son and I'm proud of you."

As an adult, Shane became a very talkative fellow who spent a lot of his time making sure everyone around him was happy. He was a people-pleaser who always put everyone needs before his own (recreating/adverse reaction). He wanted to be accepted by everyone and to feel as if he fit in everywhere. He made sure everyone was happy because this was the only thing that made him feel good about himself (external locus of control).

As the years passed, Shane became a successful businessman. He worked as an accountant in a large corporation. His dream was to one day become the president of the company he worked for. So Shane set out to make his supervisor think he was the best employee they had ever had. He spent several long months doing this, working 12 to 14 hours a day. Then the day came when Shane's supervisor placed him in charge of a very important project. He just knew if he could this well, he would be promoted and would be one step closer to being president. Shane spent hours and hours on this project, making sure every aspect of it was perfect.

Six months later, Shane handed in the very important project to his supervisor. He was very proud of the work he had done and knew he would finally get the praise and credit he deserved for all his hard work. However, days went by and nothing was said. There weren't any, "Job well done" speeches and no pats on the back. There were no memos praising him for his excellent project skills. The more Shane thought about this, the angrier he became. He began feeling unappreciated and ignored.

About a month later, Shane's supervisor called him into his office. He thought, "Well this is the day he's going to tell me how well I did on the project. This is day I will get my promotion. I can't wait to hear how proud he is of the work I did."

During the meeting, Shane's supervisor talked about everything but the project. As Shane sat there, he began feeling sad and unappreciated again (parallel processing). He wanted to ask his supervisor if he was proud of the job he had done on the project. He wanted to get the praise he deserved. He wanted to say something, but he couldn't. He just sat there, feeling overwhelmed with inadequacy and a lack of appreciation.

Shane's supervisor noticed he was quiet and withdrawn, and asked, "Shane, what is wrong with you? You act like something is bothering you, what is it?"

Shane could feel his heart starting to beat fast with fear. His stomach getting tied into knots with panic. He wanted to tell his supervisor how he felt and what he wanted from him, but he couldn't get the words to come out of his mouth (not speaking his truth/child ego state).

When the meeting was over, Shane didn't think he had the energy he needed to go on with his life, and to keep feeling unworthy of people's praise or attention. He was devastated. So he walked down the street to the local bar and got drunk (adverse reaction). In his drunken stupor, Shane made the decision to quit his job and curse his supervisor for not appreciating him (splitting). He was hurt and angry and was going to make sure his supervisor knew it.

After several long hours of drinking, Shane went home. When he walked into the door, he could tell his wife was angry because she was screaming, "Where have you been all evening?"

This caused Shane to remember what had happened at work, that he hadn't stood up for himself and that he had gotten drunk because his boss didn't praise him for the job he had done on the project. However, he was so embarrassed that he decided he couldn't tell his wife about anything that had happened. Instead, he towered over her and yelled, "It's none of your business. Why don't you just leave me alone?"

Not knowing how to respond, Shane's wife told him, "You can just sleep on the couch tonight, and maybe from now on. I'm tired of you being nice to everyone else but me. You don't talk to me or let me in (recreating relationship he had with his father)."

The next morning, Shane woke up with a terrible hangover. He was ashamed of himself. He wanted to tell his wife everything that had happened but he didn't know how. This caused Shane to feel even more worthless as a human being.

As he contemplated everything that had transpired, Shane came to realize that he couldn't deal with being the kind of person who couldn't speak his truth, and who let people walk all over him. He couldn't stand always wanting to please everyone when no one seemed to be concerned about his happiness. So Shane decided he needed to talk with someone who could help him figure out why he was this way and who could teach him how to speak his truth. Shane did what was needed and made an appointment with a therapist.

Shane spent the next several months in therapy with a therapist who knew how to do Cognitive Emotional Restructuring Therapy. He learned the cognitive techniques so things would become more tolerable for him, especially at work, and so he could start changing the way he thought about things. His therapist then started the emotional restructuring work with him. Shane learned about parallel processing and splitting. He learned that he had problems with his supervisor because his supervisor reminded him of his father. He found his secret place and the little boy who lives inside of him. He then identified all the people who had hurt him and did the Resolution Exercise with each of them. For Shane, the primary person he did the Resolution Exercise with was his father.

As a result of Shane's hard work and the Resolution Exercise, he was able to forgive his father for how he had treated him. He was able to let go of his need to please everyone and was able to please himself. He was able to let go of the anxiety and anger that went with his feeling unappreciated and worthless. He was able to replace those feelings with a healthy sense of self-esteem and confidence he acquired as a result of developing a relationship with himself (individuation). He was able to take his supervisor out of the role of being his father and thus could deal with him as the person he was, his supervisor.

About six months after Shane was finished with therapy, he changed jobs. He got another accounting job at another large corporation. In the beginning he was very happy with his new job even though it was causing him a lot of stress. He was under constant pressure to perform, and this resulted in him working extremely long hours. After a while, Shane was working almost seven days a week and didn't have any time for himself or his family.

One evening as Shane walked into the door of his home around midnight, he found his wife sitting on the couch waiting on him. She looked at him and said, "We need to talk."

Shane sat there and listened to her as she said, "I can't live this way anymore. You are never home and you are never there for me and the kids. I have to do all of the housework, take care of the kids, do the grocery shopping and pay all the bills. I want out. I want a divorce."

Shane sat there shocked, not believing what his wife was saying. He felt his heart start to race. His stomach got tied into knots just like it used to. His face became hot and turned bright red with anger. Without thinking, he glared at his wife with hate and slapped her while saying, "How dare you tell me I'm not doing good enough. How dare you not appreciate all my hard work. You are nothing but ungrateful. I hate you. If you want to leave me then go ahead. I don't care anymore. Nothing I do is good enough for anyone (parallel processing/splitting)."

That night Shane slept on the couch.

The next morning, Shane's wife approached him to talk about what had happened the evening before. She was concerned about how angry he had gotten and that he had hit her, especially since he had never done that before. Shane was so embarrassed and ashamed that he just sat there and stared at the floor. He didn't know what to do or what to say. He didn't understand why he had felt like the little boy all over again who was in trouble, especially since he had resolved his childhood issues (child ego state).

So the questions become, "If Shane had already been through therapy and had done the Resolution Exercise, did his behavior mean that he didn't obtain healing or get anything out of his therapy? What happened to him that caused him to become the old Shane again? And, how can Shane handle this difficult situation with his wife using the new plan?"

Just because Shane momentarily resorted back to some old behavior doesn't mean he did not obtain healing or recovery. It doesn't mean his therapy wasn't effective. It just means that he allowed something in his present day life to momentarily cause him to parallel process back to something in his childhood. This is perfectly normal for any survivor. However, in order for Shane to maintain his healing and recovery, he will have to make the choice to work the new plan so he can resolve what he is parallel processing back to and resolve the issue with his wife.

In order to begin working the new plan, Shane has to first recognize his body's signals that something is wrong (step 1). He has to recognize his heart is beating fast, his stomach is tied in knots, and his face is hot with anger. This is his red flag. It is his body's way of signaling him that his wounded child is being tapped into, that his wife has pushed one of his emotional buttons and is causing him to move out of the adult ego state.

He then asks himself, "Can I stay in this situation or do I need to remove myself from it?" (step 1A)

If Shane decides he has the ability to remain in the situation, he would work the plan just like he had always done (just like in Chapter 9). However, based of Shane's overreaction and hitting his wife, it would only make sense that in real life he would have made the decision to remove himself from the situation (1B). This situation was obviously too emotionally charged for him. It was also abundantly clear that he didn't understand why he got so angry, why he yelled at his wife and hit her.

The next step Shane needs to take is to look at his wife and say, "If you don't mind, I need some time to think about what happened. Can we talk after I get home from work tonight?"

This is removing himself from the situation. More than likely his request will be all right with his wife.

The next thing Shane has to do is to find a quiet place where he can begin doing his diaphragmatic breathing (step 2). While doing his breathing he will ask himself, "What am I parallel processing back to in my childhood? What do these feelings remind me of from my past? When do I remember first feeling this way? What situation was I in when I was feeling this way?" (step 2A)

These questions will help Shane understand what he was parallel processing back to. They will help him to see that the way his wife had talked to him and the things she had said to him reminded him of the way his father had treated him and how his father never praised him for anything he did.

This momentarily confuses Shane because he knew he had already resolved the issues with his father in therapy and had already done the Resolution Exercise with him. So Shane asks himself those same questions again to see if anything manifests. This time he remembers something about his father he had forgotten about. He remembers something he hadn't addressed with the Resolution Exercise. He remembered something he had buried a long time ago. He remembered how his father used to hit him and knock him down when he was trying to do his best. He remembered how his father would take his anger out on him and how he used to hit him when he got angry. Those memories had gotten buried so deep in Shane's unconscious mind that he had completely forgotten about them and thus didn't address them in therapy or with the Resolution Exercise.

Now that Shane knew his wife's verbally slapping him was tapping into his old feelings about his father physically slapping him, he could close his eyes and picture his father hitting him. He could allow his hurt little boy to write a letter to his father, telling him how it felt to be hit and not loved; to be physically broken down rather than emotionally built up and appreciated.

Once he wrote the letter, Shane could then do the Resolution Exercise with his inner child and his father who had hit him (step 2B). Shane could allow his inner child to speak his truth to his father and to tell him how if felt to be hurt and not loved. He could allow his father to hear and feel his pain. He could allow his father to understand how much he had hurt him and to ask for Shane's forgiveness. He could then choose to forgive his father and to then let him go.

Afterwards, Shane's inner child could turn to his adult self and allow his adult to comfort him and to remind him that his adult was the one who would take care of him from now on. It was his adult who would appreciate him and who would never do anything to hurt him.

Because Shane took the time to look at what he was parallel processing back to and did the Resolution Exercise, it helped him change how he felt about his father. Now that he wasn't carrying around those old, unresolved feelings about the physical abuse, Shane could go back and work the cognitive part of the plan. He could now look at what role he had assigned his wife and what role he had assigned himself (step 2C). He could see how he had assigned his wife the role of being his critical, punitive father (parent ego state) and how he had played the role of the wounded child.

Shane could then go back and think about his cognitive phrases. He could choose the ones that would help him in this situation. He could repeat to himself, "**My name is Shane and I am enough. People don't do things against me they do things to meet their own needs.** So my wife not appreciating how hard I have worked and threatening to divorce me is about her, not about me. Her venting her frustrations out on me is something she is doing to make herself feel better. **Things don't bother me, it's the way I look at them that does.** So I need to take my wife out of the role of being my father and see her for who he is, my wife. This will help me treat her like my wife and like an adult. **I need to do what I need to do in order to take care of myself first** and that means **I don't need to defend myself, I just need to speak my truth. Things can change me but I don't have to let them reduce me.** So the next time I feel like I did last night with my wife, I don't need to become my father who hits people but an adult who can talk things out."

Shane's job is to keep telling himself these things over and over again until his perspective about his wife and the situation changes (step 3). Until he no longer sees his wife as his father who physically abused him, but as the person she is, his wife and the mother of his children. Until he sees that he is an adult who is doing the best he can to provide for his family no matter how frustrated his wife gets.

By changing the way he sees his wife and his perspective about the situation he can start moving toward the adult ego state. It will give him the opportunity to choose how he would like to respond to his wife when they talk (step 4). It will also give him choices and opportunities he didn't have before. He could choose to talk to his wife out of the adult ego state and apologize for hitting her. He could be truthful about what he was thinking and feeling when he hit her and why he hit her. He could share how unappreciated he felt after he had worked so hard for so long trying to make her happy with material things. He could share how she had reminded him of his father who had verbally and physically abused him.

Because Shane was able to take responsibility for the way he had treated his wife and was able to talk to her through the adult ego state, this made it possible for his wife to respond back to him in the adult ego state. It gave her permission to apologize for her behavior, to talk about what she had been feeling and to forgive him for hitting her. Because Shane had maintained the adult ego state, so could his wife.

Then, after everything was over and forgiven, Shane needed to complete his new plan by going back to his quiet place to meditate on how he had handled the situation, what he had learned from it, how he could have handled it differently and to then journal it (step 5). This will help him to see how well he did, to feel the joy that comes from stepping out of the child ego state to handle a difficult situation like an adult. It offers him a way to feel the tremendous amount of pride that comes from being the one who sees his past trying to sneak up on him again and doing what it takes not to allow this to happen. It gives him the opportunity to look at the areas he could have done better in. It also gives him the chance to evaluate what he learned from this experience so he can apply it to the next similar situation that comes along.

As you read through all the steps Shane had to work through to understand why he responded to his wife the way he did and to change the outcome of his situation, you might be thinking, "That is an awful lot of steps to have to take for one situation. I don't know if I can do all of this every time I am faced with a difficult situation."

The good news is you only have to work the steps of the plan this thoroughly in the beginning. As you practice the steps of the plan, the process will get easier and faster.

If you are faithful in the beginning and practice the plan with any and all situations that cause you to parallel process, you will quickly learn what you need to do to handle each one of those situations through the adult ego state. So the next time a similar situation presents itself, you will be able to skip things like the Resolution Exercise because you will already know what you are parallel processing back to and will have already resolved it. You will already know what cognitive phrases to use, how to change your perspective and what you need to do to respond to that situation through the adult ego state. Thus, all you will end up having to do is recognize when you need to work the plan and then make sure you briefly address each step of it.

Let's go back to Shane for a moment. The next time his wife yells at him (verbally slaps him) and/or he feels unappreciated, Shane will be able to remember the things he learned from this last situation with his wife. He will remember this kind of situation causes him to parallel process back to his father physically and verbally abusing him. He will remember that he plays the role of the child and assigns his wife the role of the parent. He will remember which cards he needs to use to change his perspective. And, he will remember from the last situation what he needs to do in order to handle this new situation through the adult ego state. Thus, it will take him less time to work through the entire plan.

After a while, the way you respond to any and all difficult situations will become a habit and automatic. You will get to the place where you won't have to think about how you want to respond, you will just do it. You will automatically respond in the adult ego state.

This goes back to the analogy of driving through a green light without having to think about it. Because you have driven through so many green lights for so long, you don't have to stop and think about driving through them anymore, you just do it. This is the same way the plan works. As you faithfully work the plan it, too, will become automatic. The old, automatic ways you used to handle situations (child ego state) will be replaced with new, automatic ways (the plan and adult ego state).

Like Shane, practicing the new plan is the only way you will be able to maintain the progress you've made. It will be this new, comprehensive plan, which incorporates not only the cognitive tools of recovery but also the emotional ones as well that will keep you in the adult ego. It is the way you will be able to continue growing and handling life's difficult situations. However, in order to do this you will have to continue being committed to yourself and your own recovery process. You will have to continue putting yourself first and doing whatever you need to do to take care of yourself first, and that includes practicing and working the plan in any and all difficult situations.

THE NEW PERSPECTIVE PARADIGM

What makes the plan so great is that it still gives you a choice as to how you want to handle your life and the difficult situations which will come along. It gives you responsibility for how you choose to handle difficult situations.

For you and most survivors this is a very foreign concept. When you were being abused, neglected and/or traumatized as a child, you didn't have the luxury or freedom of making choices for yourself. You couldn't choose to make the abuse stop. You couldn't choose to make your father stop hitting your mother. You couldn't choose to make your parents love you. You couldn't choose to make your uncle stop drinking and molesting you. You couldn't choose to feel a different way about being neglected. You couldn't choose not to be raped. Thus, you were locked into a lifestyle of not being able to choose how you want your life to look—that is until now.

By participating in your own recovery process and working the techniques outlined in this book, you are giving yourself a new lease on life. One that is filled with choices and decisions you can make for yourself each and every day. Whenever you encounter a difficult situation today, you are the one who can now choose how you want to deal with that situation. Whenever you get upset about something, you can now choose how you want to handle it. When you feel overwhelmed or unappreciated, you now have the ability to choose how you want to respond. When you begin parallel processing or falling back into the child ego state you can now do something different if you choose to. The choices you can now make and the new perspectives you are developing about your life can be illustrated by something I call The New Perspective Paradigm. It looks like this:

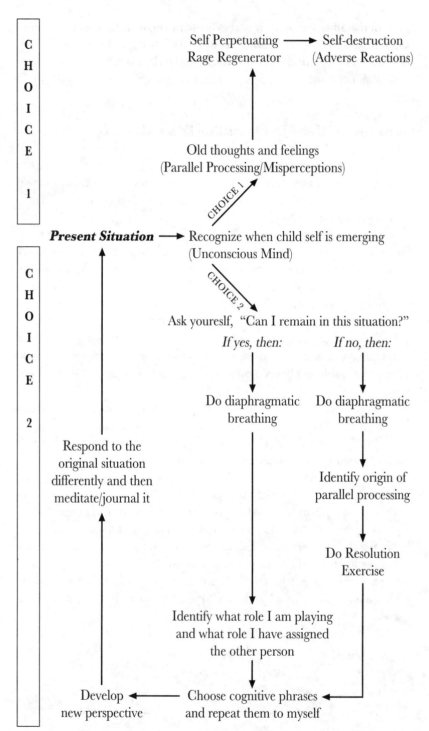

Before you, or anyone else who is in recovery can choose to do something different, you first have to understand that there are all kinds of situations you will encounter as you move through your life. And, what makes a situation difficult is when that situation causes you to parallel process back to something from your childhood. When you find yourself in one of those difficult situations this is when you, as the person who is on the road to recovery, has a choice to make. You can choose to ignore what you have learned and ignore the plan. You can succumb to the old thoughts and feelings of your wounded child, fall back into the Self-Perpetuating Rage Regenerator and engage in your old self-destructive behaviors. This is a right you and all survivors have.

On the other hand, you can choose to recognize your wounded, inner child is being tapped into and then choose to work the plan. If you do this then you are choosing to take the people and the situations you are parallel processing back to and choosing to develop a new perspective about them using your plan. This choice will allow you to respond to your present day situation in a healthier way and through the adult ego state.

You, and only you, can choose to recognize when you are parallel processing and then change your perspective about the things that are happening in your life today. Only you can choose to develop a new perspective and operate out of an internal locus of control and the adult ego state. You possess all the tools you need to develop this new perspective. You have all the tools you need to set your past free and to be happy. The choice to keep using what you have learned and to maintain your new perspective is yours and yours alone.

Chapter 19

Becoming Your Own Therapist

Now that you have worked your way through the emotional restructuring exercises, have modified the plan, and are practicing the new plan, it is time for you to practice being your own therapist. In many ways you have already been doing this.

It really isn't as difficult as you might think.

As with anything new, you will have to be educated about what it means to be your own therapist. You will have to know what tools, skills and abilities are required in order for you to be able to take care of yourself and to resolve your own problems.

So the question you have to ask yourself is this, "Do I possess this information and do I have those skills and abilities to be my own therapist?"

The answer to these questions is, "Yes." You have spent a great deal of time working your way through this book. You have been practicing what you have been taught and are quite familiar with how to take care of yourself in difficult situations. You have also been taking yourself through your own recovery process using the tools and information that have been provided to you. You have been walking yourself through each step of the recovery process. Thus, you already have been playing the role of the therapist. However, it is time for you to set time aside each day to practice your therapy skills once you have finished this book.

I recommend you make regular therapy appointments with yourself. This means you take at least 15 to 30 minutes every day and at the same each day to go to your quiet place. For some of you this is going to be a difficult task because of spouses, jobs, children and so forth. But, as discussed throughout this entire book the one thing you have to do to ensure your progress is to make yourself a priority. You have to put yourself first and to do whatever you need to do to take care of yourself first. This might mean that you get up 15 to 30 minutes earlier each day, put your children to bed a little earlier each night or use part of your lunch break to meet with yourself for your therapy appointments. Do whatever you need to do to find this time. It can be found if you deem this an important part of your recovery.

As you sit in your comfortable couch or chair in your quiet place, close your eyes, do your diaphragmatic breathing and think about how your day went. Think about how you felt as you went through your day. Remember all the positive things that happened and how those positive things felt. Did they remind you of how good it feels to be the new you? Did you see how you are continuing to use and apply your recovery tools?

Then, take a moment to reflect on how you handled each difficult situation you encountered that day. Did you use your plan and maintain the role of the adult? If so, how did that feel? Or, did you momentarily resort back to the child? If so, then what caused you to resort back to the child and what did you do, if anything, to get back to the role of the adult?

Then, look at your day in general and ask yourself, "What could I have done differently today to have made my day better and to have handled things better?"

Once you have finished reflecting on both the positive and negative aspects of your day, take the time to journal your reflections. Be free in your journaling. Talk to yourself just like you would a counselor. Try to resolve your own problems using all the tools you have been provided. Write until you have written all the way through to the solution.

When you have finished your journaling, take another five or so minutes and do your diaphragmatic breathing once again and then go directly to bed. Be sure to do this second set of breathing before you go to bed. It will help keep the things you journaled from infiltrating your dreams.

The reason why you need to practice being your own therapist each and every day is this: It will help you to spend time with yourself so you can look at your difficult situations and objectively evaluate how you are handling things on a daily basis. If you are addressing your issues every day as they come up then you are proactively handling them rather than letting them go unresolved. If you are resolving your issues the same day as they occur, then you are giving yourself the gift of starting each day with a clean slate. Equally true is that if you don't stop to look at and resolve your issues as they come up, then what happened in your past will happen again. Things will begin building up until they become overwhelming and too big to handle. Then, at some point they will tap back into your wounded child and will cause the Self-Perpetuating Rage Regenerator to start cycling all over again.

You have the ability now to choose to do things differently. You have acquired all the tools you need to resolve whatever happened in your childhood and whatever happens to you from this day forward. So be kind to yourself, use your tools and practice being your own therapist each and every day.

Chapter 20

The Challenge

WELCOME TO THE LAST CHAPTER of this book and to the final quest that lies before you. Surely it is a relief to finally be at this stage in your recovery process and to feel as good about yourself as you do. Before embarking upon this last quest, let's take a moment to reflect on how far you have come and how much progress you have made on your journey of healing.

Admiration and congratulations need to be offered to you for all of the hard work you have done. You choose to honor yourself by completing your recovery process rather than settling for the old you and your old way of life. You have worked hard and have demonstrated an amazing amount of courage to save yourself and your inner child.

I know it hasn't been easy, but you did it. Hopefully you are pleasantly surprised with how resolved everything feels and how free you feel for the first time in your life. You gave yourself a new lease on life and now know the freedom that comes from living in the present moment and having a meaningful relationship with yourself. You know the pride that comes from being able to take care of yourself and to meet your own needs, not to be afraid anymore, and to be happy to be alive.

There aren't many people who actually follow through with recovery. They don't even get as far as making the conscious decision to start looking at what happened to them as a child, the people who had hurt them and how those things affected them as a little boy or girl. But you did. You made the decision to feel the pain of your past and the feelings your inner child had carried around for so many years. You decided you were ready to help your inner child heal, to re-parent the little boy or girl inside you and to begin living a life where you could embrace what happened to you. You decided to take responsibility for your own healing; to open yourself up to a future that could be filled with happiness; and to feel a love for yourself you never thought possible. You found your secret place and the freedom this place holds for you. You found the one place no one can ever take away from you.

Not only did you find your secret place, but you also allowed your inner child to resolve the issues with the people who had hurt you. You allowed your inner child to tell them how it felt, what you had needed from them, and did what was necessary to get your needs met. You gave your inner child the opportunity to own what happened, to say everything that wasn't allowed to be said and to reveal the family secrets. You stood up for yourself and allowed your inner child to have a voice and to speak your truth. Your gave your inner child permission to resolve the abuse and the emotions associated with the abuse. You helped your inner child to let go of the pain. Because you did this, your inner child now looks to you, and only you, for ongoing comfort and support so he/she can continue emotionally growing up.

Your life and emotions are no longer being controlled by outside forces, but by you the adult. You are handling the difficult situations life sends you in a way you never thought possible. You are using your plan to make sure you never go back to the person you once were. Your bad days aren't as bad. Your life doesn't seem so overwhelming. You don't get as upset as you once did. You feel yourself evolving into the person you have always wanted to be. You have become the adult.

You have truly made a lot of progress. You have been true to yourself and your desire to recover. You have done what it takes to look at yourself and the pain you have carried around all your life. You have been faithful in your desire to heal no matter what it has taken to do so. You have given your best and your best has paid off and is continuing to do so.

Please allow yourself to reflect often on how well you have done and how well you will continue doing, as long as you use your tools. Pat yourself on the back for the progress you have made; for allowing yourself to heal and recover. And, don't forget to continue praising yourself as you continue growing and changing into the person you have always dreamed about becoming.

Now that you have reflected upon your progress and journey of healing, it is the time to look at your last quest. Hopefully this quest and chapter will feel different to you. Hopefully they will be exciting and refreshing.

What you are about to embark on is the fun part of recovery. This is where you will be provided with four challenges to complete and hopefully ones that are exhilarating to the new you. These challenges will help you in many ways. They will spark your thoughts about things you may not have ever considered as being a part of recovery. So let's begin.

Challenge #1: 90 Days of Recovery:

As mentioned time and time again, the most important task that lies before you now is practicing everything you have learned throughout your recovery process. It goes back to the concept of being your own therapist so issues in your life get resolved as soon as they appear. However, it is up to you to make the on-going practice of your skills fun and enjoyable. So be creative.

Your challenge is to practice everything you have learned for 90 consecutive days after finishing this book. If you miss a day, then the 90 days starts over. The purpose of the 90 days is to help the things you have learned to become a lifestyle, an integral part of who you are. This will help keep you from resorting back to the old you.

In detail, what this means is this: You get up every morning and start your day off with your diaphragmatic breathing. As you breathe, you think about the positive aspects of the day ahead and who you want to be as a person. As you go through your day, you continue doing your breathing while keeping your cognitive phrases in the forefront of your mind. You handle any difficult situations you encounter using the new, modified and comprehensive plan. It also means you do one nice thing a day for yourself and make time for just you and only you. Then, in the evening you keep your therapy appointment with yourself. You do your diaphragmatic breathing and then reflect on the positive and negative aspects of your day and how you could have done things differently. Afterwards, you journal your day and any noteworthy experiences. You then take another five or so minutes to do your diaphragmatic breathing once again and then go directly to bed.

If you can maintain a daily routine of journaling, breathing, using your cognitive phrases, working your plan and so forth, then the chances of you being successful and maintaining the adult ego state will be greatly enhanced.

At the end of the 90 days, do yourself a favor and read back over your entire journal. Notice the changes you have made and continue making. Notice the areas you need to continue working on. Then, treat yourself to something nice. Reward yourself for maintaining your commitment to yourself and your healing.

Challenge #2: Take back everything stolen from you as a child:

As a child who was abused, neglected, and/or traumatized, a lot of things were stolen from you. It might have been the happiness that comes from knowing and feeling someone loves you. The thrill of exploring and having fun. The joy that comes from being spontaneous and carefree. Feeling like you fit in, like you belong and are worthy of someone's attention. Maybe you didn't get to do the things you had wanted to do like go to the fair, ride go-carts, have a birthday party, go to the beach, enjoy a holiday like Christmas, go on a picnic, or even sit in someone's lap. Maybe you weren't allowed to tell anyone how you felt, and couldn't share your hopes and dreams. Maybe you never got a chance to just be a kid.

If any of this sound like you, then today is your day. Now that you have walked through the fires of recovery and have emerged on the other side, it is time to take back everything that was stolen from you as a child. It's time for you to ask your inner child, "What is it that you have always wanted to do but never got to do? What are the feelings you didn't get to experience, like happiness, love and belonging? What would make you feel like you fit in? What can I do to help you to be the kid you never got to be?"

Then sit back and listen to what your little boy/girl tells you. Feel the excitement that comes over you as your inner child might want to go to the fair to ride on the roller coaster; to go on a fast boat ride across the lake; to sit outside at night and watch the stars as they glisten in the sky; to go to the movies and be allowed to have popcorn; or to have a real birthday party with cake, candles, games and friends. Then feel the desire your child might have to sit in your lap and to feel loved; to spend time with you in your secret place; and to hang out with each other watching movies on the couch in your home. Then really listen as your child tells you all of his/her hopes and dreams, who he/she has always wanted to become and how he/she feels every day.

As your inner child shares all of these things with you, write them down in your journal. Then be kind enough to yourself and your inner child to allow both of you to experience every single thing on your list. Check them off as both of you do them and journal how those experiences felt to both of you.

You may notice that with each experience your child feels more loved and becomes more willing to grow up. Don't do as the people in your childhood did to you, and don't ignore your inner child. Be the parent you had always wanted. Treat your inner child the way you had always wanted to be treated. This is your chance to go back and recreate the childhood you had always wanted.

Challenge #3:   Restore the parts of your life that were lost:

A large number of people who were abused, neglected and/or traumatized as a child didn't get a chance to develop the various aspects of themselves: the physical, emotional and/or spiritual. They were taught to ignore these parts of themselves. Thus, they didn't get a chance to explore who they were as children growing up. This is probably true for you as well. Maybe you were beaten so often that you learned to tune out your physical pain and to ignore your body. Maybe your feelings were negated and invalidated so often that you began to question if what you felt was really true. Maybe your family was so caught up in alcoholism you never got a chance to experience what church was about. Maybe you didn't get the opportunity to really meet God and to know what spiritual support feels like.

You, as a recovering survivor, now have the opportunity and the ability to make sure every aspect of who you are is taken care of. Because you have let go of your past and now live in the present, you can start all over with learning about your body and how to take care of it. You get to start over emotionally and have acquired the skills to do this. You now know how to take care of your inner child and the new adult you. You can also discover how you feel about God and how you want to go about establishing a relationship with Him. You can decide what church you want to go to and how you want to pray.

As you look at the various aspects of yourself that were ignored or lost, make it fun. Choose to look at this like an adventure, like a new quest. You can now become the explorer who tries out all kinds of things until you figure out what fits for you. Allow yourself to go buy books on your body and body language; buy self-help books or tapes; take classes; and visit a bunch of different churches until you find one that works for you. The possibilities are endless. The only person who can limit you today is you. So enjoy the freedom you now have to experience anything and everything you have ever wanted to experience and to develop each and every aspect of yourself to the fullest.

Challenge #4:   Spread the word through healing circles:

One of the only ways you will be able to keep the spark of your recovery alive is by sharing what you have learned; by telling (others who are hurting just like you used to hurt) how you recovered; by telling your story. One way all survivors can do this is by agreeing with one another to establish and participate in what I call **healing circles**. A healing circle isn't a complicated thing or something that will require a great deal of your time. It is you, and other survivors, getting together once a week (or at least once a month at a minimum) to support each other as you continue on your journey of healing; to help each other as you face life's challenges and difficult situations. More importantly though, to help those who are just starting their journey of healing. As you know, they will need a lot of support and a place where they know there are other people who are just like themselves.

In the healing circles, you will sit in a circle facing the people who are on the same journey as you. A circle is warm and round, not square, cold and rigid. This is your circle of safety outside of your secret place. In your healing circle you can share your experiences, knowledge and hope with other survivors. You can talk about the things that helped you to obtain the progress and healing you have attained. You can celebrate with each other the milestones in your recovery and how your inner children are growing up. You can talk about the difficult situations you are working through and get support. You can share how you are able to deal with the world as an adult and how you are becoming the person you have always wanted to become. You can also start learning how to have fun with other people and enjoy how it feels to finally fit in somewhere.

If you decide to start a healing circle in your area, please make sure you email me with the name of your healing circle, where it is, when you established it, the day and time you meet and any other information you would like to share. I will place the information on my website (www.sandyriggin.com). This list is important as it will help abuse survivors to know what healing circles are available in their area and where they are located.

Finally, it is time for you to continue your journey of healing outside the confines of this book. It is time for you to find your healing circle and to continue your journey down the path of healing. Enjoy the rest of your journey and know you are not alone anymore. I wish you the best of luck and pray God will bless you. Just remember who you are and remember your worth as a human being and as one of God's children. Remember your tools and your inner child. If you do these things, you will be more than fine. God bless you

SECTION III

APPENDICES

Appendix A

Steps of the Resolution Exercise

1. Recognize in your body in your body when your inner child is coming to the surface because this is a sign you are parallel processing back to something traumatic in your childhood. This is your clue to begin working the plan (Step 1 of the plan).

2. Go to your quiet place and:
   - Sit on your comfortable couch or in your chair;
   - Close your eyes and begin doing your diaphragmatic breathing (Step 2 of the plan).

3. While doing your breathing ask yourself these questions and write your answers in your journal:
   - When do I first remember feeling this way as a child?
   - What was happening when I was feeling this way?
   - What situation was I in?
   - Who was the person I was having difficulty with or who was hurting me? (Step 2A of the plan)

4. Once you recognize the person (and situation) you are parallel processing back to, this tells you with whom you need to do the Resolution Exercise (Step 2B of the plan).

5. Once you know who you need to do the Resolution Exercise with, then:
   - Close your eyes again and envision this person, as they were when they had hurt you. See how they had hurt you. Feel what they did to you. Feel all the things you had wanted and needed to say to them. Then open your eyes and allow your inner child

to write a letter to that person. Please know you must allow the child who lives inside you to write the letter, NOT the adult. The letter is to contain anything and everything your inner child has ever wanted to say to that person, but was too afraid to say. It should spell out in great detail the pain your child felt and the secrets he/she has been holding on to. It's to be an exhaustive letter, and one that allows your inner child to speak all of his/her truth to that person.

6. Once your inner child has finished writing the letter, do NOT mail the letter to the person who hurt you but complete the Resolution Exercise by doing the following:

- Place an empty chair in front of your couch or chair.
- Sit down on your couch or in your chair and close your eyes again.
- Begin doing your relaxation technique visualizing your entire body relaxing from the top of your head all the way down to the tips of your toes.
- In your mind's eye, see your child self who wrote the letter and describe what your child looks like out loud.
- See the person you wrote the letter to standing in front of your child self and describe that person out loud and in detail. Verbalize how it feels to be standing in front of them.
- Then tell the person in front you that you have a letter you would like to read to them and you need them to listen to you. As you do this, notice the expression on their face conveys they are willing to listen to you.
- Then open your eyes and see the person sitting in the chair across from you and allow your INNER CHILD (not your adult) to read your letter to them.
- Once you have finished reading your letter, set it aside. Close your eyes again and see the person you wrote the letter to standing in front of your inner child.
- Allow your child to say anything else he/she needs to say or anything that was left out of the letter. Tell them what you had needed from them but didn't get.
- Then allow yourself to look at the expression on the other person's face and verbalize out loud what you see. Notice if they are sorry for hurting you, if they are apologizing to you or asking for your forgiveness. Allow yourself to feel what it feels like for them to be sorry and to want your forgiveness.

- Then take a moment to respond to their apology and to tell them whatever it is you need to say.
- The next step is to decide if you are ready to let go of the pain you have been carrying around. If you are, then look down at your hands and see that you are holding a bunch of boxes. Notice the boxes are several different sizes and shapes. See that each one of the boxes is filled with all the pain, hurt, sadness, and anger you have been carrying around all of these years. Describe what your boxes and pain look like.
- Allow yourself to notice how heavy the boxes are, to feel your pain that is in the boxes and really breathe into that pain.
- Then become willing to allow the person standing in front of you to feel the pain you have been carrying around. Hold out your hands with your boxes of pain in them. Feel the other person's hands as they move underneath yours and feel their hands touching yours. Tell them you want them to hold on to your boxes for a moment and feel the pain you have been carrying around all these years.
- As they hold onto your boxes of pain, see the expression on their face change as they begin to understand what you have been feeling all of these years.
- Notice if both of you are willing to let go of the pain so you can move on with your lives. If you are, then on the count of three both of you throw the boxes of pain into the air. See them as they float above you and breath out anything that needs to disappear with the boxes.
- When all of the boxes have disappeared, look at the person standing in front of you. Notice there isn't anything standing between you any more and notice how that feels. Notice how it feels to have forgiven them.
- Now that all of the pain is gone and forgiveness has taken place, it time for both of you to move on with your lives. Say your good-byes to each other. Then allow the other person to turn around and walk off into the distance, knowing it is all right because you have forgiven them.
- Then allow your inner child to turn around and see your adult self standing before you. Your adult wants to hear everything that just happened, so allow yourself to do this.
- Allow your adult to comfort your child in whatever way your inner child needs. Allow your adult to tell your child whatever it he/she needs to hear and breathe into it.

- Then look around and notice that you and your adult are sitting in your secret place with each other. Bask in how good this feels and how safe your child feels. Allow your child to marvel in how wonderful it feels to be loved and taken care of.
- When you are finished enjoying the company of your adult, find the path that leads away from your secret place. Allow your adult to take hold of your child's hand (or pick him/her up) and for both of you to start walking down the path together. With each step you take allow your adult to feel how wonderful it feels to have helped your child and to have comforted him/her through this experience. Allow your child to feel how wonderful it felt to be loved and supported.
- With each step you take feel your child starting to merge inside of your adult until he/she is completely inside of you, living in your heart. Describe how that feels out loud.
- Allow yourself to continue walking down the path until you find yourself walking back into the room you are sitting in.
- See yourself sitting on your comfortable couch or in your chair, take three really deeps breaths and blow out anything that is left over.
- When you are ready open your eyes and take a moment to reflect on what you just experienced.
- Journal your experience.

7. Once you have completed the Resolution Exercise, complete the rest of the plan, which entails:

Step 2C - Look at what role you are playing and what role you have assigned the other person(s).

Step 3 - Choose which cognitive phrases go with the situation and repeat them to yourself until you have developed a new perspective.

Step 4 - Choose to respond to the situation differently and do so (adult ego state)

Step 5 - Afterwards: Meditate on how you handled the situation, what you learned from it, how you could have handled it differently and journal it.

Appendix B

Script of the CD

Track 1: The Secret Place Exercise:

As you sit in your quiet place, I would like for you to close your eyes and remember to breathe in through your nose, and hold it and breathe out through your mouth. Breathe in through your nose, and hold it and breathe out through your mouth. And I want you to remember that relaxation starts at the top of your head and it moves its way down your body until it reaches the tips of your toes. It feels warm as it moves through each part of your body. So feel the relaxation as it starts at the top of your head and it moves it way down past your forehead, down past your eyes, down past your cheekbones and all the way down into the muscles of your jaw. And your face and jaw have become so relaxed that your mouth drops slightly open and it stays that way allowing it to be easier for you to breathe. Feel the relaxation as it moves its way down into your neck and throat and all the way down into your shoulders. And your shoulders have become so relaxed that they just let go; physically feel them as they let go. Feel the relaxation as it moves it way down into your arms and your hands and all the way down into your fingers. And your arms and hands and fingers have become so relaxed that they feel as if they are floating. Feel the relaxation as it moves its way down the back of your neck, down past your shoulder blades and all the way down into your lower back. And your shoulder blades and back have become so relaxed they just sink into the couch or chair. Feel the relaxation as it moves its way down into your chest and stomach. And your chest and stomach have become so relaxed that your breath and breathing has become effortless. Feel the relaxation as it moves its way on down into your hips and pelvis, and all the way down into your thighs. And your hips and pelvis and thighs have become so relaxed they just sink into the couch or chair. Feel the relaxation as it moves its way on down past your knees, down past your calves and all the down into your feet and toes. And your legs and feet and toes have become so relaxed that you can barely feel them. Now, feel what it feels like to be relaxed, to be in this state and I would like for you to pick one word that would describe how you feel at this very moment and tell me what that word would be.

Now in your mind's eye, I want you to imagine a place, preferably outdoors. It can be any place: a beach, a mountain top somewhere, a field of flowers, a waterfall with a pool at the bottom of it, or even a meadow that is hidden in the middle of the woods. It doesn't matter where the place is as long as it's a place that feels good to you; a safe place. Now picture that place in your mind and describe it to me in detail (pause).

Now, I want you to feel the sun as it shines on your face, and feel the light breeze as it brushes as across your cheek, and smell the scents that are in the air. Feel what it feels like to be in this place and just breathe into that feeling (pause).

Now, I would like for you to allow yourself to just sit in your secret place or maybe even allow yourself to play there for just a moment…do whatever it is that you feel like doing right now and tell me what you see yourself doing and how it feels to you (pause).

Now, allow yourself to put into words how it feels to be in your secret place and tell me what those words would be (pause).

Now, I want you to think of a name for your secret place and tell me what name you have chosen (pause). Good, that's a great name.

Now, I want you to look around your secret place one last time before it's time to go. And as you do, I want you to remember this is a place you can go when things become too difficult for you, when you feel the need to escape or when you just want to relax. Remember you can come here any time you want. Just breathe into that for just a moment (pause).

Now, I want you to look around and find the path that leads away from your secret place. Do you see it? Good. And I want you to start walking down that path, and with each step you take, I want you to feel how good it felt to be in your secret place today; to have found a place that's all your own; to have found a safe place. And I want you to keep walking down that path until you find yourself walking back into the room you are sitting in. See yourself sitting in your chair or on your couch and I want you to take three really deeps breathes (pause).

And when you are ready I want you to open your eyes and take a moment to reflect on what you just experienced and then continue reading the rest of the chapter.

This is the end of track 1.

Track 2: Introductions Exercise

As you sit in your quiet place, I would like for you to close your eyes and remember to breathe in through your nose, and hold it and breathe out through your mouth. Breathe in through your nose, and hold it and breathe out through your mouth. And I want you to remember that relaxation starts at the top of your head and it moves its way down your body until it reaches the tips of your toes. It feels warm as it moves through each part of your body. So feel the relaxation as it starts at the top of your head and it moves it way down past your forehead, down past your eyes, down past your cheekbones and all the way down into the muscles of your jaw. And your face and jaw have become so relaxed that your mouth drops slightly open and it stays that way allowing it to be easier for you to breathe. Feel the relaxation as it moves its way down into your neck and throat and all the way down into your shoulders. And your shoulders have become so relaxed that they just let go; physically feel them as they let go. Feel the relaxation as it moves it way down into your arms and your hands and all the way down into your fingers. And your arms and hands and fingers have become so relaxed that they feel as if they are floating. Feel the relaxation as it moves its way down the back of your neck, down past your shoulder blades and all the way down into your lower back. And your shoulder blades and back have become so relaxed they just sink into the couch or chair. Feel the relaxation as it moves its way down into your chest and stomach. And your chest and stomach have become so relaxed that your breath and breathing has become effortless. Feel the relaxation as it moves its way on down into your hips and pelvis, and all the way down into your thighs. And your hips and pelvis and thighs have become so relaxed they just sink into the couch or chair. Feel the relaxation as it moves its way on down past your knees, down past your calves and all the down into your feet and toes. And your legs and feet and toes have become so relaxed that you can barely feel them. Now, feel what it feels like to be relaxed, to be in this state and I would like for you to pick one word that would describe how you feel at this very moment and tell me what that word would be.

Now, in your mind's eye, I want you to see your secret place and describe what you see to me in detail (pause).

Now, I want you to feel the sun as it shines on your face, and feel the light breeze as it brushes across your cheek, and I want you to smell the scents that are in the air. Notice how wonderful it feels to be in your secret place, how safe it feels, how comfortable.

Now, I want you to look off into the distance and I want you to notice there's a small, bright, white light hovering in the distance. It's beautiful and warm (pause). Can you see it? Good.

Now, I want you to notice the bright, white light as it begins to move toward you, very slowly and invitingly. Somehow it feels familiar to you. As it moves closer and closer to you, I want you to notice that the light begins to take on a shape, and it's that of a small child. However, it's not any child you already know in your real life. Allow yourself to see who the child is and tell me who the child is (pause).

Yes, you're right, it is you. Now, I want you to notice how old your child is, what color your child's hair is, and what he/she is wearing and then describe those things to me in detail (pause).

You may notice you may be feeling a lot of different emotions as you stand in front of your child self; you may be feeling some sadness or maybe even some confusion. Your child has been looking for you for a very long time. You may notice that you may even feel like crying. If so, it's okay. I just want you to take a moment and feel what it feels like to be standing in front of your child and tell me what you are feeling (pause).

Now, I want you to look at the expression on your child's face and tell me what you see (pause).

Now, allow yourself to feel what your child is feeling and tell me what those feelings are (pause).

Now, I would like for you to ask your child out loud why he/she is feeling this way and tell me what your child is saying back to you (pause).

Now, I want you to take a moment and ask your child-self what it is that he or she needs from you at this very moment. Does your child need to hear that you love'em or that you'll never leave'em again? Or does your child need a hug and to know how much you have missed him/her? Tell me what your child needs from you right now (pause).

Now, I want you to allow yourself to give your child whatever it is that he/she has asked of you and tell me what is happening (pause).

Now, allow your child to feel what it feels like to get what he/she needs and has needed for such a long time (pause). Can you feel it? Good.

Now, I would like for you to tell your child-self anything else you want to say. You might feel the need to apologize for abandoning your child such a long time ago, or to tell your child how much you love'em, or maybe even promise that you will never leave'em again? You can say anything you want, so go ahead and say it now (pause).

Now, look and see that your child believes what you are saying and just breathe into that. Just feel how wonderful that feels (pause).

Now, I want you to take one last moment to bask in how good it feels to have found your child today and for your child to have found you.

Feel how good it feels for your child to believe in you. And just breathe into it (pause).

Now, you have a choice to make, you can either allow your child to remain in your secret place, or you can take your child with you to live in your heart. Take a moment to choose what you would like to do (pause). If you choose to let your child stay in your secret place, then tell your child now that it's okay to stay and to play because you will be back to get him/her later (pause).

However, if you choose to take your child with you, then I want you to pick your child up and to hold onto him or her. And I want you to feel your child merging inside of you until he/she is living in your heart and you have become one. Tell me how that feels to you (pause).

Now, I want you to look around and find the path that leads away from your secret place. Do you see it? Good. And I want you to start walking down that path. And with each step you take I want you to feel one last time how wonderful it feels to have found your child today and allow your child to bask in how good it felt to be found (pause).

Now, I want you to continue walking down the path until you find yourself walking back into the room you are sitting in. See yourself sitting in your chair or on your couch and I want you to take three really deeps breathes (pause).

And when you are ready I want you to open your eyes and take a moment to reflect on what you've just experienced and then continue reading the rest of the chapter.

This is the end of track 2.

Track 3: Resolution Exercise

As you sit in your quiet place, I would like for you to close your eyes and remember to breathe in through your nose, and hold it and breathe out through your mouth. Breathe in through your nose, and hold it and breathe out through your mouth. And I want you to remember that relaxation starts at the top of your head and it moves its way down your body until it reaches the tips of your toes. It feels warm as it moves through each part of your body. So feel the relaxation as it starts at the top of your head and it moves it way down past your forehead, down past your eyes, down past your cheekbones and all the way down into the muscles of your jaw. And your face and jaw have become so relaxed that your mouth drops slightly open and it stays that way allowing it to be easier for you to breathe. Feel the relaxation as it moves its way down into your neck and throat and all the way down into your shoulders. And your shoulders have become so relaxed that they just let go; physically feel them as they let go. Feel the relaxation as it moves it way down into your arms and your hands and all the way down into your fingers. And your arms and hands and fingers have become so relaxed that they feel as if they are floating. Feel the relaxation as it moves its way down the back of your neck, down past your shoulder blades and all the way down into your lower back. And your shoulder blades and back have become so relaxed they just sink into the couch or chair. Feel the relaxation as it moves its way down into your chest and stomach. And your chest and stomach have become so relaxed that your breath and breathing has become effortless. Feel the relaxation as it moves its way on down into your hips and pelvis, and all the way down into your thighs. And your hips and pelvis and thighs have become so relaxed they just sink into the couch or chair. Feel the relaxation as it moves its way on down past your knees, down past your calves and all the down into your feet and toes. And your legs and feet and toes have become so relaxed that you can barely feel them. Now, feel what it feels like to be relaxed, to be in this state and I would like for you to pick one word that would describe how you feel at this very moment and tell me what that word would be.

Now, in your mind's eye I want you to see your inner child who wrote the letter. Notice how old your child is, what your child looks like, what he/she is wearing and tell me what you see? (pause).

Now, I want you to see the person you wrote the letter to standing before you and tell me who that person is (pause). I want you to picture that person at the age they are in your letter and describe that person to me in detail (pause).

Now, I want you to feel what it feels like to be standing in front of this person and tell me what you are feeling (pause).

Now, I want you to hold onto the vision of this person and what it feels like to be standing in front of them as you open your eyes and see that person sitting in the chair across from you (pause). Can you see them? Good.

Now, I want you to look at the person sitting in the chair across from you and I want you to tell them that you have a letter you would like to read to them and all you want is for them to listen to you. I will wait as you tell'em this (pause).

And I want you to notice the expression on their face and see that it conveys that they are willing to listen to you. Can you see this? Good.

Now, I want you to take out your letter, pause this CD and allow your inner child to read your letter out loud to the person sitting across from you. When you have finished reading your letter to them, resume this CD.

PAUSE THIS CD NOW!!

Now, I want you to set your letter aside and close your eyes again and see the person you wrote the letter to standing before you; standing before your inner child. I want you to take this moment and tell this person anything else you need to say, anything you may have left out of your letter, and anything you need to say one last time. Say what you need to say to them now (pause).

Now, allow yourself to tell this person what you had needed from them as a child but didn't get (pause) .

Now, I want you to look at the expression on this person's face and tell me what you see (pause).

Now, I want you to tell me what they are saying back to you (pause).

Now, I want you to notice if they are sorry for hurting you or if they wish they had done something differently back then. If they are I want you to tell me what they are saying to you (pause).

Now, I want you to feel what it feels like for this person to have apologized to you. Just feel how good that feels and breath into that (pause).

Now, I want you to say whatever it is that you want to say back to this person in response to their apology and say it to them now (pause).

Now, the question is this: Are you ready to let go of the pain and to accept the apology of the person standing before you? Are you ready to forgive them? Good. Then I want you to look down at your hands and see that you are holding a bunch of boxes. And notice the boxes are several different sizes and shapes (pause). And I want you to see that each one of the boxes is filled with all of the pain, and hurt, and sadness, and anger you have been carrying around all of these years. And I want you to describe to me what your boxes and pain look like (pause).

Now, I want you notice how heavy the boxes are and I want you to feel your pain that is in the boxes and really breathe into that pain (pause). Can you feel it? Good. Now, I want you to notice if you are ready to let the person standing in front of you feel the pain you have been carrying around all of these years. Good. Then I want you hold out your hands with your boxes of pain in them and feel the other person's hands as they move underneath yours. Feel their hands touching yours. And I want you to tell them that you want them to hold on to your boxes for just a moment and to feel the pain you have been carrying around all of these years. Allow yourself to do this now (pause).

Now, I want you to look at the expression on their face and see that they are willing to do this. So I want you to feel the pain and the hurt as it moves out of your boxes into your hands and feel it as it moves into their hands, up their arms and into their heart. And I want you to see the expression on their face change as they now understand what you have been feeling all of these years and tell me what you see (pause).

Now that they know the pain you have been carrying around, are you ready to let go of the pain? Good. Then tell this person that you are ready to let go of the pain and then ask them if they are ready to let it go of it, too (pause).

Notice that they, too, are tired of carrying around all of this pain and are ready to let it go. So, on the count of three, I want both of you to throw your boxes of pain up into the air. One-two-three. Throw your hands up and throw the boxes into the air together, blowing out anything that is left over. And I want you to look up and notice that the boxes are drifting above you and see them as they disappear one by one and continue blowing out any else that needs to disappear with the boxes (pause).

Now, when all of the boxes have disappeared, I want you to look at the person standing in front you and notice there isn't anything standing in between you anymore. Tell me how that feels (pause).

Now, I want you to see if there is anything you need or want from this person right now, like maybe a hug? If so, then allow yourself to get what you need from them right now and tell me what is happening (pause).

And I want you to just breathe into how good it feels to get these things from this person (pause).

Now that you have forgiven this person it's time to let them and this part of your life go so both of you can move on with your lives. So I want you to take a moment now to tell this person that it's time to move on and that it's all right (pause).

Now, I want you to see the person in front of you turning around and slowly beginning to walk off into the distance. See them walking and walking until you can't see them anymore. Feel how for the first time in your life it is all right for them to be going because you have forgiven them and because you know they have finally heard you and because things between you are now resolved. And just breathe into that (pause).

Now, as you know it is your adult's job to take care of your inner child, so I want you to turn around and see your adult standing before you. Your adult is waiting for you to tell him/her everything that has just happened. See yourself doing this now and tell me what you are saying (pause).

Now, allow your child to tell your adult what you need from him/her at this very moment and allow your adult to give you what you asked for and tell me what is happening (pause).

Now, I want both of you to look around and notice you are sitting in your secret place. Feel your adult comforting you in a way you have always wanted. Feel what safety and security feels like. Feel what it feels like to be loved. Know your adult-self will always be there for you. Just take a moment and marvel in how wonderful all of this feels; how healing it is and just breathe into that (pause).

Now, is there anything you, the child, would like to say back to your adult? Do you want to thank your adult-self for being there and for loving you? If so, then do it now (pause).

Now, it's now time to go. So I would like for your adult and your child to look around and to find the path that leads away from your secret place. Do you see it? Good. Now, I want your adult to take hold of your child's hand and for both of you to start walking down that path together. And with each step you take I want your adult to feel how wonderful it feels to have helped your child today and to have comforted him/her through this experience. I want you to feel how much your child trusts you and believes in you. And with each step you take I want you to feel your child starting to merge inside of you until he or she is completely inside of you, living in your heart. Tell me how that feels to you (pause).

Now, I want you to continue walking down the path until you find yourself walking back into the room you are sitting in. See yourself sitting in your chair or on your couch and I want you to take three really deeps breathes (pause).

And when you are ready I would like for you to open your eyes and take a moment to reflect on what you just experienced and then continue reading the rest of the chapter.

This is the end of track 3.